# BRIGHT LIGHTS

## The Stevenson Engineers
### 1752-1971

[1] *Robert Stevenson (1772-1850), Civil Engineer and his wife Jean (1779-1846).*

# BRIGHT LIGHTS

## The Stevenson Engineers
## 1752-1971

Comprising:
FAMILY RECOLLECTIONS
by JEAN LESLIE
and
A SERIES OF PROFESSIONAL ASPECTS
by ROLAND PAXTON

'. . . In the afternoon of time
A strenuous family dusted from its hands
The sand of granite, and beholding far
Along the sounding coast its pyramids
And tall memorials catch the dying sun,
Smiled well content . . .'

R.L.S., Underwoods, XXXVIII.

Edinburgh: Published by the Authors
1999

Published by Prof. Roland Paxton, Civil & Offshore Engineering, Heriot-Watt University, Edinburgh EH14 4AS

First Published 1999

Conversion Factors

| | |
|---|---|
| 1 inch | 2.54cm |
| 1 foot | 30.48cm |
| 1 yard | 91.44cm |
| 1 mile | 1.61km |
| 1mph | 1.61km/h |
| 1 ton/in$^2$ | 15.44 MPa |
| 1 lb/ft$^2$ | 0.05kN/m$^2$ |

ISBN 0 9535514 0 7

Origination and cover design by Origin Reprographics, Leith
Artwork by Creative Link, North Berwick, East Lothian
Printed by Gibson Print Ltd, Livingston, West Lothian

## Introduction

This book, stems from the *Stevenson Family of Engineers Symposium* in 1994 held at the Royal Museum of Scotland in Edinburgh. It is the result of a collaboration by Mrs Jean Leslie, a direct descendant of the Stevenson family, and myself. From our completely different aspects and knowledge came the idea to produce a work based largely on family records which sheds new light on one of the world's most remarkable engineering families - the Stevensons, no less than seven of whom achieved fellowship of the Royal Society of Edinburgh.

The book covers their lives and work over a period of more than two centuries, from the birth in 1752 of Thomas Smith, first Engineer to the Commissioners of Northern Lighthouses, to the death in 1971 of D. Alan Stevenson, the last in the continuous succession of civil engineers. Particular attention has been given to the foundation of the Stevenson firm of civil engineers by Robert Stevenson which, with changes of partners from time to time, continued in service for over 140 years. Collectively the contribution of the Stevenson engineers to the infrastructure of the nation was extraordinary.

Our book is arranged chronologically in chapters, taking each member of the family involved in engineering work in turn, and with reference to such less obvious participants as Robert's daughter Jane, who took down at dictation his classic *Account of the Bell Rock Lighthouse*, and R.L. Stevenson, the famous writer, known as Louis (pronounced Lewis). Within each chapter are two sections. The first written by Mrs Leslie is a compilation of family recollections and is based on her great interest in the family and extensive knowledge of its activities as Charles's grand-daughter. The second section entitled 'A professional aspect' and the appendices are by myself and consist of information and historical engineering comment to provide an indication of the style, scope and activities of each engineer from his own writings and work.

The verse on the title is taken from R.L.S's 'Underwoods', a poem which at once reveals Louis's awe and wonder at the engineering feats of his family and yet his own sense of guilt on turning away from their achievements to his own lesser talents!

We are pleased to acknowledge the valuable help received from Ronald Birse, Adele Paxton Mierzejewski, Ann Paxton, Quentin Stevenson, John Peploe, Pamela Godfrey, Rosemary Swallow, Willie Johnston and the many contributors mentioned in the list of illustrations and source notes. It is hoped that the book will make the fascinating lives and achievements of the Stevenson family of engineers better known and understood.

Roland Paxton

# The Stevenson Family of Engineers

*'The flashes of amateur ingenuity have paled their fires before the steady luster of brighter lights and surer guides. The voice of a commercial people demanded aid for daring enterprise and grand designs. Men like Smeaton and Brindley answered the call'.*
To these names can surely be added those of Watt, Telford, Rennie and Robert Stevenson.

[From Francis Egerton (Earl of Ellesmere, 1800-1857)'s *Essays on history, biography, geography, &c, contributed to the Quarterly Review,* 1857. For this most apt quotation the authors are indebted to Professor Sydney Ross of Rensselaer Polytechnic Institute, Troy N.Y., U.S.A., Chairman of the James Clerk Maxwell Foundation].

# CONTENTS

## LIST OF ILLUSTRATIONS

Note: Sources and acknowledgments are included in this list and not under the illustrations in the text.

[Front Cover] 'Bell Rock Light House during a gale from the south east.' Engraved by W. & D. Lizars from a sketch by W. Lorimer & J. Steedman. [1816].

[Back Cover] Davie and Charles aged 4 and 5 years. Family source.

### Family recollections

In Ferryport-on-Craig, Fife, a small village opposite Dundee, Thomas Smith was born in 1752. That same year a pamphlet [ti]tled *Proposals for carrying out certain public works in the city [of Ed]inburgh* was published. He was born into an era of reform [whi]ch future generations could build a new and better life in [capita]l of Scotland. The pamphlet was explicit about the [physica]l limitations of the existing city and its unhealthy [conditi]ons. Expensive and far reaching plans were made [for expan]sion of the capital and during the next eighty [years a]ctually carried out. An outstanding need to [drain the] Nor' Loch was obvious. Equally important, [bridges would b]e engineered and built to take the citizens [out of] the ancient city to their beautiful New [Town ... ] national and international trade made [ ... ] place in which to stay in spite of the [ ... f]ew hours of daylight during the [ ... ] need was the improvement of

[ ... ]n of new lighting round the [ ... ]t. Seafarers for generations ha[ ... ]their various trades and the [ ... ] of ships that never reache[d ... ]

It mu[st ... ]s, as a small child, to have wr[ ... ]f his father, also called Thom[as ... ] daughter of a prosperous se[ ... ]on a good education local[ly ... ] him to a Dundee metal-wo[rker ... in]genious

and able to express himself well. In 1770, when James Craig's plans for Edinburgh were well under way at the East End of the New Town, Thomas arrived in the city. He lodged at first with his Kay relatives and took employment with an established metal-worker. In 1781 he was trading as a tinsmith from Bristo Street[1], where he manufactured oil lamps, brass fittings and fenders. By 1790, when his workload had increased, he had moved to premises in Blair Street[2] where he was able to employ a larger workforce. This talented young man found immediate success; for a time he was a partner in a concern called the Commercial Shipping Company.[3] His descendants possess a silver cup inscribed to him thus:

BEING A SMALL TOKEN
OF THE SENSE ENTERTAINED
OF HIS GREAT EXERTIONS AS A PARTNER
IN THE ORIGINAL ESTABLISHMENT OF THE CONCERN,
AND HIS UNWEARIED ATTENTION TO THE
INTEREST OF THE COMPANY

In 1787 he secured the contract from the Town Council to provide street lamps for the Old and part of the New Town. His tender was the most attractive, and he had designed a new oil lamp which had a parabolic polished metal reflector behind it. The result was a stronger light than any of his rivals and a considerable income for years to come. He expanded his business to take on the contract for the lighting of Glasgow twelve years later at the same price of sixpence per lamp. By 1807 he was contracting to light the streets of Perth, Stirling, Ayr, Haddington, and Aberdeen, and in 1810 to light Leith as well.

Thomas realised that with further refinement his new lamps

could also be used to guide sailors safely home to port. Seamen everywhere had to rely on visual landmarks and occasional coal fires which blew out in wind or rain and were totally obscured in fog. One example was the beacon on the Isle of May, at the entrance to the Firth of Forth which was still virtually unchanged since it was first lit in 1635. Scattered rocks and islands are in the path of the main shipping lane up to Edinburgh and beyond to Stirling. Increasing trade brought about by the Industrial Revolution meant more wrecks, bringing demands for better navigation lights, and as a result the Northern Lighthouse Trustees (later the Northern Lighthouse Board) was established in 1786 with authority to build four lighthouses on the Scottish coast.

Kinnaird Head, North Ronaldsay (Orkney), Eilean Glas (Outer Hebrides) and the Mull of Kintyre were chosen as sites for the first four lights. Parliament had asked for them to be completed in four years but Thomas did so in three. Access to Kintyre, although it was on the mainland, required a hair-raising scramble over 12 miles of rough trackless moorland and mountains, over bogs and through poorly mapped country.

Each light presented a separate challenge; land had to be bargained for, suitable keepers found and trained, and storm-proof dwelling houses built for their families. Different lighting requirements were also needed for each site. From November probably to May each year work had to be abandoned because of impossible weather conditions, and the time was spent planning and constructing the lamp parts in Edinburgh.

Great physical strength, business acumen, courage, ingenuity and a passionate dedication to the job in hand were gifts Thomas had to the full. None of the family of engineers who followed

[2] *Miniature painting of Jane Lillie*

him probably achieved anything so difficult as the lighting of these first four lighthouses.

In 1778 Thomas married Elizabeth Couper, daughter of a Liberton farmer; a daughter, Jane, was the first of five children. By 1786 his beloved wife Elizabeth and three of their children had died. A year later he married Mary Jack, daughter of a Stirling builder, and they had one girl. While enjoying a steady success in business ventures, he had a saga of domestic tragedy. With Mary Jack's death he was left with three small children to care for at a time when he was required to travel to remote corners of Scotland on lighthouse work. Two more lights had been erected, at Pladda and on Little Cumbrae in the Clyde estuary. Greenock was handling several hundred ships daily from the American cotton and tobacco run, and the work was urgent. The situation was desperate for him, but a close friend and neighbour who had known both his former wives offered to care for his home and children while he was away. She was called Jane Stevenson or Hogg.

Jane was born in Glasgow on November 21st, 1751, the seventh child of David Lillie, who was shortly to be Deacon of Wrights in that city, and his wife Isobel Miller. [2] Her elder sister Bethia Lillie, married George Laurie, the merchant founder of Laurieston, later known as Gorbals.

We know nothing of Jane Lillie's youth except that she attended a private girl's school in Edinburgh, possibly Mrs Hannay Robertson's Young Ladies School of Arts, for her father and mother were comparatively well off. At the age of 19 she married a young merchant, Alan Stevenson, six months her junior, the son and grandson of Glasgow maltsters (or brewers), both named Robert Stevenson. There is no record of this marriage but it is said to have occured in 1771, and the first and only child of this union, Robert, was born in Glasgow on June 8th, 1772.

Robert's father, Alan Stevenson, worked as a storekeeper for a Glasgow firm trading in the West Indies. He died from fever on the Island of St Christopher, now St Kitts, in 1774 while in pursuit of a thief, leaving Robert fatherless from the age of two. It was many years before his mother Jane (née Lillie) saw any money from her young husband's estate and, as her own father and mother died at about the same time, she was left in a condition of great want.

Robert Louis Stevenson wrote that there was 'something romantic' about his great-grandparents' marriage[4] and as there had been no Lillie or Stevenson witnesses at Robert's baptism it was probably an elopement without family approval on either side. This could also account in part for Jane Stevenson's poverty after the death of her husband.

Years later Robert wrote a 'Memoranda' for the information of his family and said:

'My mother's ingenious and gentle spirit amidst all her difficulties never failed her. She still relied on the providence of God, though sometimes, in the recollection of her father's house and her younger days, she remarked that the ways of Providence were often dark to us.'[5]

In spite of her deep religious convictions this well-educated girl made the same mistake twice and she conceived a son with another young Glasgow merchant called James Hogg. He was variously described as a weaver, hammerman and manufacturer. Jane was three months pregnant at the wedding on April 19th,

1777 and the child arrived in October. Three years later Jane and James Hogg moved out of Glasgow to Milton of Balgonie in Fife. On December 7th, 1780 they had another child, again a boy. The Hoggs moved to Edinburgh where James deserted his wife and vanished into England. What happened to Robert's two half brothers is quite unknown they may have been taken by their father or they may have died in infancy. All his long life Robert respected his mother's privacy regarding this second marriage.

Jane was herself living in the High Street of Edinburgh, and she had as a close neighbour Thomas Smith. She was a friend to Elizabeth Couper, and then to Mary Jack. She moved in to his home to look after his remaining three children after Mary had died and Thomas was called away on urgent lighthouse business. Referring to the 'dark days of her life' before she had met Thomas Smith, Robert, in his 'Memoranda', again, tells us:

'The Bible, and attendance on the ministrations, chiefly of Mr. Randall of Lady Yester's Church, afterwards Dr. Davidson of the Tolbooth, and at other churches, where I was almost always her constant attendant, were the great sources of her comfort.'5

Thomas proposed marriage to her but she was still married to a man who had now disappeared. In 1792 James Hogg was traced to Orton in Westmorland and, anxious to marry Thomas Smith, Jane started divorce proceedings. Robert was 20 years old when he and Thomas, together with Jane's lawyer John Easton, who lived in Allan's Close, Edinburgh, travelled south to appear as witnesses for her. The divorce was almost certainly obtained with a bit of bribery.

Written in his own hand into a family Bible starting with his grandparents Robert gives dates for the entire family with births, marriages and deaths. There was not a word of his mother's second marriage to James Hogg. None of the children of Robert and Jane Stevenson knew of their deeply religious grandmother's moral indiscretions. Robert Louis Stevenson, two generations later, certainly did not, and if he had he would probably have applauded the lady's courage and turned the whole saga into a magnificent melodrama with heavily disguised names!

Thomas Smith and Jean Stevenson were able to marry on the 14th of November 1792 and their marriage was a happy one. They had one little girl whom they named Elizabeth after Thomas's first wife. Betsy, as she was called, died suddenly in 1803 aged seven. She was much loved by Robert, who wrote in a letter [now lost] to a friend, 'I am sure there never was a greater appearance of health and a finer girl of her age.' They had deeply felt religious beliefs; although Thomas had left the Church of Scotland to join the Baptists in mid-life, he returned to his original faith because he could not reconcile the Baptists' peaceful views with his activities as a militiaman. Thomas had become a member of the Loyal Edinburgh Spearmen, later the Royal Edinburgh Volunteers, in 1793 together with Walter Scott. [3]  As a Captain, Thomas was on duty during the troubles associated with the trials of the political radicals Muir and Palmer in that year.

A letter written in 1794 from Thomas Smith to Jeanie, and addressed to her at 4 Blair Street, Edinburgh, survives and shows his concern for his third wife.

'Glasgow 10th Augt. 1794
Sunday

My dear Jeanie

I arrived here this day in good health and will be home tomorrow night, God willing. I have seen our Friends and was in time for the afternoons Church. I hope you will not have any more of your low spirits. You ought to be very thankful that I am safe landed. I was very near to be taken by the French squadron. They will be chaced off the coast before Bob comes home. I am happier tonight in the hopes of seeing you and all the children than I have been since I went away.
I am Dear Jeanie your ever faithful and affectionate husband

Thomas Smith.'[5]

Jane's son, Robert, had been brought up from his arrival in Edinburgh aged six as a playmate with the Smith children. He was apprenticed first with a gun-smith called Innes, who died. As he grew up he was frequently in Thomas Smith's busy workshop. Thereafter he knew where his great interest and real talent lay. Thomas found him an invaluable assistant and apprenticed him formally. By 1797 he was established as a business partner.

Thomas Smith's oldest daughter Jane married Robert in the last year of the century. She had been his step-sister for many years. Robert was twenty-seven and Jane twenty years old.

Those looking at the family tree have to digest the fact that Robert's father-in-law and step-father were the same person!

[4] *Thomas's house, Baxter's Place, Edinburgh 1804.*

Thomas's second surviving daughter, Janet, had to wait until 1816 before she could marry an Edinburgh engineer called David Swan. He came from a Scottish provincial family living in Kirkcaldy. The Swans had given Thomas Carlyle a helping hand when he was in Kirkcaldy Academy by engaging him for a while as a tutor. For some reason, lost in the mist of time, Robert's wife, Jane objected to the marriage of Janet who accused her of delaying it for six long years. In the event they had one son called William. Janet lost her husband when their child was only three years old.

The century ended with Thomas making a magnificent gesture to the Lighthouse Commissioners–he gifted them a sloop that was ready to be launched from the yards in Elie. He had her fitted out with special comfort for the crew and workmen. This was the second *Pharos* in a long line of lighthouse inspection vessels.

He had been elected to the Edinburgh Guild of Hammermen in 1789, becoming its Master and a City Magistrate in 1802. He had bought an extensive feu in the tiny village of Greenside, part of the New Town beside the Calton Hill. Here at what is now Baxter Place he built a splendid house, with five stories facing North and six to the South with a large garden and apple orchards. [4] It stood well back from the quiet road that led down to Leith. A ground floor side entrance opened directly into Greenside Lane and both Thomas and Robert were able to conduct the Lighthouse business from there for the duration of their partnership. Thomas' manufacturing business continued in Blair Street and he was to devote time to brokerage and insurance. Men of enterprise and wealth were his friends and he was a very successful businessman. For holidays the family would go to Mayshade, a villa in the country just ten miles south of the heart of Edinburgh, owned by the same Baxters from whom Thomas had bought his town feu. The oldest building still stands today.

The Napoleonic wars raged throughout most of his life. Although an ardent volunteer soldier and always ready to take up arms if the call came, he never actually had to fight for his country.

Three generations of Stevensons including Louis have looked in vain for the likeness of Thomas Smith. A description of him was given to Louis by an ancient sailor, who remembered seeing him as a stout man coming ashore with a gun under his arm. A portrait may have existed, as Robert left pictures in his will to his son Alan. He died in Baxter Place in the same year as the Battle of Waterloo and his wife, Jane, five years later.

**A professional aspect**

Thomas Smith had taken an interest in improving lighthouse illumination even before the Board of Commissioners of Northern Lighthouses was formed and had appointed him as

their *Engineer* on 22 January 1787. In May 1786 he had proposed to the Chamber of Commerce at Edinburgh that reflector lights be substituted for the coal light at the old private lighthouse on the Isle of May, but old traditions die hard and they were of the opinion that the coal light should be continued.[6]

Thomas did not give up his idea and on 16 June 1786 he prepared a statement entitled *A comparative view of the supperior advantages of lamps above coal light when applyd to light houses, in which he confirmed that he had constructed 2 small reflectors & lamp with a view to demonstrate by experiment what has been only laid down in theory.*[7] In July 1786 he petitioned the Board of Manufactures in Edinburgh on the utility of reflector lamp lights for lighthouses, of which he had *already made several small ones, one of which has been seen and much approved of by several gentlemen, who have expressed a desire to see one executed on a larger scale, and placed on Inchkeith. The Board resolved to allow twenty pounds towards the expense of making the model and trying the experiment upon Inchkeith.*[8] Although this trial seems to have been successful, his proposal of reflector lights for the Isle of May lighthouse was never adopted. It was not until the year after his death, by which time the Northern Lighthouse Board had acquired the old lighthouse from the Duke and Duchess of Portland, that the present structure was completed and became operational with silvered-copper reflector lamps.

From early in 1787, Thomas enthusiastically set to work on providing Scotland's new lighthouses even though he does not appear to have received any salary for about six years. In 1793 he was awarded a salary of £60 per annum over and above his expenses. His lack of building experience was not regarded by the Commissioners as an impediment to his appointment as their Engineer, as such skills could be and were brought in under his general direction. He was not however their first choice for this post. In September 1786 the Board had invited Ezekiel Walker of King's Lynn, who had introduced improved lighting at Hunstanton lighthouse in 1779, to erect their first four lighthouses. Walker had declined this invitation but offered instead to erect one lighthouse, give directions for the other three and, for fifty guineas, to instruct their representative in the *whole of his principles and improvements*. The Commissioners evidently had confidence in Thomas as they took up only the last part of Walker's offer. Within a matter of weeks Thomas was in Norfolk receiving the proffered instruction.

On 21 March 1787 the Board was informed that Thomas was *fully instructed in the whole principles of constructing Light Houses by lamps and reflectors and also directions from Mr Walker for constructing the Light houses. The clerk informed that he had employed Mr Kay Architeck to make drawings of the different light houses as well as elevations and sections agreeable to the directions of Messrs Walker & Smith.*[9] During the next two decades, commencing with the conversion of Kinnaird Castle into a lighthouse [5], Thomas was responsible for providing or improving the illumination at no less than thirteen lighthouses, mostly at remote locations.

The technical aspects of Thomas's work were essentially confined to the overall planning and illumination of lighthouses. This is confirmed in his report to the Lord Provost of Glasgow in 1792 *anent erecting an oil light with reflectors on the Cumbra Lighthouse* [Little Cumbrae, Bute]. He wrote, *I really am not a judge what these temporary erections might cost and indeed I never had anything to do with the mason work of the tower or keepers houses in the Government* [N.L.B.] *Lighthouses. I confined myself wholly to forming the plan and only executed the parts that belonged to my own business. However, by the annexed states of the supposed expence you may be able to judge nearly of the necessary expences excepting the tower, the keepers house and store house which are not included and which I could not undertake.*

*If the work goes forward I shall give every assistance in my power, and shall pay particular attention to the sufficiency of it ... As to the light on the Strone point* [at the entrance to the Holy Loch] *it will not cost near so much on account of the number of reflectors being reduced. About twelve may be sufficient, and this will also render its annual expence two thirds less. The one with 36 reflectors may cost about £50 and the one with 12 about £16 annually. George Sheills, a very careful* [Edinburgh] *mason, built three of the lighthouses* [Mull of Kintyre, Pladda and Eilean Glas]. *He was furnished all the materials and had so much a week for his work and trouble in overseeing the other workmen. If you think proper to follow this method I dare say I can procure him to do your work.*[10]

Some idea of the broader scope of Thomas's work can be gleaned from his lighthouse inspection voyage in the *Swift* of Elswick from June to September 1793. At the Mull of Kintyre he found the lighthouse in very good condition but the keeper *... much molested by the Moil Company* [the Mull Company; tenant farmers of the Duke of Argyll?] *who insist that he shall not keep a dog or gun, which I think is necessary as the place is infested with wild cats which are dangerous.* He then visited Scalpay [Eilean Glas] and was supportive of the keeper's request to graze a cow and about a score of sheep, but the landowner *absolutely refused to grant this liberty in terms very disrespectful.*

[6] *Register Office, Edinburgh, with street lighting, c. 1804.*

The situation at Scalpay was as nothing to what he found at North Ronaldsay. The lighthouse was in *a tolerable good state of repair excepting some glasses which were tore out of the reflectors by the carelessness of the keeper in cleaning* [but] *the keeper had acted the most dishonest and infamous part that can be imagined, he has by his own confession before a number of witnesses, sold the oil sent to him in very great quantities throughout the whole of North Ronaldsha and the neighbouring island of Sanda so that his conduct is notorious. A great deficiency being still in the number of his casks he endeavoured to make it up by saying that he had a great number stolen by the people of the island, he mentioned eight in one night, this I believe to be an entire falsehood to cover his knavery. I have dismissed him.* At Kinnaird lighthouse he proposed strengthening the light from the south by *putting in another sash & adding six or seven reflectors.* He also recommended waterproofing the light platform.[11]

At Inchkeith, one of the Board's most attractive-looking lighthouses completed in 1804 Thomas is commemorated above the door as its *Engineer.* [7,8] Independently of the Board, he was also responsible for harbour lights at Leith, Portpatrick and on the rivers Clyde and Tay. [9] His last major lighthouse, another fine-looking building, was Start Point, Orkney. Robert formally succeeded Thomas as Engineer to the Board on 12 July 1808.

From 1797 Thomas delegated and allowed almost complete autonomy in lighthouse matters to his energetic mature apprentice, Robert. This enabled him to concentrate on lamp manufacture and the expansion of his other interests, not least his general and

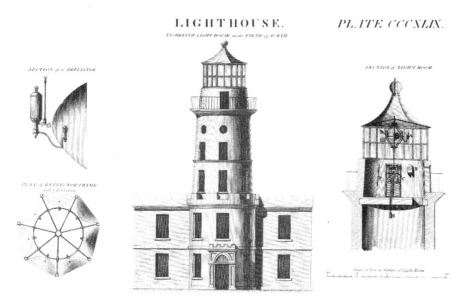

[7] *Inchkeith Lighthouse, 1804. From Robert's article 'Lighthouse' in the Edinburgh Encyclopedia, 1818.*

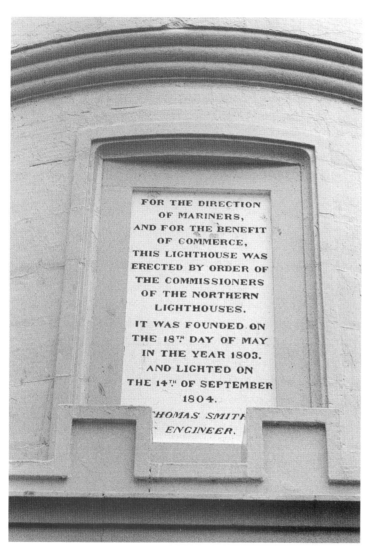

[8] *Inchkeith Lighthouse tablet.*

LEADING LIGHTS of TAY.

[9] *Tay leading lights, Buddon Ness. From Robert's article 'Lighthouse' in the Edinburgh Encyclopedia, 1818.*

21

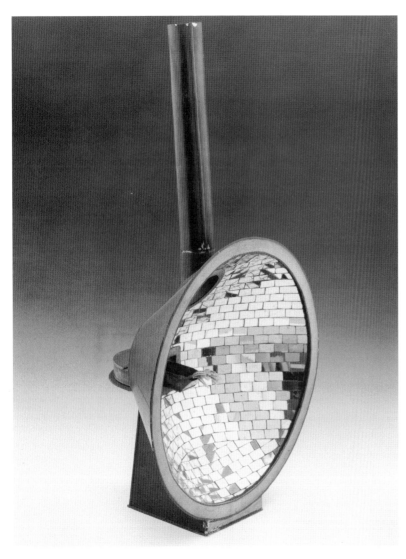

[10] *Model of Thomas Smith's reflector lamp.*

street lighting business, an idea of the extent of which can be gauged from his extensive correspondence with the Carron Company from 1787 to 1807. By the early nineteenth century his lamps were lighting much of eastern and central Scotland. In 1804 he was the public lighting contractor for both the *Old* and *New* towns of Edinburgh. [6] Thomas is understood to have retired from the firm in 1808, which was then carried on by his son James.

In terms of technical innovation Thomas deserves recognition for improving the intensity of illumination in Scottish lighthouses by means of the catoptric or reflector system. He developed and made arrays of parabolic reflector oil lamps of his own design. Each lamp had a light source at its focus and a curved reflector formed of small pieces of mirror glass set in plaster which produced a beam of light. [10] Because the reflector was made of glass rather than metal it had the advantages of being more resistant to distortion and the wear occasioned by the frequent cleaning it required before the use of wicks enclosed by glass chimneys. However, because of its joints and less accurately formed curved surface, his apparatus could not reflect light as perfectly as the silvered-copper reflectors already in use in France and soon installed elsewhere in conjunction with Argand lamps with glass chimneys.

Thomas's first operational light was installed at Kinnaird Head. It had an intensity of about 1,000 candlepower, which although very feeble compared with 690,000 candlepower for its modern counterpart, it nevertheless represented a worthwhile improvement on coal lights. He continued to adopt glass facet reflectors for new lights until 1801, after which he and Robert made and installed Argand lamps with silvered-copper reflectors, beginning at Inchkeith lighthouse in 1804 with reflectors of 21-inch diameter. Most existing installations with glass facet reflectors continued in operation until the 1820s.

Details of Thomas's practically derived reflectors became more generally known from an article *Reflector for a light-house* in the supplement to the *Encyclopedia Britannica* (1801).[12] In it Thomas is described as *an ingenious and modest man* [who] *has carried* [his inventions] *to a high degree of perfection without knowing that something of the same kind had been long used in France.* This tribute is omitted from later issues, including the last carrying the article (1823), after the editor had learned of Walker's prior development of the glass facet reflector concept. Reference is also made to the superiority of Thomas's reflectors over *obviously wrong* continuous metal ones! His change of mind by 1804 in favour of metal reflectors in conjunction with Argand lamps [7], a considerable improvement, was almost certainly due to Robert's influence.

The Lighthouse Board was later criticised by Sir David Brewster for not having applied a more scientific approach to lighthouse illumination in 1787. Whilst there is probably some truth in this charge Thomas's ingenious expedients undoubtedly represented the most practicable means of achieving an immediate improvement before the Argand lamp, patented in 1784, was eventually applied to this purpose.

Thomas deserves to be remembered chiefly for improving lighting in Scotland and for laying the foundation of the Stevenson dynasty of engineers. He achieved the latter by encouraging and sustaining the training and education of Robert, by ensuring his succession to the engineership of the Northern Lighthouse Board and by providing at least some of the financial support necessary to sustain Robert's civil engineering business through its formative years.

Although further research is required into the details and extent of Thomas's practice and that of others, there is little doubt from the depth and scale of what is already known that he has a good claim to be regarded as Scotland's first lighting engineer.

# Chapter Two
## Robert Stevenson 1772-1850 - Erector of the Bell Rock lighthouse

### Family recollections

Beside the parish church of Neilston, a flat gravestone is marked simply 'NETHER CARSEWELL'. [11] It covers the dust of some of the family's early progenitors. Some miles away a farmhouse called Nether Carswell stands in the beautiful low green hills of Renfrewshire. It is 16 miles from the city of Glasgow. Above the lintel of one of the old buildings the initials of James Stevenson and Marion Andrew with the date 1695 have been cut and recut. On another old barn, above the door, the date 1791 has been incised. It was a prosperous farm in the 17th century and home to their seven children. Generations of farmers worked the land here, turning an inhospitable and unimproved moor into a productive hill farm.

[11] *Family gravestone at Neilston, Renfrewshire. 17th century.*

Directly descended from James and Marion Andrew is Robert Stevenson, the first of the family to become an engineer.

Robert's early education was at a free charity school in Edinburgh. Later he attended classes at the University in Glasgow. He acknowledged the debt he owed to its founder in a manuscript memoranda:

'It was the practice of Professor Anderson kindly to befriend and forward the views of his pupils; and his attention to me during the few years I had the pleasure of being known to him, was of a very marked kind, for he directed my attention to various pursuits, with the view to my coming forward as an engineer.'[5]

The appearance of many men of great technical ability in Scotland was assisted by the enlightened attitudes in the centres of learning.

One of his old friends who had been his class fellow in Glasgow was Henry Duncan, of Ruthwell, who was the founder of savings banks. Subsequent winters gave him a further opportunity to study at the University of Edinburgh, where he attended the class of Professor John Robison. The Professor's assistant, whose name was Thomson, made him a double barometer, which was left to his son Thomas in his will.

Robert did not receive any academic degree, but he mastered all he needed to know for the practice of civil engineering. He wrote 'I was prevented from following my friend Mr Neill for my degree of MA by my slender knowledge of Latin, in which my highest book was the Orations of Cicero, and by my total want of Greek.'[14]

Robert and Jean, had 13 children but only five-Jane, Alan, Robert, David and Thomas lived to grow up.

With Robert leaving home for such long periods much of the early upbringing of the children was of necessity in Jean's hands. As they came along, she was required by Robert to listen to their lessons, take them for educational trips to Leith, and make sure that they did not get 'over-heated' with their high spirits! Together with Robert's mother she ran a school for the local poor children in Baxter Place for some years. There may have been a lot of religion taught but presumably reading, writing and arithmetic were included. Robert's wife kept herself in the height of fashion and went forth from her house wearing five feet of gold chain round her neck, her deeply embossed gold watch, gold vinaigrette and pearl brooch. As part of her dowry she brought much fine furniture and a wealth of family linen of strong make with an exceptionally elaborate design. The tablecloths, for instance, were embroidered with hunting scenes, and her maiden name was woven in. Her boys too were very fashionably dressed on suitable occasions. In some of the original letters that Robert wrote every few days to his wife when he was separated from her, although many contain only day-to-day events, he included news of his business transactions and gave her an idea as to the date of his return. Some have striking descriptions of fashions current in London or Paris. Writing from London in April 1815 he describes the Princess Royal as:

'dressed in a Pelisse and Bonnet of the same colour of cloth as the boy's dress jackets-trimmed with blue satin ribbands-the hat or bonnet Mr. Spittal said was a Parisian Sloutch-and had a plume of three white feathers.'[15]

She also shared quietly in her children's laughter, and nursed them devotedly through their many childhood ailments. Robert had lived for twelve years with Jean, his step-sister, before he married her, and he certainly must have known that housekeeping and coping with hiring competent staff to run Baxter Place would not be easy for her. She devoted too much of her time to religion, and judged everyone she met by the yardstick of her own deep religious convictions. RLS in his book *Family of Engineers* writes hilariously of the strong words used by Robert when meals were burnt by the cook.

Education started for the family as soon as they could talk. Later the boys all attended the High School of Edinburgh. As their time at school or university was ending each of his sons received a letter from their father formally asking for their decision as to what career they wished to follow. All of them were taken on lighthouse voyages with Robert from 12 or 13 years old and were required to take careful notes showing their daily activities. Robert read and criticised them at home. Their travels extended to many parts of Scotland, England, Ireland and France. Janey, who was so much older than her brothers and his only surviving daughter, had an especial place in her father's heart and he gave her every educational opportunity that money could buy. He took her with him when she was 17 years old on his two lighthouse voyages to France. She showed great ability as an artist and her father printed an engraving of one of her drawings in his Bell Rock book.

Robert must have found leaving his home and children behind him very difficult at times. On 31st August 1806, he wrote:

'Carskey Bay. On board the Canal Packet.
Sunday morning 31st August. 1806
My dearest Jeannie,

I am sure from the attention of our friend Mr. Leitch that

our sister Mary and you would have a very pleasant Journey and from the state of the weather you must have found the Journey home much more agreable than in coming west. At home I trust you found our dear little Family and all our friends well, and as I hope Mr. Leitch gave up his intention of staying at Mr. Halls you will all be very happy; as for myself I feel as well as on former occasions of the like absence from my Family and friends, and comfort myself with the prospect of good weather and a short voyage, which will lead to a happy meeting with you My Dear Jeanie- you would observe that I sailed in the afternoon but owing to the heavy swell of the sea and the wind increasing against us we were obliged to return to our old anchorage about midnight after getting a little below the Cumbraes - had I waited till the middle of the day I might have landed and again taken leave of you, but as this is rather an unpleasant thing I rather got under weigh in the morning and as we stood over to the Island of Bute I dare say you might have observed the vessel. I looked anxiously for the Coach about the hour of its setting off. ...'5

When the boys were small they received letters separately written in a large printed script, which they could read themselves, and which were full of instructive but interesting facts from which they might profit.

'London 26. May 1816.

My dear Boys,
After writing to you from the Isle of Man, Mr. Neill & I sailed in the Yacht, over a broader part of the sea than the Frith of Forth, & came to a town called Liverpool. Which has more ships than Leith. The inhabitants of Liverpool are very fond of education, they have many large rooms full of Books, and also a large Botanic Garden, full of curious Plants from all parts of the World. Some of these Plants were brought from Arther's [sic] Seat, & other mountains in Scotland, One which Mr. Neill & I admired much, the Banana, was so large, that it would reach higher than from the floor to the Roof of the Dining room, and one leaf of it would cover James & Mary from head to foot. This plant was brought from the Sandwich Islands, in Captain Cook's Ship, by Sir Joseph Banks. ...'5

In this next letter Robert uses his exceptional powers of observation:

'On Board of the Light House Yacht, Off Kirkwall the Capital of Orkney, Wednesday 31. July 1816.

My Dear Boys
At the towns of McDuff, Banff and Portsoy, many of the houses are built of marble, and the rocks on this part of the coast, or seaside, are marble. But my Dear Boys, unless marble be polished & dressed it is a very coarse looking stone & has no more beauty than common Rock. As proof of this, ask the favour of your Mother to take you to Thomson's Marble Work, in South Leith, & you will see marble in all its stages, & perhaps you may there find Portsoy marble. The use I wish to make of this, is, to tell you, that without education, a man is just like a block of rough unpolished marble. Notice in proof of this, how much Mr. Neill, & Mr. McGregor know, & observe how little a man knows who is not a good schollar [sic]. Be sure that you shake hands with

Mr. Neill when you see him, & make my compliments to him.

On my way to Cullen, a small but pretty little town, I saw a windmill-tower, which a gentleman caused to be erected on his estate, but the people there did not know how to stop the windmill, when it was going very fast, & the whole machinery was broken to pieces. ...'[5]

Robert Stevenson's life is well documented both by himself and his sons, and later by his grandson Louis. He was an elder of the Church of Scotland and once represented Cupar at the General Assembly. Together with his eldest son Alan he set a pattern of family services for lightkeepers; bibles were provided at every station, and missionaries were asked to visit, and later to take books and help with the education of lighthouse children. From Thomas Smith's time religion gave the family of that generation, and the next, a deep compassion for other people. If one of Robert's workmen had an accident he would arrange for a pension to be paid to the widow. During the years of terrible unemployment after the Napoleonic wars he organised the construction of walks on the Calton Hill, an early job-creation scheme.

Robert also seems to have had second sight, or extra-sensory perception, as did his father-in-law Thomas. Thomas arrived at his mother's bedside in Broughty Ferry just a few hours after she had appeared to him in a vision, and just before she died.

Louis writes:

"In the early part of the [19th] century the foreman builder was a young man by the name of George Peebles, a native of Anstruther. My grandfather had placed in him a very high degree of confidence, and he was already designated to be foreman of the Bell Rock, when, on Christmas-day, 1806, on his way home from Orkney, he was lost in the schooner *Traveller*. The tale of the loss of the *Traveller* is almost a replica of that of the *Elizabeth* of Stromness; like the *Elizabeth* she came as far as Kinnaird Head, was then surprised by a storm, driven back to Orkney, and bilged and sank on the Island of Flotta. It seems it was about the dusk of the day when the ship struck, and many of the crew and passengers were drowned. About the same hour, my grandfather was in his office at the writing-table; and the room beginning to darken, he laid down his pen and fell asleep. In a dream he saw the door open and George Peebles come in, 'reeling to and fro, and staggering like a drunken man,' with water streaming from his head and body to the floor. There it gathered into a wave which, sweeping forward, submerged my grandfather. Well, no matter how deep; versions vary; and at last he awoke, and behold it was a dream! But it may be conceived how profoundly the impression was written even on the mind of a man averse from such ideas, when the news came of the wreck on Flotta and the death of George."[4]

Louis goes on in his *Family of Engineers* to relate that Robert took care of George Peebles' widow and brothers, and was still trying to cope with helping the family as late as 1839 when he finally gave up.

In the first draft of Louis' book *Family of Engineers* he gives a great insight into family life in Baxter Place:

"In this house, Baxter Place, for the better part of half a century, my grandfather led a life of inimitable regularity, only broken by his continual displacements. He rose very early in the morning, it seems about half past five, put on a shawl-patterned dressing gown, carefully lathered his face, and set off on a round of bed-side visits to his sons. From the innocence of sleep, these were wakened to the dread consciousness of his displeasure, and must listen, from his soapy countenance, to the enumeration of their own misdeeds. This duty performed, and the lather now well soaked in, he would leave his sons to go to sleep again if they were able, return to his own room, shave, and employ himself with his industrious pen till seven. Then he made his usual round of the Calton Hill, and was back by eight for breakfast. From breakfast to dinner he sat close in his office dispatching affairs. Only during the winters of the Bell Rock, was this iron rule relaxed; in those four years, he returned every afternoon to the house and went to bed for an hour's sleep. At five o'clock dinner was served. Up to that hour he was an abstainer from drink; but at dinner port wine made its appearance. 'Of this,' says Mr Swan, 'the old gentleman would take a large allowance, and was never seen to be the worse of it.' He had an evening walk which was no less stereotyped than that of the morning, to the 'Green Tree' some half way to Leith, wrote from seven to nine, and read the London Standard, then about three days old and just about to hand by the mail, till it was time for supper. 'The Baxter Place suppers,' says Mr Swan, 'were very usually of prime cheddar cheese and old Porteous excellent wheaten bread.' A large silver tankard, which had originally been my grandfather Thomas Smith's, was charged initially with two bottles of porter. As the bread and cheese was being consumed, the tankard passed grandly round the table, and when the level of the contained fluid was becoming inconveniently depressed, it was from time to time replenished by a fresh bottle drawn for that end. At length, when all had taken enough bread and cheese, hot water and 'fine old Jamaica rum' were brought in, and each man, if so disposed, had his tumbler of rum punch. My uncle declared 'there was not a headache in a puncheon of this rum!'

The only surviving child of his widowed mother and educated at home, Mr Swan had a standing invitation to spend the day and dine at Baxter Place on Saturday. If other guests chanced to be present, he and my grandfather, who were about of an age and fast friends, dined by themselves at a side table, enjoying their single glass of port in peace, and were remitted from the obligation to pledge the company by name and in a series."[13]

Robert belonged to many of the clubs and societies which existed in his time-the Wernerian, Smeatonian, Astronomical, Highland and, of course, the Royal Society of Edinburgh. In 1814 he was a co-founder and director of the Scottish Equitable Insurance Company. Later he was a director of the Sea Insurance Company until 1837, when his son David took over.

The Waterloo Coffee House at the East End of Princes Street was opened in 1820 and was a favourite place for him to meet his large circle of friends.

Robert had a special relationship with Sir Walter Scott whom he first met through the Edinburgh Volunteers of 1795. He invited Scott to accompany him on the *Pharos* for the annual tour round the Scottish lights. They landed on the Bell Rock where Scott inscribed in the visitors book the 'Pharos Loquitor.' Walter's gift to Robert at the end of the voyage was a volume entitled *Some account of the voyage of James V round Scotland, under the conduct of that excellent pilot, Alexander Lindsay*, first printed in Paris in 1583. The following year Robert invited him again and received this letter of regret:

'Robert Stevenson Esq  Architect  Edinburgh
Abbotsford  20 July -- [1815]

My dear Sir
I am much obliged to you for thinking so kindly about my voyage and I assure you that the pleasure I promise myself in visiting France under the present extraordinary circumstances scarce compensates for that which I anticipated in our gallant yacht & with my kind friends. But time is precious with me & I have already formed a party for Flanders[,] Waterloo being one of our great objects. It therefore only remains for me to hope that we will one day have another Lighthouse Voyage & to wish you as much happiness & fun & as little sea sickness as the circumstances will admit of  Believe me Dear Sir Very much your obliged & faithful

Walter Scott.'14

Robert, so methodical in the keeping of his business ledgers, letters and diaries, neglected to preserve his written communications with his friend:

'I at one time had many notes and letters of Sir Walter's, but they have somehow or other got out of my hands.'5

In June 1828 Robert and Jean's daughter Jeannie  married Dr Adam Warden. This wedding was a very important event for the Stevenson family. Adam had studied surgery in the hospitals in Paris. Later he was appointed aurist to Queen Victoria, probably because he invented an ingenious medical instrument using lenses for looking into ears. The technical knowledge for this had in fact come from his brother-in-law Alan. Adam Warden was only 25 when he married Jane who was two years older than her husband. They had two daughters and two sons. In Robert's lifetime they lived with their own front door in an extended part of the family house in Baxter Place. Sadly Adam was to die at the height of his distinguished career when he was only 47 years old and only two months before Robert. In his will, extending to over 100 pages, Robert left Jeannie and her children very substantial property. She was to live on until 1864.

Robert saw much of his Warden grandchildren in Baxter Place and mentions them individually in his will.

A most charming letter written by Robert's granddaughter, Jane Warden, thanks him for her birthday present when she was ten years old.

'Edinburgh Feb. 21st. 1840

My dear Grandpapa
I am much obliged to you for the desk and the beautiful Seal which Mama was quite surprised at. I hope to be able to keep it in order, and improve in my writing, and I will be able to write you when you go away in the ship. Mama says I must go to bed as it is near nine O'clock. I remain your affectionate grandchild

Jane Warden.'5

Robert's most important work was the building of the Bell Rock lighthouse. He left an interesting account of it in a quarto volume of 500 pages written by dictation to his daughter Jane. [12] He was 52 years of age before he found the time to write it.

At the age of 77 he started writing about his work from 1811 to 1847 and his unwavering handwriting marks many of the entries. When he tired he dictated this too to Jane. By March 1850 they had completed eight volumes which he presented to his sons with a letter stating 'I set out in this work with the intention of reading each report and marking memoranda after perusal, but I found this irksome and too laborious. So I trusted to my memory. It should all be gone over with a very careful hand.'

In 1842 Robert's wife, Jean, died. He sailed once more on the annual inspection voyage before his official retirement in 1843. The officers and lightkeepers of the Northern Lighthouse Board presented him with a silver tureen inscribed:

AS A MARK OF THEIR RESPECT
FOR HIS STRICT AND IMPARTIAL EXACTION OF DUTY
AS THEIR CHIEF OFFICER
AND ALSO OF THEIR HIGH ESTEEM
FOR ALL THE PRIVATE VIRTUES
WHICH DISTINGUISH HIM AS A MAN

It has a silver lighthouse as a handle on the lid and was left in Robert's will to his eldest son Alan. He did not retire from the separate family business of general engineering until 1846 and he left his three sons as partners.

He wished his sons to be able to conduct themselves like gentlemen, and educated them accordingly. They all had a natural gift of being able to meet and enjoy the company of the men who worked under them. The servants of the Northern Lighthouse Board who came to Edinburgh were always welcomed to breakfast at Baxter Place where they were treated by Robert with exactly the same hospitality that he gave to his personal friends.

Robert Louis Stevenson had a passionate interest in everything that concerned his grandfather and his grandmother. Although Louis never knew his grandfather, his writings offer a revealing insight into Robert's mind:

'There is an ominous creak of my grandfather's utterances to his grandchildren and nephews which testifies to a mind little at ease. A profound underlying pessimism appears upon enquiry to be the last word of the Stevensons. It does not usually depress them; they are cheerful enough; they have a great gift of enjoyment, but their sense of the tragedy of life is acute and unbroken. My grandfather with his unrivalled digestion, his active regular habits, his eminently detached and mathematic views of religion, may have appeared to an outsider the very type of the sanguine character. But the vulture was within, and almost from the beginning he seems to have regarded the prospects of his sons and nephews with despair.'[4]

Robert never properly understood the great need two of his sons had to express themselves in writing on matters other than engineering. Both Alan and Thomas had to hide much of what they wrote from him. Although he would have loved the strange little boy Thomas produced he would have been terribly shocked at the wild behaviour of the teen-aged Louis and would have urged Thomas to be more effective at disciplining his son. He would have been astonished to know that this grandson who refused to follow his own profession would only forty years after his own death carry a name that is a thousand times better known than his own. Today, few people except engineers know who built the Bell Rock lighthouse or indeed any of the Scottish lighthouses. The initials R.L.S. are known in households round the world.

Robert is recorded as being able to whistle in perfect time while dancing in Baxter Place with one of his beloved grandchildren in his arms. Louis himself missed this experience as he was born only three months after his grandfather's death. The 'time capsule' was wrong.

When the children were very young, summer holidays were spent only a mile away on the clean sandy beaches of Leith. Later, Portobello became the fashionable place. The only holiday that Robert himself is ever known to have taken was spent in Holland. The letters he sent back to his young daughter Janey are an absolute delight. They were printed in the *Scots Magazine* from 1818-21. That he did combine business with pleasure and the civil engineer is evident in much of his notebook. A separate edition dedicated to Janey was privately printed in 1848 containing a facsimile of the gold medal presented to Robert in 1829 by the King of the Netherlands **[13]** and a neat coloured diagram of Bonaparte's 'Fly Bridge over the Scheldt.'

In his first letter to Janey, Robert was looking back on the town he loved so much as the ship took him down the Firth of Forth. He wrote that no one could be said to know half its beauties who had not seen it from the Roads of Leith, or from the walk round Calton Hill. He said good-bye to the town when the evening sun began to be reflected from the windows of Queen Street as if by ten thousand mirrors.

25th July 1817.
'As seen from the Firth of Forth, the city appears to be set down in an immense amphitheatre, encircled by a range of

**[13]** *Medal presented by the King of the Netherlands, 1829. From Robert's Journal of a trip to Holland, 1848.*

mountains. On the west we have the hills of Corstorphine, which seem to be separated from those of Fifeshire, as if by some sudden dislocation, to admit the waters of the Forth to empty themselves more freely into the sea. Towards the South the Pentland range holds a commanding place, while Salisbury Crags and Arthur's Seat are seen sloping towards the East, and fall into the sea at the bay of Musselburgh; and still to the Eastward we have the Moorfoot Hills, Traprain Law, and St Abbs Head on the brink of the German Ocean.'[15]

A fine breeze carried the vessel down the Forth, tacking towards the Fife coast, and affording views of Kirkcaldy, Wemyss and Anstruther-passing Fidra, the Lamb and Craigleith, the town of North Berwick, and the Bass Rock. At nightfall a view of Dunbar Castle was before them. The trip that Robert took in these six weeks was formidable and he transports Jane and the family with superb use of the written word to dozens of places in England and Holland that were foreign to them. Robert referred to his fourteen letters having been, at times, irksome for Jane to read, so much of them being concerned with engineering and similar matters, but there are also many interesting passages, such as these excerpts on the dress of the inhabitants of Rotterdam and of Scheveningen:

'Rotterdam, 6th August.
The most remarkable peculiarity in the dress of the people you meet with in the streets, when compared with the costume of England, consists in the men very commonly wearing cocked hats, large metal buttons, and large shoe and knee buckles; the fashions of Holland having all the appearance of being about thirty years behind those of England. The women wear ear-rings, from the size of a pea almost to that of a middle-sized plum; some of the better sort, particularly those from North Holland, have not only ear-rings dangling upon their shoulders, but bands or plates of gold round their foreheads, passing behind the ears and back part of the neck. They generally wear black or white stockings of cotton or silk, with a black or red high-heeled slipper, without any quarter-leather for the heel. They are in general, very cleanly in their apparel.

Hague, 7th August.
Here, instead of the simple English muslin cap, it is common to wear a large straw-hat, measuring about two feet and a half in diameter, suited for all the purposes of the eastern parasol and the northern umbrella, under which they certainly ogled very prettily, with their handsome decorations of large drop ear-rings, pearl-pins at the breast, and not a few with the gold-plate or clasp of North Holland encircling their foreheads and their ears, even to the back part of the head.'[15]

Robert's three engineering sons held different views of their talented father. In his *Biographical sketch of the late Robert Stevenson, Esq.*, Alan wrote:

'He was a man of sincere and unobtrusive piety and had perseverance, fortitude and self-denial and an enthusiastic devotion to his calling. Add to this a deep quiet sense of humour and great physical strength. Only once was he known to 'have a cold' and the Doctor said he had to stay inside for a couple of days ...

He hated parties, except in his own house, had a fiery temper, easy to arouse.' [14]

Several portraits exist of Robert in his lifetime, and at least two busts were made. One was placed in the library room in the Bell Rock to his honour and stands now in the entrance hall at the Northern Lighthouse Board, George Street. It was sculpted in marble by Samuel Joseph and was considered by experts to be a perfect piece of sculpture. The face has always seemed to be almost alive. Two passports of 1820 and 1834, issued in France, describe him thus: 'chestnut hair, grey eyes, large nose and generous mouth, round chin in an oval face, ruddy complexion, clean shaven and about 170 centimetres high.' A portrait of him can be seen in the mural cavalcade of the nation's famous men and women, painted by William Hole in the entrance hall of the National Portrait Gallery, Queen Street. He is marching along in good company, and carrying a model of the Bell Rock! Two memorial windows exist, one in St Giles Cathedral, Edinburgh and another in Glasgow Cathedral.

Robert Stevenson is buried in the New Calton Cemetery in 'The Gated Cell' beside his wife. He enlarged the family vault:

'The Tomb or Burying Ground belonging to me in Calton New Burying ground already occupied in part by my own immediate family-and the Co-lateral family of Dr Warden-may in the opinion of the Recorder of the Burying Ground be found sufficient for the several members of my family viz: Mrs Warden, Alan, Robert, David, and Thomas Stevenson-yet to render this more certain and from the earnest desire which I feel, that it should be so-and that we may continue to unite in "Peace" at death, as we have happily done through life-I am endeavouring to acquire the enlargement of the said Burying ground toward the west, and to extend the present enclosure in that direction-as the ground on the south and North is already fully occupied by others. For the particulars of this Burying ground see my private Ledger folio 74.'[5]

Robert had moved the graves of his family to the new site when he successfully fought the battle to get an extension east from Princes Street and Waterloo Place to carry the road through the Old Cemetery and round the sweep of the Calton Hill along what is now Regent Road to London Road. It was a tremendous engineering task to build up the road and carry it safely over the ravines and round what was called 'The Panoramic Highway.' Lord Cockburn said: 'The effect was like the drawing up of the curtain of a theatre.'[16] The Regent Arch is a colossal bridge of stone, a processional way fit for the capital. It is also a successful effort to build public works in the Roman manner, before new large structures, such as the Crystal Palace and the London underground railways, were realised in iron and steel.

There is a Disposition and Settlement of Robert's Estate on the 13th December 1850.[17] The house at Baxter Place was furnished with every comfort and luxury available at the time as we can see from the individual bequests he left for his children and grandchildren. Although he disliked attending 'social' events, dinner parties from his own mansion were given in fine style. Guests were required to use the 'finger glasses' that his daughter had asked him to get while she was still unmarried. Several sets of silver are mentioned, silver salvers and also silver handled dessert knives and forks, also best sets of tea and coffee cups. To all the family went numerous pictures, wall mirrors, carpets, sofas, coffee tables, wine decanters and of course his well filled wine cellar. He owned several hundred books in individual book-cases all round the house and he gives the titles of many. Some were very rare when Robert bought them and they would be priceless now. To David he left his *Universal history* in sixty-seven volumes, including two volumes of supplement and a folio of maps; 'This book,' the will states, 'is rarely to be met with in a complete state-it was purchased by me while attending the Natural Philosophy class in the College of Glasgow, I think in 1791.'

The great scope and variety of his children's general knowledge and varied interests in life are revealed in the list of the literature he owned. He had more books on literary subjects, including travels, novels such as *Don Quixote,* and Scott's *Lord of the Isles*, than any other. Several histories, both Maitland's and Kincaid's histories of Edinburgh, and almost as many of a scientific or philosophic nature such as Newton's *Works,* Serres's translation of Bougard's *The little sea torch light,* and *The skilful pilot,* and Barlow's An exact survey of the tide. He also owned a number of religious titles. Other technical books which he possessed were considered the property of the firm and kept separately at the office.

Dr Bob [Robert] was remembered equally with the others by his father and was left enough articles of every variety to furnish a whole house. Thoughtfully he added in the will: 'In case my dear son Robert should not have retired from the army at the time of my death some of the foregoing articles bequeathed to him may be considered cumbersome, and others may not be thought to be soon found useful to him: But let him consider, that the less bulky articles can be taken charge of by his sister Mrs Warden and the rest being carefully packed and labelled can be sent to the Lighthouse Store, Leith, to lie for him as was done with the late G. C. Scott's books etc where they lay many years, in good order, waiting his return from Italy.'

Bob did in fact die tragically only one year after his father. He had contracted a fatal illness in India but got back home to Edinburgh in 1851. Robert Alan Moubray Stevenson, Robert Louis Stevenson and Robert [Bob] Stevenson were the only descendants of the dynasty who did not enter into the world of civil engineering.

**A professional aspect**

Robert, in common with other engineers of his generation, was a largely self-taught civil engineer of the practical school. He gained an engineering related education by part-time attendance at professor John Anderson's classes in natural philosophy at Glasgow University in 1792-94. From 1800-04 he attended classes in natural philosophy, mathematics, chemistry and natural history at Edinburgh University. By the time he had completed these studies he was 32 years of age. Before embarking on an engineering career he had been apprenticed to an Edinburgh gunsmith and was himself described as such until c. 1791 when he began to work in Thomas Smith's lamp-making business. By 1794 he had gained experience of lamp installation at Portpatrick harbour and on the erection and illumination of Pentland Skerries lighthouse. From 1796-1802 he was formally apprenticed to Thomas as a tinsmith. In this capacity, but with much more responsibility than was usually undertaken by an apprentice, he continued to specialise in lighthouse work, making reflectors, installing lamps and assisting with arrangements for the erection of lighthouses.

In 1797 Robert was entrusted by Thomas with the installation of the lamp at Cloch lighthouse. On its successful completion he was allowed much greater autonomy in lighthouse work. By 1800 his progress was such that Thomas took him into partnership, even though he was technically still an apprentice. At the same time Robert was also trying to gain approval for building a lighthouse on the Bell Rock, eleven miles off Arbroath. This was an outstandingly difficult engineering challenge made even greater by the fact that the rock was submerged to a depth of not less than about 12 feet during every tide.

In 1799 Robert proposed a beacon-style lighthouse on cast iron pillars for the Bell Rock. However, in 1800, after seeing the rock, and considering the possible damage to such a structure by ships, he abandoned this idea in favour of a stone tower following the general concept of John Smeaton's Eddystone Lighthouse completed in 1759. As part of the design and promotional process for the project he had both proposals accurately modelled, a practice which he often employed subsequently on important maritime and bridge works. Soon after the models were made he showed them to John Rennie (1761-1821) a leading engineer on maritime work, who expressed a decided preference for a stone tower.

Following the failure of a parliamentary Bill for the provision of the lighthouse in 1803 and because of the project's hazardous and unprecedented nature the Board, on Robert's advice, secured the services of Rennie. With his support, the necessary Act of Parliament was obtained in 1806[18] and on 3 December the Board resolved that the lighthouse *shall be erected under the direction of John Rennie, Esq., Civil Engineer whom they hereby appoint chief engineer for conducting the work.* He was requested to furnish plans, visit quarries and to report back. At a meeting of the Board on 26 December 1806, Rennie and Robert reported jointly on quarries, and the Board agreed to Rennie's proposal *that Mr Stevenson should be appointed assistant engineer to execute the work under his superintendence.*[19] The lighthouse, completed in 1811, was to prove Robert's most important engineering achievement.

Although the above terms of reference seem clear, the relative roles of Rennie and Robert in creating the Bell Rock lighthouse subsequently became a controversial issue between their families. The matter came into public prominence in 1848 when the Stevensons objected to Sir John Rennie's assertion, in his book on Plymouth Breakwater,[20] that his father had *designed and built* the lighthouse. Robert's sons lost no time in claiming this merit for their father through the columns of the *Civil Engineer & Architect's Journal.*[21] The issue was still very much alive at the time of D. Alan's death in 1971. On several occasions both he and the late James Rennie FICE urged the author that if he ever wrote about this matter he should make it very clear that is was their forefather who designed and built the lighthouse!

It would be inappropriate to enter into lengthy details of this issue here, except to say that from 1806-1810 the Rennie - Stevenson combination proved excellent for the success of the project. With Rennie's experience and direction and Robert's energy, ability and assiduous superintendence throughout the design and erection of the lighthouse, a remarkable achievement evolved which reflects great credit on both engineers, particularly on Robert for overcoming the exceptional difficulties of its execution.

Rennie's role was however much more significant than it came to be portrayed by Robert's sons and others influenced by them, that is, as only an *advising engineer in case of emergency.*[22,23] It is now evident from a study of the early records that Rennie competently exercised his role as chief engineer throughout the duration of the work by means of meetings, visits, reports and a large correspondence. Contrary to the impression given by the Stevensons,[24] he inspected the works at least twice during the crucial early construction of the tower. His notebook records him at the rock on 25 November 1808 *ordering* the replacement of Roman Cement to masonry joints.[25] He is also said to have been at the works on 29 September 1809,[26] when the tower was about 30 ft. high and in a report of 2 October 1809[21] [omitted from Robert's *Account* of 1824], informed the Commissioners of his directions in respect of fundamental design features, including the internal construction of the tower.

Rennie's main design contribution was, in general, to adhere more closely to Smeaton's Eddystone design which had stood the test of time rather than Robert's laterally undovetailed proposal of 1800 used in obtaining the Act in 1806.[15] In determining the external shape of the as-built tower Rennie adopted much greater curvature near the base than in both Smeaton's and

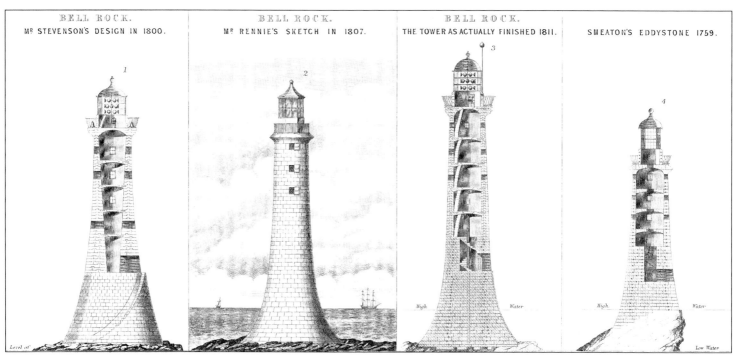

BELL ROCK.
Mʳ STEVENSON'S DESIGN IN 1800.

BELL ROCK.
Mʳ RENNIE'S SKETCH IN 1807.

BELL ROCK.
THE TOWER AS ACTUALLY FINISHED 1811.

SMEATON'S EDDYSTONE 1759.

**[15]** *Bell Rock and Eddystone lighthouse designs compared. From the Civil Engineer & Architect's Journal, 1849. Note the similarities between the as built tower shape and Rennie's initial design and between the as built interior and Smeaton's.*

Robert's designs, which by directing the waves upwards dissipated their energy more effectively. The narrower tower in the wave action zone tower also had the advantage of reducing the area upon which the waves acted. From the illustration **[15]** it can be seen that the sides of Rennie's initial design, and the lighthouse as built, rise from the rock at about 40 degrees from the horizontal, compared with about 70 degrees for Smeaton's and Robert's designs.

Rennie also incorporated greater lateral strength in the tower by means of horizontally dove-tailed masonry throughout its base to a height of about 45ft, and also, to the centres of the apartment floor cantilevers above, the latter being a modification to what was essentially an innovation of Robert's. **[16]** Within Rennie's broad parameters and direction Robert carried out almost all of the detailed design for the project.

This involved making many decisions on his own initiative and he undoubtedly had autonomy in the matter of fixtures and fittings **[17,18]** and was solely responsible for planning and executing the impressive shore base and signal tower at Arbroath.

Remarkable engineering innovations introduced at the works under Robert's direction and which greatly facilitated construction included, the temporary beacon barrack, and elevated cast iron railways for transporting materials across the rugged surface of the rock. **[19]** Also, ingenious and highly efficient moveable jib cranes and an iron balance crane, the latter, with a moveable counter balance weight, being a forerunner of the modern tower crane.

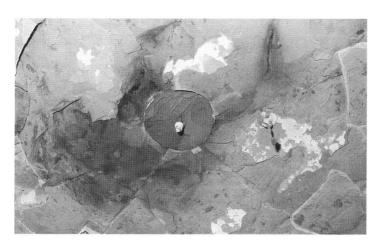

[16] *Bell Rock Lighthouse - kitchen roof after the fire in 1989. Note the cantilever end dovetailing. This was a modification by Rennie to what was essentially an innovative feature of Robert's design of 1800.*

Robert may have conceived the idea of some or all of these innovations and certainly superintended their provision and use, but there is evidence from the clerk of works David Logan (c.1786 - 1839), who later became a chief engineer, that the cranes used were invented by foreman millwright Francis Watt and that he also designed and made the beacon and probably the railway.[29] This attribution attracts support from a letter of January 1808 in which Robert wrote to Watt, *so soon as you have got a proper draught of the crane, of the rock and railway, and of the wooden house for the beacon - come this way* [to Edinburgh].[30] [20] Robert does not seem to have specifically claimed the *invention of the cranes* for himself or to have acknowledged this to Watt, but did claim that they were made from his designs, perhaps he meant in a proprietary sense. In time he became credited with their invention.[31,32]

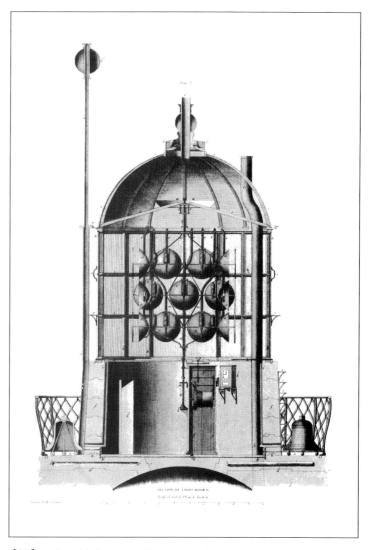

[17] *Bell Rock lightroom with fixtures and fittings to Robert's design. From Robert's Account, 1824. XX.*

[19] *Bell Rock works, August 1810, showing stones being transported from railway to tower top. From Robert's Account, 1824. Foreman millwright Francis Watt can be seen giving instructions at the beacon base.*

Robert's definitive *Account of the Bell Rock Light-House,* in which the various operations and intricate machinery and equipment used on the work were described and profusely illustrated by the best artists and engravers, was eventually published in 1824. The work took thirteen years to come to fruition, and it was perhaps not a coincidence that its publication occurred three years after Rennie's death as he is most unlikely to have approved of it.

As befitting a great achievement, the book was dedicated to King George IV, with a frontispiece from a specially commissioned, and since it was acquired by the National Galleries of Scotland now well known, watercolour by J. M. W. Turner, for which the artist asked Robert 30 guineas.[33] The book also generated an input about the use of the word *situate* from Walter Scott resulting in a *miscorrection* considered by Louis to *blot the page*[A] of the dedication, a verse written by Scott in 1814, and a ballad about *Sir Ralph the Rover* by Robert Southey. Although only 300 copies were printed, the book was widely distributed to influential recipients and, in addition to being a valuable work of reference, added lustre to Robert's reputation and gained him a gold medal from the King of the Netherlands [13].

Robert was perceived in some quarters, as having not sufficiently acknowledged the contributions of Rennie and foreman millwright Francis Watt. This led to unfavourable comment in various publications,[27] which eventually reached a much wider readership through Smiles' *Lives of the Engineers.* Smiles commented, with some justification, that the credit for the lighthouse was *almost exclusively* given to Robert, because Rennie was *in a great measure ignored* in Robert's *Account of the Bell Rock Lighthouse* and concluded that he *should not be deprived*

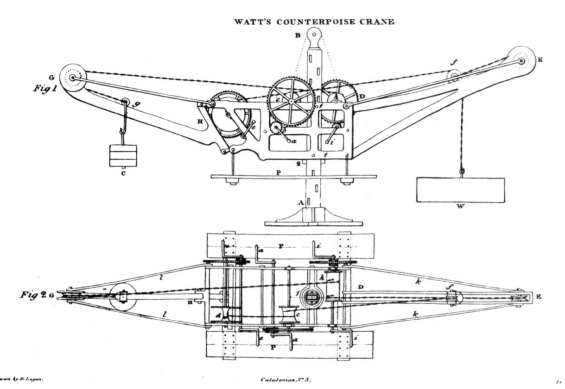

WATT'S COUNTERPOISE CRANE

*Fig 1*

*Fig 2*

Drawn by D. Logan.

Caledonian Nº 3.

[20] *Watt's counterpoise crane used at Bell Rock Lighthouse.*[26] *From a drawing by David Logan published in 1821. Its design differs in detail from that shown in* [19],

*of whatever merit belonged to him as chief engineer.*[28] David seems to have disputed with Smiles that Rennie had not acted as chief engineer for the work, but did not manage to persuade him of this and Smiles' comments were repeated in subsequent editions of the *Lives* down to the present time. This perhaps helps to explain the lack of interest by historians outwith the family in the broad ranging achievements of the Stevenson engineers until recently.

The successful completion of the lighthouse enabled Robert, from 1811, to establish within a decade, an indigenous civil engineering practice of sufficient importance to make modest inroads even into the work of the London based practices of Telford and Rennie. The firm which he founded, with changes of partners from time to time, practised continuously until 1952.

To create an engineering dynasty which flourished for nearly a century and a half required the extraordinary talents which Robert undoubtedly possessed. His success was based on his ardent acquisition, application and promotion of largely self-taught practical knowledge, combined with shrewdness, ambition, determination, hard work, outstanding entrepreneurial flair and managerial ability and a good financial start. In engineering terms his strengths related to maritime work, river improvement and inland communication, particularly bridges. His theoretical and mechanical engineering attributes were less remarkable. In 1825 when invited by the scientist David Brewster (1781-1868) to write the article *Steam Engine* for the *Edinburgh Encyclopedia* he replied *I should be afraid of disappointing you every way*[34] and offered him instead an article on suspension bridges, which was not taken up.

As engineer and, in those days, chief executive of the Northern Lighthouse Board from 1808 until his resignation in 1843, Robert can be considered to have inaugurated the modern lighthouse service in Scotland. He even had the ultimate in status symbols, his own shipping flag, the sight of which no doubt stirred many a lighthouse keeper into a flurry of activity. [21] During his period in office Robert was responsible for the design and construction of at least 23 lighthouses, of which that at Cape Wrath built by John and Alexander Gibb of Aberdeen is a fine example in the north, [22] and the rebuilding between 1821 and 1830 of five of the early lighthouses including Mull of Kintyre. In the field of lighthouse

[23] *North Berwick Harbour, improved c. 1812. Robert's specification for rebuilding the destroyed north pier (on right) is dated 5 Aug. 1812. The extent to which it was implemented is uncertain.*

illumination he improved on Thomas Smith's work and brought the catoptric system, that is using silvered-copper parabolic reflectors and Argand lamps, to a high degree of perfection. In order to distinguish between the ever increasing number of lights he invented *intermittent* and *flashing* lights, distinctions which are still in use.

With the possible exception of bridges, maritime and river engineering represented the largest and most successful element of the firm's general practice. From 1838, when David entered the partnership, Robert's contribution to the firm diminished and ended with his retiral in 1846. The numerous harbours upon which the firm reported under Robert's stewardship, and in many cases improved, included Stonehaven, Dundee, North Berwick [23], Rothesay, Grangemouth, Leith, Peterhead, Lossiemouth, Fraserburgh, Ayr, Aberdeen, Kirkwall, Sunderland, Ballyshannon, Perth, Granton and Chester. The firm became pre-eminent in river engineering in northern England and Scotland having worked on navigational improvements for the Tay, Forth, Severn, Ribble, Lune, Dee, Tees, Wear, Erne and the Dornoch and Pentland firths.

State of the art maritime work by Robert included the design and construction in 1821 of a sea wall at Trinity, near Edinburgh, with a cycloidal curve vertical profile which represented an improvement on common walls. Rennie had drawn his attention to the advantage of this profile in November 1806 in connection with the curvature of the Bell Rock lighthouse. Robert also made experiments on the destruction of timber by the *limnoria terebrans* which influenced the general adoption of greenheart for marine timberwork. For most of his professional life he had a consuming interest in coastal erosion and its causes based on a study of the bed of the North Sea. [24] This interest resulted in papers to the Wernerian Society and British Association from 1816 (See Appendix 1).

In the early years of the firm Robert engaged extensively on canal, road and rail-road projects, often adopting a promotional role. Before 1818 he had made proposals for a canal between

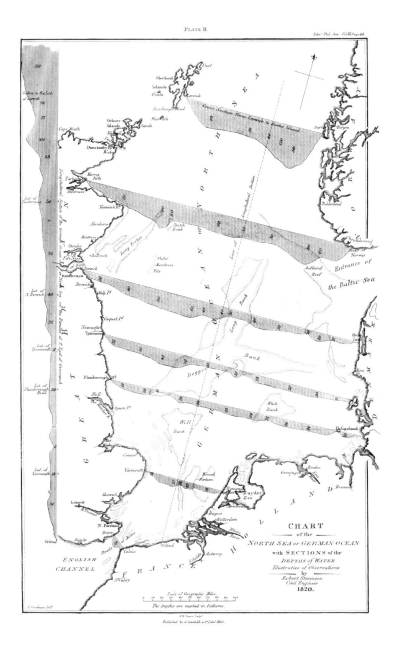

[24] *Chart of North Sea, 1820.*

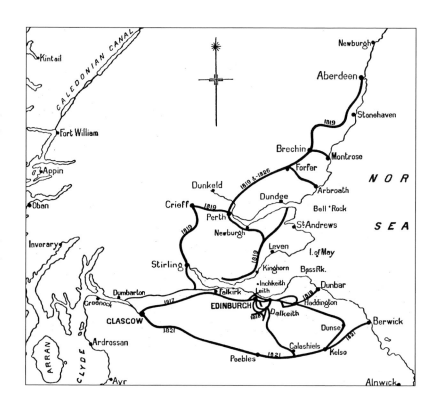

[27] *Plan showing Robert's railway proposals in Scotland, 1817-36. From David's Life of Robert, 1878.*

Edinburgh and Glasgow estimated to cost nearly £½m and another from Forfar in the Vale of Strathmore to Arbroath. The former had the feature of being on one level between the two cities, but with a connection to Leith locking down through Princes Street gardens or alternatively down the valley of the Water of Leith. [25] Robert's ruling design practice for canals was to keep lockage to the practicable minimum. In 1828 his reputation was such that he worked with Telford and Alexander Nimmo, on an extensive proposal for a new harbour at Wallasey and a ship canal across the Wirral to the Mersey. For various reasons, often their high cost, most of his schemes were not executed. Those that were tended to be for roads and bridges.

Several substantial lengths of road were executed under Robert's direction and it is evident that his road-making, probably influenced by Charles Abercrombie's improvements,

was at the forefront of national practice. His road making was similar to but more substantial than that advocated increasingly by John L. McAdam from 1811. Robert's specification for nearly a mile of new road from 16-20 feet wide at Marykirk, Kincardine, dated 12 February 1813 read, *The Reporter makes some alterations upon the common and ordinary method of breaking and laying road materials by reducing the road metal to a more uniform size and using a [3 inch] course of gravel if it can be procured or even of clean sharp sand as a bottoming for the [10 inch layer of] broken stones [which were to be blinded with a 2 inch layer of gravel].* He addressed the *evil of incompetent roadmaking* and emphasised the importance of seeing *that new roads are formed and executed upon proper principles.*

Robert further advised that *A road composed of stones of various sizes can never be brought into that smooth and uniform surface which is so much (sought) after, for the moment the pressure*

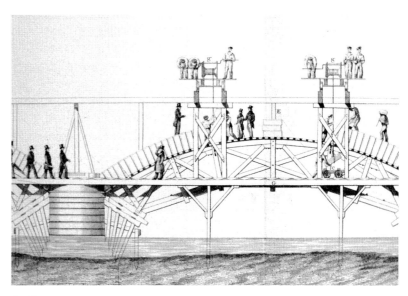

**[29]** *Hutcheson Bridge works, 1832. With inspection by Robert and party. Note the Bell Rock works influence in the use of railways for transporting stones and moving the winches transversly. From Weale's Bridges, 1843.*

**[28]** *Hutcheson Bridge, Glasgow, 1834-68. From Weale's Bridges, 1843.*

[**33**] *Regent Road approach via Calton Hill into Edinburgh 1815-19. Note the massive retaining wall required in front of the new High School. Engraving of a drawing by G.M. Kemp, 'Calton Hill . . . with the National Monument as it would appear if completed,' 1843.*

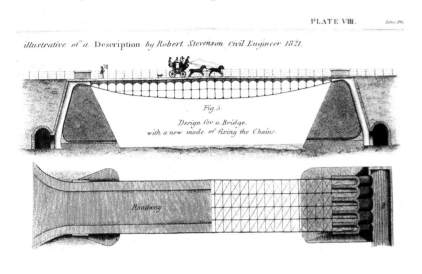

[39] *Underspanned suspension bridge proposal for crossing the r. Almond, near Edinburgh, 1820.*

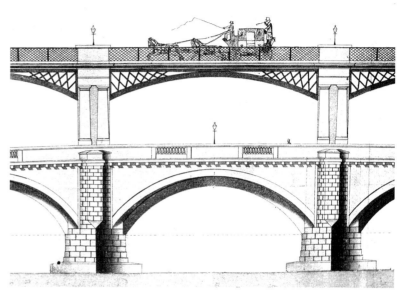

[37] *Proposed cast iron roadway on existing bridge at Newcastle-on-Tyne, 1828.*

[38] *Model of proposed laminated timber arch bridge at Dornoch Firth ,1830.*

*is brought upon one or other of these out-sized stones it must either be crushed under the wheel or be forced by repeated attacks into the road and thereby displaces the surrounding stones and in either case admission is given to the surface matter, a pit is immediately formed and every succeeding wheel widens the breach untill the road is reduced impassible. To counteract this very common effect arising chiefly from the very vague manner of defining the dimensions of road metal by bulk or even by weight, the reporter provides that the Trustees shall furnish a riddle . . . of such dimensions that a stone measuring more than 1 in [38mm] upon any of its sides can(not) pass through it . . . when a pressure is brought upon any particular part of the road it acts with a perpendicular force in the direction of gravity and tends to compress the whole regularly.*[35]

By 1818 Robert had become convinced of the superiority of horse-drawn railways over small canals for inland communication and proposed the *Edinburgh Railway* to connect with the Midlothian coalfield.[36] In 1819 he proposed a railway between Montrose and Brechin. **[26]** His reputation was now such that he was called in as a consultant to advise on proposals such as the Stockton & Darlington Railway and the Elgin Railway extension.[37] About this time he also edited for publication, with *Notes,* numerous *Essays on Rail-Roads* submitted to the Highland Society. In 1823 when consulted by Sir John Sinclair about an inland communication between Edinburgh and London, Robert advised that a *railway was not only much more practicable but more commodious and useful for general intercourse than a canal.*[36]

By 1836 the lines of railway proposed in Robert's various reports traversed Scotland from the Tweed valley north to Perth and Aberdeen and from Edinburgh westwards to Stirling and Glasgow, more or less on the lines of the eventual network. **[27]** However, the estimated costs of his proposals were considerable and the financial climate for their execution was unfavourable. As steam locomotion developed, Robert lost his pre-eminence in this field in Scotland. His only railway proposal executed was the short Newton Colliery line from Little France on the Dalkeith road near Edinburgh, although his *Edinburgh Railway* work **[35]** to some extent facilitated the successful *Edinburgh & Dalkeith Railway* in 1831.

Robert's design practice for railways was basically the same as for canals and followed the traditional practice of Jessop, Rennie and Telford. He proposed lines as near level as practicable, avoided the use of heavy rolling stock to reduce track damage and designed inclined planes with stationary steam engines to overcome differences in level. As early as 1818 he advocated the adoption of 12 ft. long malleable iron edge rails in preference to the short cast iron rails then in common use.

In 1821 George Stephenson (1781-1848), in acknowledging Robert's influence on Birkinshaw's epoch-making malleable iron forerunner of the modern edge rail, paid him the tribute, *you have been at more trouble than any man I know of in searching into the utility of railways.*[36] However, by the following year his son Robert Stephenson (1803-59) who had conferred with Robert as consultant for the Stockton & Darlington Railway was rather less complimentary. After learning by enquiry *that Mr Stevenson had surveyed an immense quantity* [of railways] *but had not had the good fortune to get them into action,* he wrote to William James, projector of the Liverpool & Manchester Railway, *If he has executed any railway it must be of very trivial consequence. I hope we shall be able to keep him out of the Liverpool concern.*[38]

Robert's bridge engineering and highway planning in Scotland were more successful. His many projects, by no means all of which were executed, included two large bridges over the River Clyde at Glasgow. These were Hutcheson Bridge (1834-68) [28,29] and the 32ft. wide 14-span timber bridge (1832-46) erected at Portland Street [30] to accommodate traffic whilst Broomielaw Bridge was being built under Telford's direction. This timber bridge, one of the largest of its type in terms of width, proved so convenient for pedestrians that it was retained in use until 1846. Hutcheson Bridge erected by Robert's former assistant John Steedman as contractor for about £24,000 was considered one of the best examples of the segmental masonry arch bridge type in Britain. Unfortunately the bridge had a life of only 34 years because deepening of the river for navigation purposes undermined its piers.

Another fine example of Robert's work is the bridge over the River Forth at Stirling (1829-32) constructed by Kenneth Mathieson for about £17,000 and for which he also planned its town approach. The bridge still carries main road traffic. [31] This approach is not as imposing as Robert's earlier London and Regent Road approaches into central Edinburgh skirting Calton Hill, his proposals for which included sketch elevations of housing terraces [32] and open parapets at Regent's Bridge to enable its users to enjoy the fine views. From 1815-1819 he engineered the Regent Road approach, a work of particular difficulty because of its line and level, severance of Old Calton cemetery, extensive rock blasting and requirement of a massive retaining wall in front of the new High School. [33,34] He also provided the engineering input to Regent's Bridge for which the architect was Archibald Elliot.

Segmental arches characterise the style of Robert's masonry bridges, other fine examples of which still exist at Marykirk 1814 [35], Annan 1827, Allanton 1842, and on a smaller scale at Kearvaig 1828 executed by Alexander Gibb of Aberdeen on the Cape Wrath lighthouse access road. [36] The impressive Stannochy bridge c. 1824 near Brechin, if not by Robert, was almost certainly influenced by the design of Marykirk bridge. Similar arch profiles were adopted in his proposals for the Bridge of Don at Old Aberdeen 1823, Canonmills Bridge 1812-34 on a new northern approach to Edinburgh and in using iron for increasing the traffic capacity of existing bridges at Newcastle-upon-Tyne [37], Perth 1827 and North Bridge, Edinburgh 1832. State of the art designs by Robert for other bridge types included a slender laminated timber arch for Dornoch Firth in 1830 [38] probably influenced by John Green's work and, in 1820, a new type of underspanned suspension bridge. [39]

This new type of suspension bridge, which was originally intended for crossing the River Almond at Cramond near Edinburgh, was novel in that its roadway superstructure, a cast iron framework, rested on the chains rather than being suspended from them. This proposal together with Robert's authoritative accounts of other suspension bridges was publicised throughout Europe in his *Description of bridges of suspension*, 1821. Although not executed, several underspanned suspension bridges were erected in Europe and India by 1870 and in Britain numerous small spans on the truss principle which developed from the concept, the earliest by Robert being Abbey St. Bathans, Berwickshire c.1834, His publication encouraged the development of suspension bridges generally.

After Rennie's death for about two decades Robert can be

considered second only to the Telford-Gibb combination as the leading bridge engineer practising in Scotland. By c. 1830 his office library of bridge books was probably second to none in Britain. Robert's bridge practice of all types was further disseminated in a major contribution to the most comprehensive and influential work of its day, Weale's *The theory, practice and architecture of bridges* published in London from 1839. This work carried Robert's portrait as a frontispiece and five of his bridges were illustrated on 18 plates. His executed work, amounting to more than twenty bridges, was basically of state of the art traditional rather than innovative design.

More unusual tall structures than lighthouses upon which Robert advised in his private practice were the severely cracked tower of Montrose church (1811), Arbroath Abbey ruins (1815) and, his tallest memorial, the magnificent Melville monument which adorns St. Andrew Square, Edinburgh.

Engineers rarely receive the credit they deserve for their often essential contributions to the structural integrity of notable buildings. It was ever thus. The Melville column, except for the brief mention in David's Life of his father, is almost invariably considered to be the work of architect, William Burn, but let us look at Robert's role. In March 1821, together with Burn, he examined the 31 feet square foundation pit for the column, which was then 8 feet deep, and reported that as the monument was upwards of 140 feet high and weighed about 1,500 tons, it *becomes necessary to obtain the best foundation . . . such considerations naturally suggest the unpleasant aspect and even dangerous state of the hanging tower of Pisa, the spire of Salisbury Cathedral and other instances of failure in the foundation of lofty buildings . . . the foundation pit should now be dug to the depth of 12 feet before any final decision is entered into.*[39]

By 23 March the foundation pit had been duly excavated to a depth of 12 feet and Robert pronounced it *in all respects sufficient for the support of the building* without timber planking or piling. After specifying the form and method of construction of the masonry from 31 feet square at its base and diminishing *by equal scarsements of 5 inches to 22 feet square,* he then considered the strength of the walls of the column itself, modifying thicknesses and staircase dimensions. He preferred the use of Craigleith stone as being *not only of a beautiful and durable quality but it is also of a considerably greater specific gravity and strength of grit* than the stone from any other sandstone quarry with which he was acquainted.

Two months later the work below ground level had been executed in accordance with Robert's recommendations. In order to fund these alterations he urged the committee *to extend the funds to £500 or £600 a sum still too inconsiderable to be put in competition with the more certain stability of a building intended to perpetuate the memory of so illustrious a statesman as the late Viscount Melville.*[39] The project did go ahead and the scaffolding and tackling for the incredibly delicate task of raising and positioning the statue were carried out under Robert's direction using an iron balance crane of the type used at the Bell Rock, perhaps even the same one. [40]

Robert had a life-long interest in gaining and promoting knowledge and his writings, which were of a descriptive and practical character, appeared in more than sixty publications. Many were engineering reports, but about one-third achieved wider circulation through leading periodicals, encyclopedias and text-books, details of a selection of which, including his ten

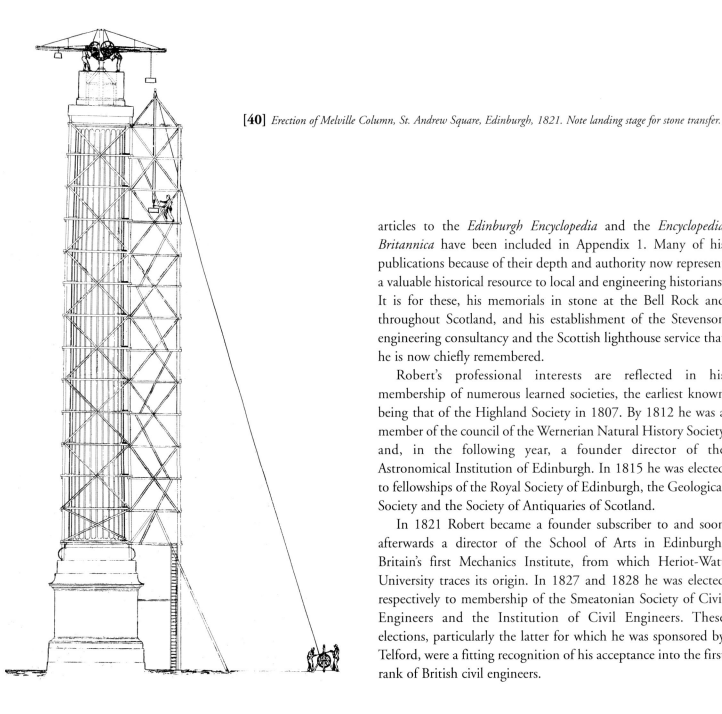

**[40]** *Erection of Melville Column, St. Andrew Square, Edinburgh, 1821. Note landing stage for stone transfer.*

articles to the *Edinburgh Encyclopedia* and the *Encyclopedia Britannica* have been included in Appendix 1. Many of his publications because of their depth and authority now represent a valuable historical resource to local and engineering historians. It is for these, his memorials in stone at the Bell Rock and throughout Scotland, and his establishment of the Stevenson engineering consultancy and the Scottish lighthouse service that he is now chiefly remembered.

Robert's professional interests are reflected in his membership of numerous learned societies, the earliest known being that of the Highland Society in 1807. By 1812 he was a member of the council of the Wernerian Natural History Society and, in the following year, a founder director of the Astronomical Institution of Edinburgh. In 1815 he was elected to fellowships of the Royal Society of Edinburgh, the Geological Society and the Society of Antiquaries of Scotland.

In 1821 Robert became a founder subscriber to and soon afterwards a director of the School of Arts in Edinburgh, Britain's first Mechanics Institute, from which Heriot-Watt University traces its origin. In 1827 and 1828 he was elected respectively to membership of the Smeatonian Society of Civil Engineers and the Institution of Civil Engineers. These elections, particularly the latter for which he was sponsored by Telford, were a fitting recognition of his acceptance into the first rank of British civil engineers.

# Chapter Three
## Alan Stevenson 1807-65 – Of Skerryvore Lighthouse fame

**Family recollections**

Alan was the eldest son of Robert and Jean to survive infancy. The nursery at 1 Baxter Place had three occupants when he was born, Jane, Thomas and Elizabeth, but a year later the twins Thomas and Elizabeth had died. Two months after their death another son Robert was born and Alan and Bob became close companions for each other.

Tutors visited the home to teach the boys until they were six when they were sent to the High School of Edinburgh. This was an ancient institution sited near the old University buildings in the Old Town. It was considered at the time to give the best education. It moved to new and splendid premises on the south side of the Calton Hill in 1829, close to the Stevenson boys' home. Alan did not leave the High School until July 1821 when he matriculated at Edinburgh University in the Faculty of Arts and in the Autumn took classes in Latin, Greek and Mathematics.

In the spring of his sixteenth year Alan received a formal letter from Robert asking for his decision as to a career. He replied as follows, written surely with his 'tongue in his cheek'!

'Dear Father, I take this opportunity of answering your letter in which you stated a desire that I would apply myself to some business and although I must confess I had a liking for the profession of a soldier, on receipt of your letter I determined to overcome this foolish wish and am happy to say I have succeeded. On further consideration I found in myself a strong desire for literary glory and I picked upon an advocate but there was a want of interest. It was the same way with a clergyman and as I am by no means fond of shop-keeping I determined upon an engineer, especially that all

with whom I have spoken on the subject recommend it and as you yourself seemed to point it out as the most fit situation in life I could desire. I only doubt that my talents do not lie that way, but in hopes that my choice will meet with your full approbation, I remain, my dear Father, Your ever affectionate and grateful son, Alan Stevenson.'[5]

He then signed a formal contract of apprenticeship to his father dated 'As from October 1822 - for learning the art and practice of a civil engineer, as exercised by him, for the space of five years, undertaking faithfully, diligently and honestly to attend to his said master's service by night and day and not to divulge any secrets which his master might entrust him.'

Alan was wrong that his talents 'did not lie that way ...' He became an engineer of outstanding ability within the comparative few working years that were granted to him. Probably the choice he made did lead to his early death. His health was never robust and it should have been obvious to his parents that the strong physique held by his father and grandfather had not been inherited by their eldest son. Travelling round Scotland to reach the distant lighthouse stations by sailing ships was still a tough and hazardous business. His mother worried constantly about him but with his mind made up Alan never looked back, and gave his heart to the job. He never at any time gave in to the messages his aching body must have been sending out to him.

Robert felt his son should learn some independence away from home, and was also aware of the limits of the Scottish environment that had been so far the whole of Alan's experience, so he arranged with the Rev. Charles Pettingal, in the London suburb of Twickenham, to receive Alan as a pupil. He gave lessons in classics and science. A report of his progress sent to his parents said:

'Mrs Pettingal and I are pleased with your son. His disposition is so mild, so amiable, so perfectly willing to do what is pointed out to him as right.'[5]

Alan had great personal charm and back home in Baxter Place he and his young brother Thomas, for whom he had a special affection, were involved in every kind of high-spirited mischief. Alan wrote parodies about the many visitors to his father's table, and could see a joke in almost any situation. To a certain extent Robert could share their laughter, but he was determined that his children should learn self-control as well as all the social skills of the day. This included, in Pettingal's words, an ability 'to bear a part in a ballroom and acquire an easy carriage.' The first quarter's account amounted to £87. 2s. and included expenditure on books and amusements. They visited the Isle of Wight, saw the Royal George stationed off Portsmouth, visited a circus, fair, and dockyard. He was much moved to see the miserable condition of prisoners who were passing through the dockyard who had been captured during the war with Denmark.

His first cousin Tom Smith, intellectually the most promising of Thomas Smith's children, joined him at Twickenham in August. Later Tom entered Pembroke College at Oxford. Alan was released from Twickenham in October as Robert wrote that 'Alan must be more of a man of business: the theory will do little for him in our way of life without the practice.' He sailed from London in the *James Watt* steam packet for Leith to attend Edinburgh University and worked for two hours daily in George Street as well where 'he was occupied to improve his hand.' In 1824 still only 17 years old he was left by his father at the Rinns of Islay where a new lighthouse was being built. Alexander Slight, one of his father's senior assistants, gave him instruction. The work was on an island exposed to the worst blasts of the Atlantic and Alan had to experience terrible conditions 'in hopes of him profiting by the practice of these works and in surveying.'

Every aspect of life was put in Alan's way by his father-including horse riding. Robert wrote to William Blackadder, his resident surveyor at Glamis, for a proposed railway.

'As I have an idle horse in the stable, and should you wish to have him in hand in going over the line, if you think that he [Alan] could be put up either with you or at the Sun Inn, I will send him from Fife next week. If you have room for him in your stable I think an hour's work in the morning and currying the horse would be excellent exercise for Mr Alan and a useful lesson through life. He would also have the advantage of riding daily-all things should be practised in youth.'[5]

Alan made himself proficient in French, Italian and Spanish with a wide knowledge of the standard literature of these languages. He had a great gift in the use of words and an appreciation of style in writing. He gave a paper to the Royal Physical Society on 'The causes of obscurity in style and the means of obviating them.' This had some original advice to authors on many aspects of writing. His great love of literature worried Robert, who feared he might take up writing as a career instead of engineering, but Alan remained faithful to his choice and read and wrote only as a relaxation in his spare time.

Travel followed in 1827 to Russia, Sweden and Holland. He

gained much insight into the working of the Russian mind. 'No country,' he wrote, 'is surely further removed from everything that is connected with liberty, happiness and religion.'

On a visit to Paris in 1834 he met Lèonor Fresnel, the eminent French scientist, who befriended and assisted him, giving him introductions to enable him to see any lighthouses he wished. Taking advantage of this opportunity he travelled extensively round the French coasts, and made full reports of all he saw which he sent to his father in a series of seventeen remarkable letters. The lights were not all in a good state of repair and efficiency, as this sad account makes clear:

'Tour de Cordouan
August 31st. 1834.
My dear Father,
Mr. Drouin the Contractor for the Lights of the Ocean landed me here yesterday with great difficulty and it has since blown an hurricane of rain and hail. You would be sadly disappointed to see this noble edifice which for want of timely repair is fast going to decay; and among other changes would miss the beautiful regal crown which surmounted the pediment of the door, but which last winter yielded to the effects of time and neglect and now lies a mass of ruins in the court. The rich carving which has been executed in a reticulated limestone of soft texture is also much disfigured. What would Louis XIV & XV say to this? The lantern alone has undergone some temporary repairs, but the storm of last night and today has forced the water through the joints and the vaulted staircase is swimming with water. I shall say nothing of the Chapel and other rooms which remain as formerly; the two altars still retaining the arcs [?] and small wooden crosses. On one of the altars I found the fragments of a broken *remonstrance*.'[40]

A visit with his brother David to undertake a survey at Lynas Point in Anglesey was to change Alan's personal life. It was there he met his future wife Margaret Scott Jones. He was 26 and Margaret 21. She lived in peaceful, beautiful green countryside at Lynon Hall, with a strict Victorian father and two sisters and three brothers. Only one rather poor portrait of Alan survives, made in his youth, but there is no doubt that he was very handsome. It was at a ball in Anglesey that he first met Margaret, and he never forgot her. It was to be eleven years, however, before Alan could return to marry her.

These eleven years were to see virtually the whole of Alan's staggering achievements in engineering. He completed Skerryvore, perhaps the most beautiful lighthouse in the world. He also made a steady progression with the mathematical precision of calculations for illuminants that were used by all lighthouse authorities.

From Alan's own account of Skerryvore, he tells us of his life in the second 'house', erected on the rock for thirty men, and how he had

'spent many a weary day and night at those times when the sea prevented any one going down to the rock, anxiously looking for supplies from the shore, and earnestly longing for a change of weather favourable to the recommencement of the works. For miles around nothing could be seen but white foaming breakers, and nothing heard but howling winds and lashing waves. At such seasons much of our time was spent in bed; for there alone we had effectual shelter from the winds and the spray, which searched every cranny in the walls of the barrack. Our slumbers, too, were at times fearfully interrupted by the sudden pouring of the sea over the roof, the rocking of the house on its pillars, and the spurting of water through the seams of the doors and windows, symptoms which to one suddenly aroused from sound sleep, recalled the appalling fate of the former barrack, which had been engulfed in the foam not twenty yards from our dwelling, and for a moment seemed to summon us to a similar fate. On two occasions, in particular, those sensations were so vivid as to cause almost every one to spring out of bed; and some of the men fled from the barrack by a temporary gangway, to the more stable but less comfortable shelter afforded by the bare wall of the lighthouse tower, then unfinished, where they spent the remainder of the night in the darkness and the cold.'[41]

On 11th September 1844 Alan and Margaret were married. She was 32 years old and they had three daughters and a son.

It is astonishing that Alan got to the church alive and in time for his wedding. In his 'day to day' diary in the month of August we realise how lucky Margaret was that he turned up!

'6th August: Off Port Patrick at 8 am in very strong easterly gale. Miserable day off Mull of Galloway and the Isle of Man, with south-east hurricane. Impossible to land at Point of Ayre because of the surf. Go to Ramsay and drive to Point of Ayre arriving at 9 pm. I am thoroughly fatigued and go to bed at 11.

8th August: Land at Cape Wrath at 6-in very heavy surf. I fall on the slippery quay and am nearly drawn back by the backdraft of the surf which wet me to the skin with some risk of injury and I got dried at the lighthouse.

18th August: (Sunday) Walk to Inverness (from Clachnaharry Loch) and attend morning and evening service. I take very ill and am forced to go to bed in the evening and take no dinner as my cough is very troublesome.'[5]

The inspection voyage he was on continued in this way until the 28th and two weeks later he was going up the aisle!

The married couple moved at once into 11 Windsor Street and then to Regent Terrace where his two eldest daughters Margaret and Dora enjoyed the large gardens that are still at the back of this beautiful street.

Alan's health was failing even before the birth of his son. He was disabled by a form of arthritis and a creeping paralysis. He handed over his work for the Northern Lighthouse Board (much of it well advanced by himself) to his brothers David and Thomas in 1853. A plea for a pension was made to the Treasury but the papers were lost and he received nothing. He moved to a smaller house in Portobello and then over to Kirkside, a house in the Angus village of St Cyrus. Thomas and Maggie, trying to be helpful, took Kathleen and Bob for a short time when they were still resident at No. 1 Inverleith Terrace, but Thomas could not handle these two gifted 'free thinking' children and Alan took them away after only a few months.

During the lonely, often storm-bound hours when he was building Skerryvore, Alan had translated from Greek a number of hymns by Synesius[42] and he sent them to the Rev. David Hogarth who lived in the Rectory at Portland in Dorset. He was an old university friend. As late in his life as 1861 Alan stayed there for three months translating Homer and Lucretius.

A friend of both Robert and Alan's wrote a letter from Portsmouth to William Wordsworth in the Summer of 1840. He was Captain Basil Hall, son of Sir James Hall, the famous Scottish geologist. The captain was, if anything, even more well-known to the public than his father, and the poet, a keen reader of newspapers, would have been flattered to receive a letter from him. In his letter he says that Alan has asked for an introduction, and that he does not hesitate to bring Alan to his notice. The letter was not sent, and some time after, the unfortunate captain was declared insane and taken to Haslar, the Royal Navy's hospital at Gosport, where he died in 1844.

Another friend, James Wilson, who knew and sometimes visited Wordsworth at Rydal Mount, did tell him of Alan, living on the most dangerous rocks off the Scottish coast, building Skerryvore. Wordsworth gave James Wilson locks of his hair, laurel leaves from his garden, and autographs, some of which were posted to Alan. James Wilson, who was a zoologist, gave a copy of one of his books to Wordsworth, *A voyage round the coasts of Scotland and the Isles,* which was published that same year.[43]

All the above contact was to take place through friends who acted as intermediaries, and Wordsworth and Alan never met. In 1848 Alan sent him a copy of his *Account of the Skerryvore Lighthouse* to which the 77-year old poet replied with a short but finely expressed letter which thanked him not only for the present of the book but for his esteemed work in making the seas safe.

'Rydal Mount
Ambleside
May 20th 1848

My dear Sir
Accept my grateful thanks for the valuable Present of your Account of the Skerry Lighthouse &c from the perusal of which I promise myself confidently both instruction and pleasur, in no small degree. Every one who think and feels must take a lively interest in your lonely situation and most important employment. This be assured I do eminently, and with sincere good wishes for your health and well-being.
I remain
My dear Sir
faithfully your
much obliged
Wm Wordsworth.'

Alan Stevenson Esq[r] &c &c &c
to the care of Mess[rs] [A. & C.] Black    North Bridge Edinburgh[5]

Alan was deeply religious and observed the Sabbath day, but during the building of Skerryvore he made an appeal for the workmen to turn out on a Sunday. They obliged him but he was to suffer agonies of remorse about it and he wrote a long letter of apology some years later to John Sinclair, then working as Assistant Keeper, Pentland Skerries, Huna, [by] Wick.

'Edinburgh 10 March 1846.

Dear Sir,
I feel it to be my duty to address a few words to you on the subject of the greatest moment, which I *habitually* disregarded while you were engaged some years ago at the Skerryvore Lighthouse works under my direction. The difficulty of the work in which we were engaged, and the

uncertainty of the weather, I at that time considered as a sufficient plea for violating the sanctity of the Lord's Day; but I have now seriously to declare my deliberate and sober conviction that, although there be works of necessity and mercy which *ought* to be done on the Day of Rest (according to the precept and example of our Blessed Lord himself), it may well be doubted whether almost any of the operations at the Skerryvore were of the kind to be so exempted; while in the great majority of the cases which occurred, no honest ground for each exemption could have been pleaded. (Jeremiah, xvii. 21, 22, 23.) ... "the Christian Sabbath was openly profaned, almost without the shadow of pretext,"'[5]

Alan was a frequent visitor to France where he became greatly attracted to the Roman Catholic religion and was a close friend of the organist at Amiens Cathedral - he would sit by him in the organ loft during the celebration of high mass. He returned to Scotland and he finally had to come to terms with the established church. When he died he did not know that his own son would be a profound agnostic, a grandson a Roman Catholic priest, and that a great-grandson would become a Buddhist!

Alan's rigorous and careful education prepared him for his life as a practising and an innovative engineer but his health was shattered at an early age. His fine mind, was equally at home with classic authors and contemporary writers as with the advancement of lighthouse lighting technology, and he collaborated with other leading engineers such as Telford and Fresnel. Endowed with great tact and sensitivity, he used his great intelligence to push forward his own knowledge gained from the close work with Fresnel without hurting his father's feelings and rigidly held opinions. He left his two younger brothers with careful far-seeing guidelines before he retired.

He was a man of astonishing physical courage against the adversity of pain. Expressed in many poems to his wife Margaret and to his children was the love he had for them.

When his mother, Jane Stevenson, died at the beginning of March 1846 Alan wrote this poem:

'ON MY DEAREST MOTHER
Of gentle soul, to all that knew her dear,
The tender mother, best of friends lies here,
Whose darling wish was comfort to impart,
To cheer the drooping, soothe the aching heart.
Love, truth, and meekness breathed in all she said;
Faith bless'd her life, hope smooth'd her dying bed.

Dearest of mothers! best of friends, farewell;
These words sincere a son's affection tell;
Through life thy virtues were his joy and pride,
In death his best example and his guide.
Our social hopes and fears, alas! are o'er;
A mother's love now cheers our hearth no more.'[44]

For the twelve years after his retirement Alan's courageous spirit never failed him. **[41]** He continued to lecture and write and the Commissioners gave him a small pension, much eroded by the expensive treatment which he hoped would alleviate his illness. The cause of death was given as 'General paralysis - 8 years.' As his father had wished, he is buried with his wife Margaret Scott Jones in the family burial ground in the New Calton Cemetery in Edinburgh.

## A professional aspect

Alan Stevenson with his classical background and M.A. degree can be considered the most intellectual of the Stevenson engineers. At Edinburgh University he had gained under Sir John Leslie the Fellowes prize for excellence as an advanced student of natural philosophy. In 1827-28, before completing his training, encouraged by and with access to the notes of his father, he compiled a list of British lighthouses with their identifying features. It was published as a pocket book for the benefit of mariners entitled *The British Pharos* and, as the first comprehensive work of its kind, proved sufficiently popular to require a second edition within three years.

In 1830, having completed his training, Alan was appointed clerk of works to the Northern Lighthouse Board working under his father. During the next three years he was engaged on several new lighthouses, including Girdleness, Aberdeen, where he may have been responsible for specifying the decorative cast-iron ornamentation including, birds, crocodiles and rustic style bamboo balustrade with animal feet. **[42]**

The Board, acting on Robert's advice, had been slow to develop the potential of Augustin Fresnel's dioptric or lens system of improved lighthouse illumination introduced in France in 1822, and was encountering criticism on this account from David Brewster and others. Alan took the lead in defending the Board from this charge and in progressing this innovation in Britain. During the summer of 1834, he visited lighthouses and workshops in France, gaining knowledge of the best French practice from the work of Léonor Fresnel, Jean-Baptiste François Soleil and Isaac-Ami Bordier-Marcet. In 1835 his influential *Report . . . on illumination of lighthouses by means*

**[42]** *Girdleness Lighthouse, Aberdeen, 1833. Ornamental ironwork. Note bamboo style balustrade and crocodiles on ladder side.*

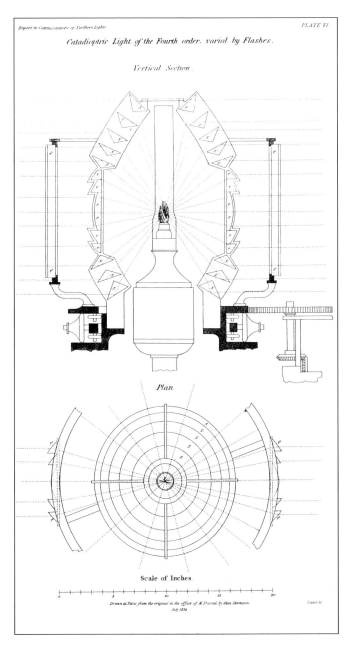

PLATE VI

*Catadioptric Light of the Fourth order, varied by Flashes.*

*Vertical Section.*

*Plan.*

*Scale of Inches.*

0      5      10      15      20

*Drawn at Paris, from the original in the office of M. Fresnel, by Alan Stevenson.*
*July 1834.*

[43] *Alan's re-drawing at Paris of a Fresnel fixed small light, 1834.*

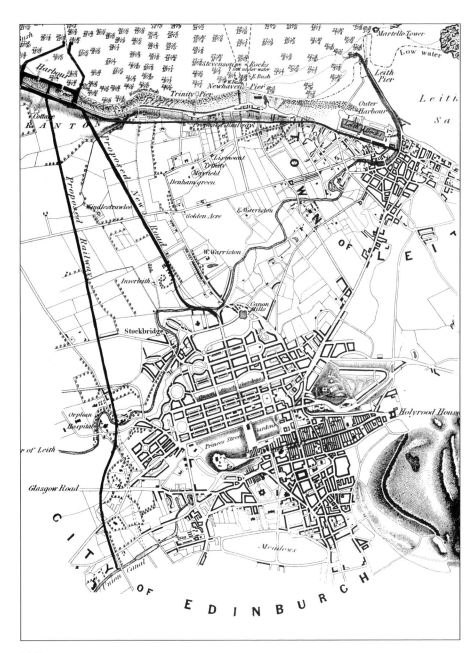

[44] *Granton Harbour proposals with road and railway routes to Edinburgh, 1834. Only the northern part of the road, now Granton Road, was built. From Robert and Alan's report.*

*of lenses* was published which included a valuable account of French practice and recommended application of the dioptric system in Scotland. [43]

The Board thoroughly approved of Alan's initative and diligence in this matter and soon afterwards the revolving light at Inchkeith and, in 1836, the fixed light at the Isle of May were converted to the new system under his direction. The result was a three-fold order of increase in brightness and the general adoption of the dioptric system in British lighthouses. In 1836 he designed and superintended the installation of the first dioptric light in England at Start Point, Devon, for Trinity House of Deptford Strond.

In c. 1832 Alan was taken into partnership in the firm by his father, the business then being known as *Robert Stevenson & Son.* From 1838, when David became a partner, until 1846, it operated as *Robert Stevenson & Sons.* Between 1832 and 1838 Alan's work included preparation of a chart of the Scottish coast, Ballyshannon harbour improvement, Granton harbour [44], plans for Edinburgh & Glasgow, Edinburgh & Dundee and Perth & Dunkeld railways, Perth harbour, and navigation improvements to the rivers Tay and Ribble. Although it must have been disappointing for Robert and Alan that their railway proposals came to nothing, they undoubtedly had a greater affinity with the maritime work which proved to be the mainstay of their business. Soon afterwards Alan wrote an authoritative account of the development of *Sea Lights,* from the earliest times until c. 1838, which was published in successive editions of the *Encyclopedia Britannica* in 1840 and 1857.

From December 1837 until August 1843 Alan was intensively and almost exclusively employed by the Northern Lighthouse Board on his most important work, the design and

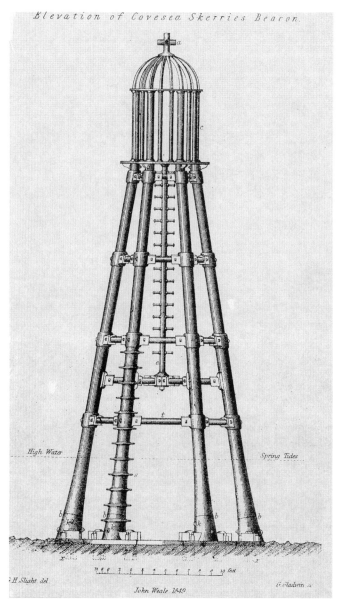

**[46]** *Covesea Skerries iron beacon, 1844. From Alan's Lighthouses treatise, 1850.*

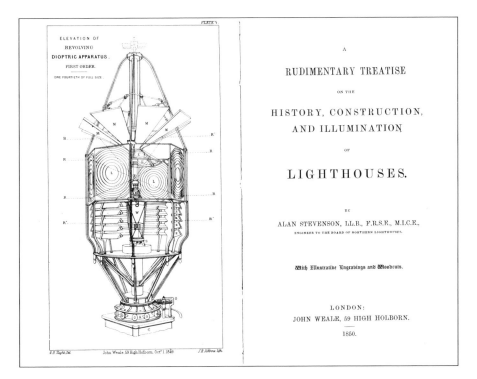

[47] *Alan's Lighthouses treatise with elevation of revolving dioptric apparatus 1st order, 1850. This apparatus was devised for and used at Skerryvore Lighthouse.*

construction of Skerryvore lighthouse. [45] It had been mutually agreed that this was too arduous a task for Robert who was by then sixty-five. In January 1843 Alan succeeded Robert as Engineer to the Board and for the next decade, until paralysis dictated his retirement, he was responsible for the design and construction of numerous other new lighthouses and a cast iron beacon at Covesea Skerries. [46]

Alan's reputation was based mainly on his design and execution of Skerryvore lighthouse, his definitive account of which, together with his notes on lighthouse illumination, were handsomely published in 1848.[41] Two years later these notes were extended and more widely propagated through *A rudimentary treatise on the history, construction and illumination of lighthouses,* dedicated to his *dear friend* Léonor Fresnel. [47] Both works were technically valuable to maritime engineers for a century.

Skerryvore Lighthouse, 155 ft. high on a dreadful storm-swept, reef exposed to the full fetch of the Atlantic 12 miles west-south-west of Tiree, was one of the world's greatest lighthouse achievements. It was erected and serviced from a purpose built harbour and base at Hynish to Alan's design. [48] The method of conducting the work was basically similar to that for the Bell Rock lighthouse using a temporary beacon barrack. This barrack erected in 1838, the first season's work, was totally destroyed by a storm soon after its completion. The eventual creation of the lighthouse by 1843, under great difficulties and at a cost of about £90,000, severely tried Alan's courage, patience

[48] *Hynish dry-dock, Tiree, Argyllshire, c. 1844.*

[49] *Skerryvore Lighthouse lamp.*

and health and fully exercised his undoubted ability.

This lighthouse was more scientifically designed than any of its predecessors, with sides curved in the form of *a solid generated by the revolution of a rectangular hyperbole about its assymptote as a vertical axis*[45] which had the lowest centre of gravity of various possibilities considered. The result was widely acknowledged to be the finest example for mass combined with elegance of outline of any rock tower. Alan's design strongly influenced that of the virtually identical Alguada reef lighthouse in the Indian Ocean from 1862-65. [119]

Skerryvore lighthouse's revolving dioptric apparatus, the optical elements of which were made in Paris under the immediate superintendence of Léonor Fresnel, was at the time the most advanced in the world. With Alan's innovation of prismatic rings instead of mirrors below the central belt its dioptric effect was greatly extended. [47] The light source was an intricate and beautifully executed oil lamp with four concentric wicks. [49]

Alan further improved the efficiency of the dioptric system by constructing refractors in rhomboidal intead of rectangular pieces of glass thus obviating obscuration in any one direction. For the same reason he introduced inclined astragals into lanterns, a practice often adopted in later lighthouses and lanterns. [96] He also introduced an improvement in fixed dioptric apparatus by converting Fresnel's narrow lenses into a truly cylindrical drum and adding prismatic rings above and below the central belt. This feature, later improved by Thomas, was a development of [47] made possible by the manufacturing skill of Messrs. Cookson of Newcastle. The drum, by equally distributing light all round, extended the dioptric action through the whole height of the apparatus.

In 1830 Alan, sponsored by Telford and other leading engineers, became a corresponding member of the Institution of Civil Engineers and, in 1838, a Fellow of the Royal Society of Edinburgh, serving as a member of its council from 1843-45. In 1840 the University of Glasgow conferred on him an honorary degree of LL.B. The Emperor of Russia and the Kings of Prussia and Holland presented him with medals in acknowledgement of his merit as a lighthouse engineer.

Alan's writings exhibit clarity and style. A confident example is his masterly critique of Smeaton's basic design analogy of the Eddystone Lighthouse tower with the trunk of an oak tree. *There is no analogy, he wrote, between the case of the tree and that of the lighthouse, the tree being assaulted at the top, and the lighthouse at the base; and although Smeaton goes on . . . to suppose the branches to be cut off, and the water to wash round the base of the oak, it is to be feared that the analogy is not thereby strengthened; as the* materials *composing the tree and the tower are so different, that it is impossible to imagine that the same opposing forces can be resisted by similar properties in both.*

*It is obvious, indeed, that Smeaton has unconsciously contrived to obscure his own clear conceptions in an attempt to connect them with a fancied natural analogy between a tree which is shaken by the* wind *acting on its* bushy top *and which resists its enemy by the* strength *of its fibrous texture and wide-spreading ligamentous roots, and a tower of masonry, whose weight and* friction *alone enable it to meet the assault of the* waves *which wash round its* base; *and it is very singular, that . . . he does not appear to have regarded those properties of the tree which he has most fitly characterized as "its elasticity" and the "coherence of its parts." One is tempted to conclude that Smeaton had, in the first place, reasoned quite*

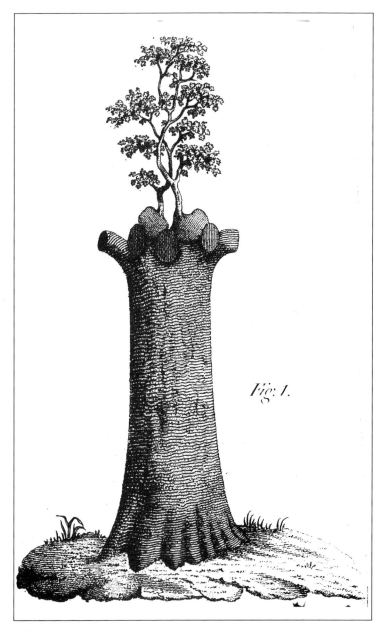

*Fig: 1.*

**[50]** *Smeaton's tree trunk analogy for Eddystone Lighthouse design. From Smeaton's Narrative, 1791.*

soundly, and arrived, by a perfectly legitimate process, at his true conclusion, and that it was only in the vain attempt to justify these conclusions to others, and convey to them conceptions which a large class of minds can never receive, that he has misrepresented his own mode of reasoning.

In the paragraph preceding that which refers to the tree 80 [64 in Smeaton's *A narrative of the building . . . of the Edystone lighthouse, 1791 -* **50**], he has, in point of fact, clearly developed the true views of the subject; and, with the single exception of the illusion to the oak, he has discussed the question throughout in masterly style. In a word, then, the sum of our knowledge appears to be contained in the following proposition - 'that, as the ultimate stability of a sea-tower, viewed as a monolithic mass, depends, caeteris paribus, on the lowness of its centre of gravity, the general notion of its form is that of a cone; but that as the forces to which its several horizontal sections are opposed decrease towards its top in a rapid ratio, the solid should be generated by the revolution of some curve line convex to the axis of the tower, and gradually approaching to parallelism with it.' And this is, in fact, a general description of the Eddystone Tower devised by Smeaton.[46]

Alan, the first member of the family to apply an academic approach to his work, proved to be a lighthouse engineer of truly outstanding ability during his short professional life. On his death the Commissioners of the Northern Lighthouse Board recorded *their deep and abiding regrets for the loss of a man whose services had been to them invaluable and whose works combined profound science and practical skill and conferred lasting honour and benefit on his country.*[47] [**51**]

Engraved by W. & A. K. Johnston.

[**51**] *Skerryvore Lighthouse's commemorative tablet. From Alan's Account of the Skerryvore Lighthouse, 1848.*

# Chapter Four

## David Stevenson 1815-1886 - River improver and consolidator of the dynasty

### Family recollections

Born in Baxter Place, like all the second generation, David went to the High School in October 1824 and spent six years there. It was then still in Infirmary Street and moved to its New Town site in 1829. He was only able to enjoy its proximity to his home in Baxter Place for one term. Lessons came easily to him and he won many prizes. His father encouraged him to study subjects other than the Latin and Greek which would have enabled him to get a university degree, and although this never appeared to detrimentally affect his career as an engineer, it was a decision he later regretted.

A natural writer, throughout his life he was to take copious notes of details on his travels useful to him to recall or make a point. He wrote a diary which his father required him to keep of his first voyage to the northern lighthouses when he was thirteen years old. The trip in August 1828 was aboard the *Regent* and lasted for a month. David's diary is neatly written, although the handwriting gets a little wobbly when the seas were rough, and it is full of lively character and keen observations. Two young cousins, Alexander and William Swan, were with him. There was no favouritism shown to the children and all the passengers were expected to lend a hand with the crew, who numbered fourteen.

[August 1828] Monday 18. Embarked at Newhaven in the Regent tender boat at six P.M. with our party consisting of Mr Moconochie, Mr Bell, Mr A. Cuningham, Mr Reid, and my companions, Mr A. Robertson, and my cousins A. and W. Smith with my father being on his annual voyage to the Lighthouses. Our gallant ship being under the command of Captain Soutar. Her cargo consisting of the aparatus for the Lighthouses now building at Cape Wrath. The Regent's tonnage is 141 tons Register though she is only at present half loaded.

On our way down the Firth we landed at the Island of Inchkeith and were very much gratified with a view of the Lighthouse. Mr Bonnyman the principal keeper was very attentive in shewing us all his apparatus. He was one of the masons at the building of the Bell Rock Lighthouse in 1809 when he had the misfortune to lose one of his fingers. We here also met with an old Lighthouse Pilot of the name of Noble who had had 20 children. On being asked by my Father how a certain pleasure boat sailed he replied "Sail Sir, how the Devil could she sail, when the party played at the *Cairts* [cards] on the sabath day." After leaving Inchkeith we had a very pleasant sail toward the Isle of May and with the help of the moon we could see the coast of Fife and before going to bed we had both the revolving light of Inch Keith and the stationary light of the Isle of May distinctly in view. Tuesday 19th. After seeing the Lighthouse [on the Isle of May] which here is upon a grand scale we took a walk round the island. The first thing pointed out to us was a precipitous part of the rock on the western side of the island where our incautious and importionate Pointer sliped his hold while scrambling for birds nests and eggs and falling into the water he was afterwards found quite dead with a severe contusion on his head. After winding up a curious *zig-zag* path we reached the top of the island and aproaching another precipitous face of rock we contrived by shouting, clapping hands, and throwing stones, to put thousands of sea gulls to flight. But although they almost darkned the sky Mr Pithie the light keeper asured us that the major part of the birds had left the island with their young so that what we saw were chiefly the herring, and laughing, gulls, the Marrot [marrott; guillemot] and Picktarnie [picketarnie; pictarnie; tern] having already migrated. In the course of our walk we visited two insulated columnar masses of rock measuring about 30 or 40 feet in height called the *pilgrims*. We also coasted round *Pilgrims bay* and went to the *Bishops well* and visited the Chapel, and then after embarked in our boat from the ship under the Pilotage and guidance of our worthy friend and galant commander Captain Soutar. In aproaching this curious and kind of sacred island we entered by *Kirken Haven* and left it by *Monks Wick*. It may be remarked that all the names such as *Altarstones* &c have reference to the church, the Chapel here having in former times been a dependency of the Monastery of *Pittinweem*. But from this and other particulars my father refers us to Sybalds history of Fife.'[5]

Towards the end of the voyage they arrived at Largs:

'Later that day we anchored opposite the church of Largs in 20 fathoms and took a view of this overgrown village. Its resident population numbers perhaps 2,000 people, for such are the facilities afforded by the numerous steamboats upon the Clyde that Largs and its immediate neighbourhood contain handsome marine villas which are occupied by the citizens of Glasgow during the bathing season. In my father's recollection it consisted of a few thatched hamlets.
At an early hour next morning the Captain and the crew were astir and set up the rigging of the ship which, owing to the continued drought, had become slack: for the support of the mast in gales of wind it is of consequence to have the rigging set tautly up. Here our forecabin friends-the Commissioners-left us with the dog Hew to join the *Albion* steamer leaving for Glasgow.'[5]

The *Regent* then sailed for the Isle of Man where the lighthouses at Point of Ayre and Calf Island; were inspected. David noted that over 300 boats were employed at the Manx herring fishing, each with 8 or 9 seamen, but that the herrings seemed to have shifted their ground and had become very scarce. On the small Calf Island

'our dog Dickie killed a rabbit, a circumstance which gave my father regret. Some of us minor folk thought a single rabbit would never be missed among the hundreds that were seen which led to some remarks tending to contradict our views with regard to the right of property.
On coming on board at the Point of Ayre we had all expressed a desire to know where we were now bound but we had the old answer of 'we know nothing on this ship'. [A standard joke in the lighthouse service.] We must confess that we now look with a certain kindliness towards *Auld Reekie* and my father acknowledges that this desire is considerably increased from a late falling off in the dessert. We have not had for some days the full display of figs, raisins, prunes and almonds, the steward having been able to supply our dessert plates with only two kinds of dried fruit. It is further charged against us that visages became lengthened when the steward announced that we had just finished the last can of jelly. Perhaps it was for these weighty considerations that the ship now turned homewards and we were happy to find that we should soon sail up the Clyde towards Glasgow.'[5]

Next year David went on another lighthouse voyage. Robert took him and his brothers, Alan, and twelve year old Tom, on the journey. Not only did they visit Scotland, but this time the boat went to Wales and Ireland as well. A storm, which kept the travellers at Lerwick and off Kirkwall for six days, would have terrified many adults let alone a 15 year old boy, but seemed to have little effect on David. He had an excellent brain, cool head and steady heart.

Robert recognised David's potential and planned for this second son with great care. He knew the value of a thorough apprenticeship and of learning from basics as he had done. In the autumn Robert took him over to Cupar in Fife, on the 'Defiance' coach, to work for a Mr James Scott, engineer and millwright. David describes how he worked 'in moleskin jacket, ... first at wood and then to some extent at iron work.' In those days much of the machinery, particularly connected with agriculture, was made of wood and so the business of millwright was often combined with engineering. He was lodged with a 'respectable widow' and installed as his 'own master.' David writes that 'a box passed to and fro' from Edinburgh once every fortnight bringing sundry edibles, but nevertheless my housekeeping in lodgings was very indifferent. I dined often on sausages or Finnan Haddock and had a headache almost every day'. David grew to a height of only 5 foot 8 inches and possibly this spartan diet had something to do with it! In the early miniatures done of him and without wearing his spectacles he was a very handsome young man, always well dressed.

It is obvious, reading from his account, that David was very homesick and therefore delighted when Mr Scott sent him off to fit up new machinery at the flax spinning mills of Malleny which were only 8 miles from home. He could walk into Baxter Place on a Saturday and return on the Monday.

He writes of two hair-raising incidents at Malleny:

'Once, on walking to Edinburgh and coming down the steep road to Currie which is bounded by hedges on either side, a gun was fired and the bullet *whisked* past me, evidently within a yard of my head. Supposing it to be some boys firing a pistol I at once sprang up on a small embankment to shew myself above the hedge and prevent another discharge, when I found to my dismay that the bullet came from two men in the field at a short distance, who were aiming at a target against the hedge, and *directly* opposite the spot where I was standing. The shooters were not less discomfited than I was and hurried up to learn the result of their carelessness. The ground was covered with snow, the road impassable for carts and I supose I myself almost the only traveller, and they had presumed that in that forlorn unfrequented farm road they might use any liberty with perfect safety.'[48]

He had a second narrow escape from death with the water wheel, 30 foot in diameter, which still stands at Malleny. Taking a short cut and trying to climb up from the wheelhouse to the flat above via the wheel using the buckets as a ladder landed him in moments of terror:

'The wheel itself was always 'ranced' as it is called, or made fast by beams put through the spokes so as to prevent it from moving while the alterations on the mill gearing were being made. I commenced to *clamber* up the side of the great wheel and had nearly reached the top, when buckets and spokes began slowly to revolve and I saw the whole enormous mass was in steady motion. I continued to tread with my feet and to clutch with my hands the revolving buckets, but no sooner were they grasped than like a prisoner in the tread mill I found them sink below me and saw that I could not possibly gain the top as the harder I worked, the faster the wheel seemed to go. After a few seconds I decided to take my chance of being able to jump off as I reached the ground. Happily for me a plank had been left across the 'ark' or chamber in which the lower half of the wheel works and I stepped off upon it unhurt. Had the plank not been left there, I must have been carried down with the wheel and if not killed outright certainly seriously hurt.'[48]

Terrified that his mates might have lost arms or legs when the wheel started to move all the heavy machinery inside the mill, David lost his nerve to confront the boss and slipped out of sight behind some trees. He observed his workmates coming out of the mill blaming each other for not rancing the wheel following some work that had been done earlier in the day! The wheel had been left standing as it had stopped with its buckets full of water, and David's weight was all that it had required to set it in motion again. Mr Scott and his men, hearing of his narrow escape, were in fact horrified at the neglect of the wheel.

His apprenticeship to Robert, like his brother Alan's, was formidable. It encompassed everything from the surveying of harbours and rivers, railway works at Coventry and railway tunnelling at Liverpool, road building in Ireland and lighthouse construction in all its various stages. At the age of 16, he was sent to the bridge works at Stirling where he was taught to dress stones [52] and later to Glasgow. But practical experience on its own was not enough. From 1831 to 1835, David also attended

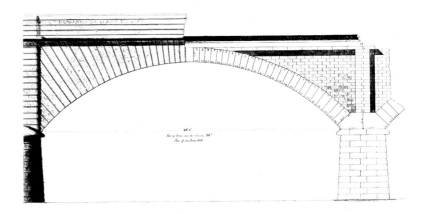

[52] *Stirling Bridge drawing from Robert's office, c. 1829, re-drawn 1841. Young David helped to dress at least one of the variable depth, greenstone, archstones.*

Edinburgh University, studying with Professors Wallace, Forbes, Hope, Jameson, Low (agriculture), and D. B. Reid (practical chemistry, etc.). In his free evenings he went for classes in drawing and mathematics, and if there was any extra time after that, he spent it in the office learning the family business. While still an apprentice, he had amassed sufficient knowledge to deliver the first of several papers to the Society of Arts in Scotland.

Two weeks later, after his apprenticeship was finished, he was appointed resident engineer in charge of the harbour works at Granton by the Duke of Buccleuch. For this, his salary was £150 per annum. At the same time he was offered a job at the Thames Tunnel in London but neither David's father nor mother relished this idea much and he accepted the job close to home at Granton.

David's appointment to the Duke of Buccleuch was not to last. Before two years were completed he had professional disagreements over the harbour plans which he felt were inadequate, and he was prepared to resign rather than compromise his views. Robert was delighted to welcome him to the office but first David decided to travel abroad. His brother, Alan, had been to Russia, but America was David's choice. Accordingly he sailed for New York in March 1837 and visited the principal places in the United States and Canada, and afterwards went to France, Italy, Switzerland, Germany and Holland. When he went to America there were no steam Atlantic packets and trips by amateurs were comparatively few. On his return to Scotland late in 1837 he extended his American notes, working sometimes to two and three o'clock in the morning. In 1838 he published the result, his book, *Sketch of the Civil Engineering of North America*. It showed the development of pioneering engineering in the States, the wonderful dawn that was flooding into the New World. He took fresh ideas from this country and came back with much that had a major impact here.

In his book, David restricted himself to professional matters concerning America. He was lucky to arrive at New York because his ship the *Sheffield*.

'was close beset by field ice off the banks of Newfoundland for about 16 hours which, as appeared when she was docked in New York, carried off her false keel and stripped away every square foot of copper off her bottom. Our Captain who had made more than 100 voyages between Liverpool and New York and had never *touched* ice before was in great fear for his ship. As it happened we got clear of ice in what has been called 'the nick of time' as we were overtaken by a hard gale; had it come on a few hours earlier when we were among the ice it would have inevitably sent the ship to the bottom.'

The voyage home was equally dangerous:

'It so happened further that I had rather an unpleasant landing in Europe on my return voyage in the Francois Premier, Captain Pell. ... The captain notwithstanding the state of the wind and sea determined at all hazards to get his ship into harbour. He spent the forenoon in arranging his plans, determining to run in and drop his anchors over the bows whenever she was within the pier heads to check her way. Accordingly having slackened our way as much as possible till high water, the Francois entered the pier heads which were crowded with people to see the sight. The signal was given to let go the anchors but no sooner had the strain come on the windlass than the whole of it gave way and was carried right over the bows of the ship and curiously enough over the head of the mate who was not in the least hurt. The ship unchecked continued her course up the harbour of Havre striking first one then another ship until she had damaged half a dozen & she herself more than any of them. It was a strange feeling to be standing on the quarter deck of a 900 ton ship under no earthly command of helm or sail, careering through a crowded harbour with tiers of vessels on either side of us. On examination the timber of the windlass was found to be quite rotten and had it been necessary on the previous night with a high sea & heavy gale to drop anchor off a lee shore it is not difficult to predict what would have been the result.'

In his Journal, written from Paris in 1837, David (aged 22) writes:

'... Of Churches, Notre Dame and the Pantheon are splendid

also La Madelene and Lorella are modern. The Louvre Gallery of pictures and sculpture is splendid. The Palais Royale and the shops and cafes which are on a magnificent scale is worthy of notice, as well as the many arcades with which Paris abounds. Taking Paris all in all I am disappointed. There is much that is magnificent combined with a far greater proportion that is wretched. With the exception of the Boulevards there is not a decent street in all Paris. The large gutters in the middle of the street, the want of footpaths and the very close contact with the nose and person with the Butcher shops, eating houses, pawn brokers, etc, makes the walking of the streets a most unpleasant and disgusting pastime. I was much struck in Paris with the seeming want of stamina that is found in the French character. They are a people pleased and delighted with trifles and the very amusements which afforded them the greatest gratification would be looked on by Englishmen as only fit for children. If a man dismounts to adjust his stirrup he will not fail to be encircled, not by a mob of boys-but bearded men gazing with open mouths and seeming quite unconscious of the absurdity either of their appearance or their conduct. Such sights as this are decidedly a characteristic of Paris and Parisians ... They may safely be said to conform to the laws of no religion for the Catholic religion at least in Paris is no religion at all.'5

When David returned to Edinburgh, he was made a partner in the family firm of Robert Stevenson and Sons. He joined his brother Alan and his father. It was May 1838, and Robert was almost 70. Alan was immersed in plans for the lighthouse at Skerryvore so David was assumed as 'managing partner.' Working well into the night he pulled the firm into profit and

also established for himself a wide reputation as a water engineer. In 1846, Robert finally retired, and Thomas Stevenson succeeded him, the firm being renamed D. & T. Stevenson. Alan had renounced his nominal partnership to concentrate exclusively on his position as Lighthouse Engineer to the Commissioners.

As Alan gradually became unable to carry out his duties as lighthouse engineer through ill-health, David and Thomas combined to take the weight of work from him. They built 29 new lighthouses round the Scottish coast between 1854 and 1880 including Dhu Heartach. The Stevenson name was now known world-wide and orders for lighthouses and technical expertise came from Burma, Japan, New Zealand, Australia and Canada. Because of David's depth of understanding of mathematics and science he was able to work in areas of new development. Besides designing heavy machinery, engineers everywhere were experimenting with gas and electricity and the Stevensons had to keep ahead. Robert's great curiosity about every aspect of life had been handed on to his sons and they tackled details of the astonishing variety of work that landed on their desks with scrupulous care. They learnt to be very careful indeed about sharing experimental knowledge with competitors and the riposte 'hush, hush' was a joke in the family for three generations.

But it was not all work for David, because by this time he was a happily married man. He had been particularly fortunate in his choice of Elizabeth Mackay as his life partner. [53] Her brother, Alexander, was a close friend of his, and the Mackay family lived nearby in Forth Street. The first mention of a close friendship between the Stevensons and the Mackay family comes in Thomas Smith's will where he appoints James Mackay, junior, Goldsmith in Edinburgh, as one of the trustees for the disposition of his estate. As teenagers, David and Elizabeth had spent much time together and had carved their initials on a tree on the banks of the River Forth at Stirling. She was 14 years old, he was 16. They became engaged before David started his job at Granton and married on 3 June 1840. There is an embossed leather album, given to Elizabeth by her mother for a new year gift in 1836, which is filled with drawings and scraps showing how much she was in love with David. Her future brother-in-law Alan has written into it several verses for her.

David and Elizabeth lived for the early years of their marriage at 12 Union Street. Their daughters, Elizabeth, Jane, Georgina and Mary were born there. Another child called Georgina Burke, a niece of Elizabeth Mackay, was adopted at birth when her father was lost at sea and her mother died a few weeks later. She was known as 'Gina', to distinguish her from Georgina Stevenson. By 1850 they had moved to 8 Forth Street and Elizabeth had the son they wanted so much, Robert James.

It was the same year as his grandfather Robert died, and also Robert Louis Stevenson came into the world for Thomas and his wife Maggie at 8 Howard Place. They all passed each other like 'ships in the night' in that eventful year marking the mid-century. Robert James was known to Louis and everyone else as 'Bo'. [54,55] He was Louis' first friend and playmate. The two little boys saw so much of each other because 'Cummy', Louis' nursemaid, walked the short distance from 1 Inverleith Terrace. They moved there when Louis was two. She could enjoy the company of Catherine Docherty, 'Cashie', who was nursemaid to the Davids, as Louis always called them. There also was Agnes Wilson, 'Aggie', semi-retired after a lifetime of service to the earlier generation in Baxter Place. The three women consumed a comforting cup of tea together and enjoyed talking in the 'Lallans', the Lowland Scots tongue that was not always comprehensible to the children. Stories of Louis' very lonely childhood have been much exaggerated. Elizabeth Stevenson [56], with six growing children, was very close to the beautiful young Maggie, newly married to Thomas, and she helped her in every way she could. Their two husbands met daily in the firm's office at 84 George Street so family news passed quickly between them.

In Maggie's famous diary are the following entries:

'January 1853. 22nd Saturday. Smout at his first party at Forth Street. He was very good and shouted with delight when he saw the magic lantern'.[49]

Next morning, on Sunday the 23rd, Smout's first words were:

'Did Uncle David show it to me?'
Tragically she made this entry on April 24th, 1854:

'David's wee boy Bobbie died to-day of intermittent fever ending in water in the head. Smout did not like to hear of it and said he 'hoped it would please God never to let him die'. He asked if Bo would be playing in heaven. Tom came home to-day for the funeral quite unexpectedly. (In Colinton.)'[49]

Elizabeth was by then six months pregnant. Three months on Maggie records:

'21st July 1854 Friday. David's second son born ... David Alan.'[49]

Maggie does not record the birth of a third son, Charles Alexander, in 1855.

David was always deeply religious and was an elder of the Greenside church where all the family worshipped. It was 200 yards from their home at 25 Royal Terrace. He was also a Secretary of the Scripture Readers Association and he wrote several small books that were published for his mission work and intended to 'direct the young to the Bible in the matter of our salvation'. He was a member of the same photographic society as David Octavius Hill and Robert Adamson. He was working in the days when there were no dry plates, no films or hand-held cameras and he was producing 'positives' before 1855. He sensitised his plates and developed them in the harness room adjoining the stables. The cap on the outside of the lens was taken off by hand and replaced by hand when the time exposure, about 4 seconds, was considered sufficient. The positives were as a rule beautifully clear and most have lasted unfaded for years.

David Stevenson died at North Berwick on the 17th of July 1886. He was the only one of Robert's children who chose a new grave site in the Dean Cemetery, on the west side of the town, probably because he knew his family were too numerous for the 'gated cell'. This letter was from R.L.S. to his parents:

'19th. July 1886.
My dear people,
This is a scratch to say my cold is better and to mention that I have heard of poor Uncle David. I don't know why I should say poor; he was won off the stage, and has been waiting his exit for some time. I fear my father will fear it; but these things are rewards to those who go; good wages I am sure. It seems difficult to think of the world without Uncle David.

Your aff[ectionate] son
R.L.S.'[50]

Maggie Stevenson replied on 31st July:

'Uncle David's death upset your father very much ... He was very low for a day or two (quite done and never to be fit for anything again) but he is a shade better to-day'.[51]

## A professional aspect

David, unlike his brothers, was single-minded about pursuing an engineering career from his early teens, and was a mature nineteen year-old when he went south to gain experience of railway work with national contractor William Mackenzie (1794-1851). He kept a memorandum book of engineering data which he updated throughout his life-time, illustrated diaries and other accounts, which make fascinating reading today. For example, during the building of Edge Hill tunnel on the Liverpool & Manchester Railway in 1834, he:

*. . . spent many a weary hour and I may say night, for Mackenzie, with whom I lived for some time, would often after finishing his pipe and glass of brandy and water, instead of going to bed, go out to one of the shafts which as ill luck would have it was close to his house and if he found by further bad luck a bucket going down he would at once say "now then Stevenson let us just jump in and see what these fellows are about down below" and I knew that on all such subterranean excursions the night was sacrificed and instead of sleeping quietly in bed there was in store a journey through dampness and darkness in a suffocating stench of gunpowder and workmen part of the way being through long narrow holes called drifts in which we had to crawl on hands & knees and the whole nights expedition terminating in making our*

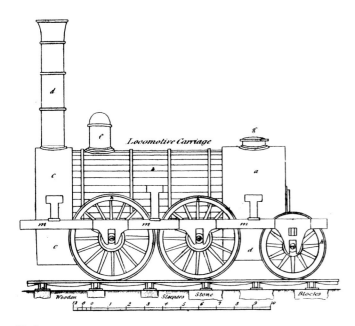

[57] *Liverpool & Manchester Railway locomotive. From David's paper in Arcana of Science and Art, 1836.*

*exit into daylight at 4 or 5 in the morning at the Hay Market (exactly opposite the spot where St. George's Hall now stands) in a state of dirt . . . I got into the way of making myself scarce when I saw a chance of a midnight visit to the works.*[48]

In his diary covering this period a wealth of detail is recorded. The tunnel, was for a double-track railway with an inclination of 1 in 96, and was 2240 yds in length, 25 ft broad and 20 ft high. It was excavated with vertical sides through soft red sandstone and a segmental arched roof was formed, one to two and a half courses thick, springing from skewbacks formed in the rock [sketch]. The void above was *firmly packed with stone slivers . . . they work at 4 faces and excavate at the rate of 22 yds per month at each face working with a day and a night set of men, all the rock is blasted and the work is done by candle light. The blasting powder costs 6d. per lb and priming powder 8d. The workmen are kept strait by wires hung from the centre of the roof to* *which they attach candles, the process of levelling likewise is performed by attaching a candle to the vane of the levelling rod. There are 3 or 4 shafts by which they bring the excavated rock to surface.*[52]

In November 1835, on completion of his apprenticeship [Appendix 3], David obtained the post of resident engineer at Granton Harbour, Edinburgh, for the construction of a pier and approach road [Granton Road]. [44] In accepting this position he had declined an invitation from Marc Isambard Brunel (1769-1849) to work as a resident engineer on the Thames Tunnel, which became one of the wonders of Victorian London and now forms part of London Underground. He described Brunel, whom he met at the tunnel soon afterwards, as *a very fine old man.*[48]

About this time David began to follow in the family tradition of communicating with learned societies and read papers to the Royal Scottish Society of Arts on two railways of which he had first-hand knowledge, the *Liverpool & Manchester* [57] and *Dublin & Kingstown.* His paper on the former earned him an honorary silver medal from the Society, as did another on the building materials of the United States six years later. In 1838 his influential and now historically valuable *Sketch of the civil engineering of North America,* encouraged the introduction into Britain of faster streamlined steam vessels with long-stroke pillar engines and, the adoption more generally, particularly in developing countries, of cost effective timber structures, including bridges. [58,59] David, no doubt encouraged by Robert, was responsible for designs prepared by the firm for an 8-span *Town* type truss crossing of the River Tweed at Norham (1838), not executed, and a 150ft. span Long's frame bridge for India.

[58] *Western Water steam-boat on r. Ohio, 1837. From David's drawing in his Sketch of the Civil Engineering of North America, 1838.*

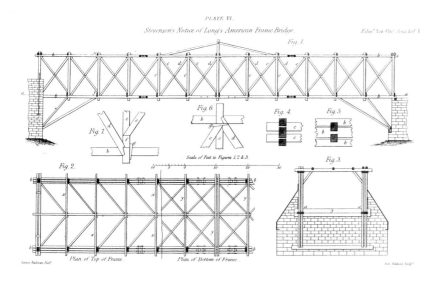

PLATE VI.
Stevenson's Notice of Long's American Frame Bridge.

[59] *Long's American timber frame bridge, 1838. Widely promoted by David as an economical and effective bridging method for developing countries. From his Sketch of the Civil Engineering of North America, 1838.*

When David entered the firm in May 1838 he immediately became responsible for the entire management of the firm's general business and acted in this capacity for the next 43 years. The firm's method for distributing its profits is of interest. Under an agreement of 8 June 1843 David became entitled to four-sevenths of any profits. From 1849 when he and Thomas became the only partners David's share increased to two-thirds, becoming three-fifths from 1854, and a half from 1872. [53] In Scotland the firm's work included navigational improvements on the rivers Forth, Tay, Clyde, and Nith, and numerous harbour schemes of which that for Peterhead was among the most notable. English projects included improvements to the rivers Dee, Lune, Ribble [60], Wear and Fossdyke and, in Ireland, the Erne and Foyle. Other work included Mullagmore and Morecambe harbours, Allanton bridge, Newfoundland lighthouses, Peebles railway, Birkenhead docks and opposing proposed railway crossings of the rivers Tay and Dee for navigational interests.

David soon developed an expertise in river engineering. In 1842, arising out of his practice in connection with the Dornoch Firth salmon fishings and Tay navigation, he defined the different lengths of a river according to its characteristics by what were to become the universally-known terms, 'sea proper', 'tidal', or 'river proper'. This work led to his paper 'Remarks on the improvement of tidal rivers' read to the Royal Society of Edinburgh in 1845, in which he argued conclusively that if the duration of tidal influence was extended, the hydraulic head would be lessened and the velocity of tidal currents decreased. He

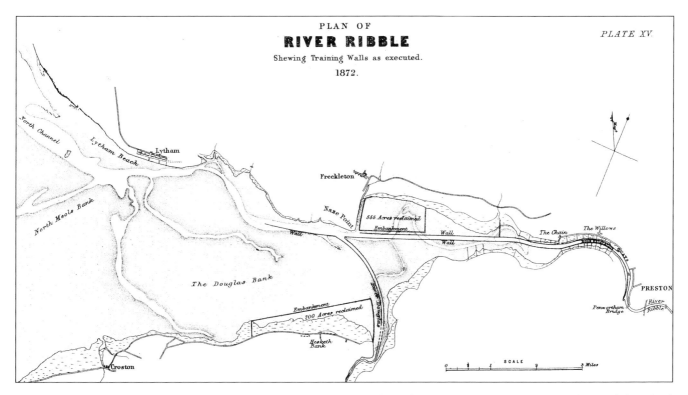

PLAN OF
**RIVER RIBBLE**
Shewing Training Walls as executed.
1872.

*PLATE XV.*

recommended appropriate measures to achieve this end. He also correctly propounded the theory of the origin of bars at the mouths of rivers and defined effective measures for their removal. In estuaries, where appropriate, he advocated the channelisation of currents between low rubble training walls, a practice which was subsequently adopted extensively.[60]

In order to encourage the collection of accurate data upon which to found river and maritime improvements, David published in 1842, *A treatise on the application of marine surveying and hydrometry to the practice of civil engineering,* which described the manner of conducting the survey of a river or harbour from beginning to end. [61] This useful work, the first of its kind, attracted excellent reviews in the technical press and, three years later was followed up with his *Remarks on the improvement of tidal rivers,* which developed into an *Encyclopedia Britannica* article and the standard reference source *Canal and river engineering,* 1858. *The Builder* considered this work, which reached a third edition in 1886 and continued in use well into the present century, *second to none* in its field.

All these and numerous other publications added to David's reputation and helped to establish him as an international authority in this branch of engineering. In 1844 he was elected both to fellowship of the Royal Society of Edinburgh and to membership of the Institution of Civil Engineers, becoming a vice-president of the former from 1873 to 1876 and a member of council of the latter from 1877 to 1883. He was also a member of the Société des Ingénieurs Civils, Paris, and had the distinction of being twice elected president of the Royal Scottish Society of Arts, in 1854 and 1869.

In 1846 during the railway mania period, David held Courts of Inquiry under the Preliminary Inquiries Act for at least twenty proposed Bills. It is understood that his findings were accepted in every case, except for the Caledonian Railway's proposed crossing of the Clyde at Glasgow which was at first opposed by the Admiralty but approved later. In 1849-1850 he reported on Fishery Board proposals for improving Lybster and Scallisaig harbours which led in 1851, on the retirement of Joseph Mitchell C.E., to him becoming, with Thomas, joint engineer to the Fishery Board for more than thirty years. He insisted on the joint arrangement, rather than a sole appointment for himself.

In March 1853 David succeeded Alan as Engineer to the Northern Lighthouse Board, after failing to persuade the Board to allow him to serve jointly with Thomas, an arrangement which he considered essential in order to safeguard the firm's private business on which its financial success mainly depended. David eventually prevailed in this, although not without considerable opposition. In March 1855 he resigned his individual appointment and *D. & T. Stevenson* took on the role as the Board's Engineers until David's retiral in 1884 after several years of ill-health. At the same time the responsibilities previously attached to the post for the general management of the whole service including lightkeepers and stores, which had become *irksome* to David, devolved on the Secretary.[48] Of the many lighthouses which they built, Dhu Heartach 1872 [62] was a work of particular difficulty, as will be seen later.

David's competent management and dedication were nowhere more ably demonstrated than in the temporary construction of Britain's most northerly lighthouse at North Unst (Muckle Flugga) in 1854, and its successful completion undoubtedly helped him to prevail in his tussle with the Board over the joint engineership issue. This had been preoccupying his mind when, as he wrote later, *the Russian war broke out & a blockading fleet was sent to the White sea. The Admiralty was of course, I suppose, consulted by the government and as there was no light to indicate the Northern and Eastern coasts of the Shetland islands it seemed desireable that when the blockading fleet left the White sea they should have something more than Sumburgh Head to tell them the position of the Shetland.*

*Accordingly the Admiralty hurriedly resolved that two lights should be exhibited on the North East coast of Shetland not later than 1st October 1854. I therefore at once sailed for Shetland on 17th February of that year to determine which were the most useful sites and what was the best method of carrying out the instructions of the Government. The weather was wretched and the passage most uncomfortable and on arriving at Lerwick on Saturday night at 11 oclock, having experienced considerable difficulty in finding the entrance to the Bay we were informed that the last mail received at Shetland from the mainland was on 1st December [1853] and that the winter had been an unusually severe one. There were no steamers trading there at that time and the poor Shetlanders who had been nearly three months without communication received our printed and verbal "news" with the greatest interest . . .*

*North Unst* [was one of the sites selected for a light] . . . *the other being Whalsey . . . our appearance off the coast at that season of the year caused no small speculation among the simple islanders. The rumour of the war too it seems had reached them . . . they all retreated to the interior leaving their houses to our mercy and we learned afterwards that they were afraid of the press gang or that we might be Russians.*

*When surveying the several sites on which we landed I had a very favourable opportunity of witnessing the effects of the storms during the recent severe winter which had left their traces in unmistakeable distinctness on every headland . . . they were particularly observable at North Unst where the deep water comes close to the rocks also at Lambaness and Balta where stones of half a ton were thrown up on the green sward at elevations of 80 to 85 feet above high water and I came to the conclusion that what I had formerly considerd as* abnormal *seas occuring at certain peculiar places such as Whalsey were in point of fact* normal *in this country being common to the whole of the North and East coast of Shetland and indeed in all other places where similar physical circumstances prevail there being deep water close in, and the exposure being open in all directions affording in fact a corrolation of my observations made on the waves of the American Lakes and their causes -* area of exposure *and* depth. *I reported that no buildings could be considered safe on any part of that coast which were not very considerably elevated above high water level . . .*

*On my return from this voyage no time was lost in getting ready apparatus and preparing temporary wooden towers for the lights and iron houses for the Light Keepers, which were erected and surrounded with rubble walls for warmth. These had all to be made and fitted up in Edinburgh - vessels had to be hired to convey them, and all arrangements had to be made for their erection at the place, for getting the Light Keepers to take charge of them - and many other needful requirements not excepting supplies of provisions for the winter the responsibily of all devolving entirely on me and to make matters worse I was by no means well . . . the preparations went on and by dint of perseverance every thing was got ready before the fleet required to use the lights. Whalsey temporary light was exhibited in September and Mr. Alan Brebner who acted as my assistant at Unst managed to get the work done in a very short time [by 11th October] . . .*

*With reference to this work I may mention that the weight of materials to be landed at the rock was 120 tons which had to be sometimes hauled through the surf, that everything had to be carried up a rock 200 feet high on the backs of men, there being no time to prepare any other appliance - and that the whole was landed, taken up, and built, in 26 days on an outlying rock the* most northern habitable spot in the British Islands. *These temporary works were visited during the winter after their erection in 1855 with severe storms from the North West and although the temporary houses and tower were 200 feet above high water the seas rose to such height and in such weight as to deluge the houses with water forcing in the doors and throwing down the walls built round the houses for protection . . .* abnormal *sea storms depending as they do on the conjunction of high winds from a particular direction, with high tides, and a long continuance of the gale, do not often occur, an interval of apparent rest being merifully granted to those, who, like myself have all my life been fighting with the sea although I must admit not always successfully.*[48] The permanent lighthouse was completed in 1857. **[63]** A good example of a minor light erected in the same year was Kyleakin, Skye. **[64]**

During the next 25 years the firm continued to flourish under David's management. When in 1858 a Royal

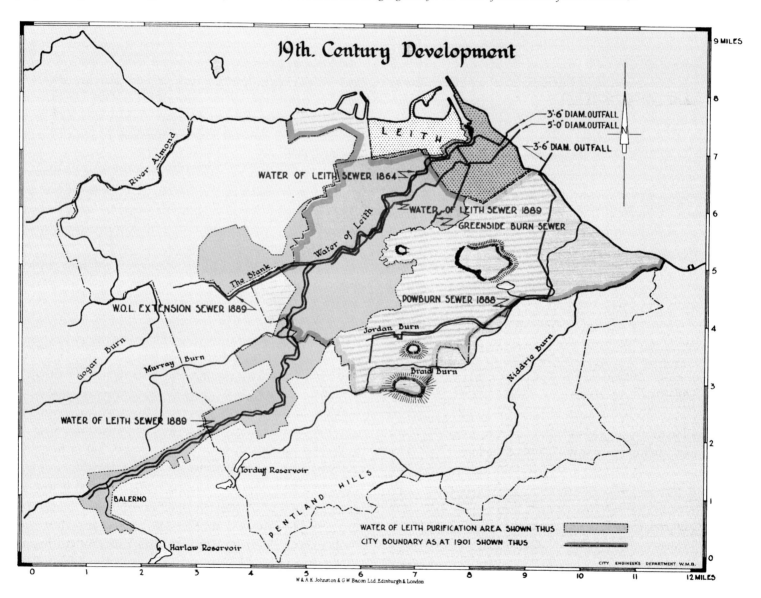

[65] *Edinburgh Main Drainage in 19th century. The Stevensons were the consulting engineers for the Water of Leith sewers of 1864 and 1889.*

19th. Century Development

9 MILES

3'-6" DIAM. OUTFALL
5'-0" DIAM. OUTFALL

LEITH

3'-6" DIAM. OUTFALL

River Almond

WATER OF LEITH SEWER 1864

WATER OF LEITH SEWER 1889
GREENSIDE BURN SEWER

Water of Leith

The Stank

W.O.L. EXTENSION SEWER 1889

POWBURN SEWER 1888

Gogar Burn

Jordan Burn

Niddrie Burn

Murray Burn

Braid Burn

WATER OF LEITH SEWER 1889

Torduff Reservoir

BALERNO

PENTLAND HILLS

Harlaw Reservoir

WATER OF LEITH PURIFICATION AREA SHOWN THUS
CITY BOUNDARY AS AT 1901 SHOWN THUS

CITY ENGINEER'S DEPARTMENT W.M.B.

0    1    2    3    4    5    6    7    8    9    10    11    12 MILES
W & A K Johnston & G W Bacon Ltd, Edinburgh & London

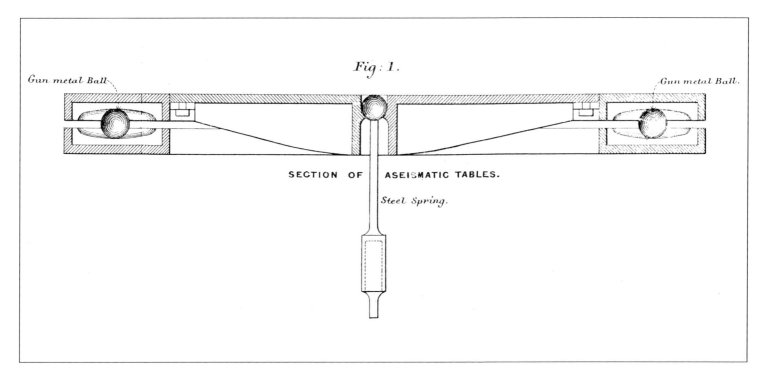

*Fig: 1.*

Gun metal Ball.

Gun metal Ball.

SECTION OF ASEISMATIC TABLES.

*Steel Spring.*

**[66]** *Aseismatic table for mitigating earthquake effects on lamps in Japanese lighthouses. The circular table which rested on 3 balls in cups (2 visible), bore an array of holophotal reflectors. The steel spring added to restrain unrequited motion was only partly successful.*

Commission was appointed to inquire into the condition of the lights, buoys and beacons of the United Kingdom, J.T. Chance commented that the lights of England and Ireland were *much inferior to those of Scotland which were under the able supervision of the Stevensons.*[54] With the passage of time Thomas also made an increasing contribution to the firm's success which is reflected in the incidence of his published reports and in 1872 David implemented an equal division of the profits between them.

During their 27-year partnership the two brothers are understood to have divided the sum of £95,000 in fees, after payment of salaries and expenses, of which about one-quarter came from the Northern Lighthouse Board.[53] In addition to maritime work, public health improvements were undertaken, including Edinburgh & Leith sewerage, the city's first such major scheme involving construction of the Water of Leith sewers of 1864 and 1889 to outfalls in the Forth. **[65]**

Abroad the firm's advice extended to lighthouses in India, China and Newfoundland, and to the lighting of the whole coasts of Japan and New Zealand. In 1871 David and Thomas were appointed consulting engineers to the Japanese Lighthouse Department. For Japanese lighthouses in earthquake zones David devised an *aseismatic joint* [66] to mitigate the effect of shocks on lighting apparatus for which he was awarded the Makdougall-Brisbane Medal of the Royal Scottish Society of Arts. However, according to Richard Brunton, Chief Engineer of the Japanese Lighthouse Department for whom the device was installed, and incidentally who had been briefly trained by and recommended for this appointment by David and Thomas, it was *ill-conceived*. The reason he gave for this opinion was that the device was based on their mistaken premise that the violence of the earthquake shock would be aggravated by the greater elevation of the building above the source of motion. Brunton commented, *precisely the reverse of this occurs actually and Messrs Stevenson, accomplished and learned as they were, came to a wholly erroneous conclusion.*[55]

The aseismatic joint was installed at only seven lighthouses. It was fitted to 8 ft. diameter tables and, although mitigating the effects of external movement, the unrequited motion which occurred during lamp cleaning and wick trimming deranged the lamps. David devised a steadying arrangement but this was only partly successful. In defence of a charge that the device had been found wanting and abandoned, Charles wrote in 1884, *there are three at present in action, and have been so for ten years, viz.*

*Mikomoto, Siwomisaki and Yesaki. At Iwosima and Satanomisaki, in the south, the tables are screwed up so as not to act, as it is reported that no earthquakes are felt at these stations. At Tsuragisaki and Kashmosaki, which are revolving lights, the steadying screws sent out with the apparatus were not put in and the tables were firmly strutted with timber to prevent any motion. These are the only two lighthouses at which any damage has been done; while those stations at which the tables are in operation have never suffered at all, although they have been repeatedly subjected to shocks.*[56]

From about 1870 David played a leading part in developing and promoting the use of paraffin in place of the widely used and more expensive colza oil for lighthouse illumination which resulted in enhanced light intensity at a lower cost and a considerable saving in cost world-wide.

By this time *D. & T. Stevenson* had become one of Britain's leading firms of consulting engineers in maritime and river engineering. Nearly all British rivers from the Dee and Trent to as far north as Donoch Firth, and many harbours, had come under its remit, including Wick breakwater, their notable failure, which will be referred to in more detail later.

David's substantial contribution to his profession and mankind through his outstanding engineering practice and in consolidating and ensuring the continuance of the firm, ranks second to none in the achievements of the Stevenson family of engineers.

# Chapter Five

## Thomas Stevenson 1818-1887 - Investigator of natural phenomena and innovator

**Family recollections**

Even if he had done nothing else of importance in his life, the fact that he produced a son called Robert Louis Stevenson would have assured Thomas a place in history. In many ways father and son were like each other, but in far more ways they were not! Their childhood circumstances were different as Thomas was brought up with considerable parental assumption that he would amount to something and his father, Robert, with great persuasion, patience and authority stuck into the project until he had achieved his aim. Thomas as a child drifted aimlessly from Mr Brown, his tutor, to the Edinburgh High School, and he appeared to have no aims or ambitions regarding the outcome of his life.

Charles remembered this family episode, told him by his father David:

'This story was told me by my father David about an incident he remembered from Baxter Place when he and Tom were still children. Tom was reported 'to be lying in bed and won't get up'. So brother Bob, who afterwards was a surgeon in the Army, was told off to examine him and as usual found it was again a case of shamming illness to escape classes at school. On completion of his examination Bob left the room and returned furnished with a pickled gherkin which he pushed up one of Tom's nostrils and then he left the room. The result was an immediate success ...' [5]

Possibly Robert's patience held out so long with him because he was the youngest, and as both his elder brothers were well settled into engineering and endowed with obvious gifts to bring to the profession, Thomas was free to choose virtually any career he wanted. The trouble was he didn't really wish to do anything

except write visionary stories, visit antique bookshops, study natural science and sleep as long as he liked in the morning! In 1834 a year after leaving school Thomas tried printing. An interest in bookselling followed, and finally a job in the publishing house of Patrick Neill. Here he stuck until complete boredom drove him to ask his father for an apprenticeship in the family firm. This meant enrolling at Edinburgh University, office work, site work in the holidays and an endless bombardment of advice from Robert.

*'From the Craven Hotel, London*
I dined yesterday where I heard on first rate authority that Walker rises at 4 o'clock every morning and has his fire and candles going all in apple pie order for business! ...
*Edinburgh 13th May. My own room, Sunday 9. p.m.*
You need not look to David as a correspondent at present. He does not trust himself to rise in the morning but sits until one or two o'clock overnight besides the day's work. Never speaks to David about rising. If he does not sit at night, he generally gets called at 6 and rises as you do. How perfectly absurd it was to hear you formerly saying 'I cannot rise, it quite knocks me up.' See where it is now! Never allow yourself as a young man to think or speak or act in this style either about rising, or sitting, or standing, or wading a water carrying a burthen, or eating this, that or t'other thing. *All trash.* Set your mind and your shoulders to the world and press onwards'. [5]

But by 21 years old life was changing for Thomas. He had shown innovative ability by designing a new set of surveying instruments. He had also supervised the erection of a lighthouse on Little Ross.

It was Alan who gave Thomas his first real break and handed over the completion of his own brain-child, Skerryvore, to him. Thomas thoroughly understood Fresnel lamps and Skerryvore still needed its lantern. His brother's confidence paid off and as Alan was ill it was Tom who saw the lamp first shine out on 1st February 1844.

Robert retired from the family firm in 1846 and Thomas was made a partner with some real money to jingle in his pocket. Time now to think of marriage. The girl of his choice was the fair haired, very elegant, tall daughter of the Colinton manse, Margaret Isabella Balfour. He met her on a railway journey to Glasgow in 1847 in the charge of an uncle and aunt. She was 18 years old and shortly after he proposed to her on a walk on the Pentlands. It was real love on both sides and Thomas was devoted to her for the rest of his life. They were married on 8th August 1848 and moved at once into their own house at 8 Howard Place. On 13th November their only child came safely into the world. He was plump, fit and well, without illness of any sort until he was 18 months old. Possibly if anyone had measured his rib cage they might have found that it was unusually narrow. All the Victorian ailments hit him hard and he scarcely had time to recover from one before he was hit by another. His mother too was considered 'delicate' and ordered to stay in bed until noon. Here Thomas showed one of the best sides of his character. He held the view that no sacrifice on the part of a man was too much to make for a woman and he cherished his wife with tender care. With Louis' nurse Cummy probably asleep on her feet after getting him alive through another night, Thomas would arrive to sit by the nursery door and hold imaginary conversations with unseen bodies in an effort to get his son to relax.

When Louis was 2 years old they moved across the road to what was then No. 1 Inverleith Terrace. The house still stands, but is No. 9 today. Like Howard Place it was found too cold and damp and the family moved again when Louis was 7 years old to 17 Heriot Row. Thomas probably bought this house with the legacy left him after the death of his brother, Dr Robert, M.D., Surgeon to the Buffs.

In 1867 Thomas leased Swanston Cottage on the northern slopes of the Pentland Hills, about five miles distant from Heriot Row. This house was a wonderful summer retreat. Louis was now 17 years old and often walked out to it, even in mid-winter. He could escape there with personal friends, away from his ever anxious parents. When Thomas was in residence a phaeton was driven into town twice daily. Thomas had flair and he lived in style wherever he went. He had long forsaken his lazy ways and he was accepted as a very successful Edinburgh citizen by the time his father died in 1850. He worked extremely hard, but his leisure hours were still spent with friends or going on long walks speaking to and feeding every dog he met, convinced that they had souls. His views on the education of children were light years away from his contemporaries. He thought that children only learnt what they wanted to learn at the time they were ready for it. It had been so for himself ... Louis in his essay on his father writes:

'Latin he happily re-taught himself after he had left school, where he was a mere consistent idler; happily I say, for Lactantius, Vossius, and cardinal Bona were his chief authors. The first he must have read for twenty years uninterruptedly, keeping it near him in his study, and carrying it in his bag on journeys.'[57]

Fate certainly dictated that Louis was to have a very erratic education, but Thomas got expert, divergent and sometimes inspired help for his son's tuition wherever they were in the world. Louis' natural mental gifts flourished like beanstalks. Thomas and his son shared a talent that was really a love of words and they were often great sparring partners both in public and private. Louis writes:

'His talk compounded of so much sterling sense and so much freakish humour, and clothed in language so apt, droll and emphatic, was a perpetual delight to all who knew him … His affections and emotions were liable to passionate ups and downs, found the most eloquent expression both in words and gestures. Love, anger, and indignation shone through him and broke forth in imagery.'[57]

Louis recognised in his father the depressive state that was mutual to them both. He also knew that, for his father, hard work and the constant need for travel in the Lighthouse Board offered an escape from what Louis called 'Troublesome humours.'

The devout belief in Christianity inherited from the previous generation was a strength that he could always call upon. When Louis declared on the last day of January 1873 that he was no longer a Christian it was a terrible blow to his father and mother.

Thomas had always given much time and money to the Church of Scotland, serving on many of their committees. He had founded a Magdalene Mission in Edinburgh, and had written and published a work on the defence of Christianity. Like many devout Christians it was impossible for him to have any insight into Louis' spiritual dilemma and equally difficult for his mother. The little family just had to ride out the storm and it blew them all into immediate illness. Eventually help came because Louis' young life was moving forward all the time, and right ahead was to be his first meeting with Sydney Colvin and Frances Sitwell. The whole world changed colour for him the day he walked into Cockfield, Suffolk, near Bury St Edmunds-he was falling in love! The letters he wrote to Fanny for the next few years of his life, most of which are published in Ernest Mehew's *Letters of Robert Louis Stevenson,* show us today the tremendous depth of a very remarkable soul. **[67]**

Another blow to Thomas was the final realisation that Louis was definitely not able or willing to follow him into the engineering world. The alternative, that he would qualify for the Scottish Bar, had to satisfy them both for the moment. Thomas wrote to David on the 19th of April 1872:

'For as my only son has, from causes to which I shall not advert, abandoned Engineering all connection between me & the business ceases at my death. Moreover Louis' fees as an Advocate are I understand about £500 & after he has passed he must expect to be a briefless Barrister for a number of years, whereas you know very well how soon your son can get a fair allowance in our profession.'⁵

A bribe of £1,000 was to be paid over on his qualification and Thomas duly paid up. Louis gave at least threequarters of it away to his friends.

Thomas and Maggie also had to face the departure of their son to America without informing them of his intention. He went to marry a divorcee, ten years older than himself with three children, one still dependent on her and only twelve years old. The very conventional Edinburgh society of their day assumed that Louis' 'unsuitable' marriage was another disaster his 'black sheep' of a son had inflicted on him. In the event when the couple arrived in Heriot Row for their extended honeymoon, Fanny Van de Grift Osbourne's charm and talents completely won over Thomas and Maggie. Both of them enjoyed and spoilt their daughter-in-law and their Stevenson relatives 'closed ranks' and put on a good face to outsiders regarding Louis' behaviour.

Thomas worked hard for his political beliefs as well as his Church. He was a Tory and every year paid into the party funds- every year until the one before his death when he forgot, and this omission probably cost him the knighthood that he coveted, and that friends were trying to negotiate for him. He had become ambitious for worldly honours and it was a bitter blow to him.

Thomas was very hard with his brother David and also his two nephews, David and Charles, regarding financial questions.

In spite of a very close successful working relationship with his brother David raised the subject of the partnership the year after Elizabeth's death and wrote this letter to Thomas:

'North Berwick 13 April 1872
My Dear Tom
I have been so much engaged with my book that I have not had time to write on business matters. I have not my letters with me but I think in my last (of which I think however I kept no copy) I said that rather than incur the *family* breakdown of a separation of the engineering firm now going on for a century old, I would acquiesce in any redivision of the future profits of the business which you proposed. After that [I] got your letter proposing that the profits in future should be *equally* divided in which proposal in terms of my letters I now acquiesce. You say that you hope our differences may *now* be ended, I hope so too; but I should not wish my *acquiescence* to be held as implying *approval* for my opinion remains unaltered. An equal division of the future profits is in my opinion carrying an *abstract principle* (the soundness of which when viewed *merely* as an abstract principle no body can dispute) to an extent which (viewing the *which circumstances* of our case as fully set forth some years ago in the first letter I wrote to you on this subject) is neither *natural* nor *just*. But having in order to avoid misconception

stated that my views as there I expressed are unchanged no more need be said on that point, as I have under the circumstances above stated given my acquiescence to the arrangement, for the commencement of which I presume some *definite* date must be fixed and I suppose the first of January last may most conveniently be named.

You say something about providing for one or other of the boys entering the business but really I dont know that there is much use in doing so. If it be requested as any equivalent for which I may give up in the division of future business profits I do not see how it can in any way be so regarded or accepted by me. I think I mentioned already in some letter that my boys are really only entering on their studies and that it seems impossible under any circumstances that Davie, for example, could take a part in the business for 6 years at least (he was 17 last birthday). No one knows what the business may then be and still less perhaps is it possible to tell whether either of them may then desire to enter it. But this we know, that both of them are entered on an expensive course of education to fit them for what even may be their profession. Besides, I confess I do not like the notion of contemplating the possibility that under any circumstances the door of our office could ever be shut against them or opened in preference to a stranger provided either of them was fitted to take a place in the business and express a desire to do so. Neither on the other hand do I see any propriety in placing you under a legal obligation to assume as a partner a person who may have no turn for general business and still less for Engineering. It is not at all a business which is carried on even to the *smallest* extent by Capital, it is entirely *head* work (the only analogous professions I know being painters &

[68] *Thomas Stevenson, PRSE.*

advocates) which cannot be bought & sold like stock in trade, but if anything were necessary on the subject a single letter builds enough credit.

I am My Dr Tom
Your afft. brother
David Stevenson

I have no paper with me here.' [5]

Thomas was a very handsome man-he was five feet ten inches tall, broad shouldered, regular features, expressive eyes, and a slightly florid complexion. With an excellent speaking voice he commanded attention wherever he went. [68]  At 84 George Street, however, they recognised David as the better engineer who gave far more attention to the business than Thomas.

All the Stevensons fought against approaching death and, except for Louis, never liked to acknowledge that it might be 'just round the corner.' Thomas was no exception and 'the reaper' caught him at a favourable moment at his own house in Heriot Row. As Louis wrote in his famous article on his father, 'He had upon the whole a happy life; nor was he less fortunate in his death, which at the last came to him unaware.' His death certificate gives the cause of death as 'Enlarged liver, 2 years. Jaundice, 2 months.' He joined his father in the vault at the New Calton Cemetery with his wife Maggie. A flat stone records the death of their only son, R.L.S., and his wife Fanny, who are both buried on the summit of Mount Vaea in Samoa.

## A professional aspect

Thomas initial reluctance to embark on a civil engineering career has been referred to already. To Robert's consternation he even indulged his interest in writing fiction after having decided

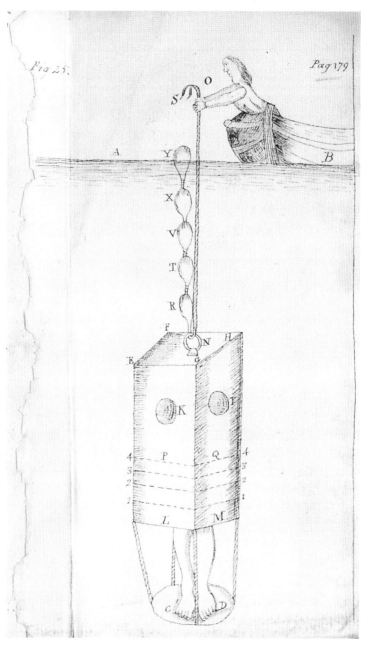

[69]  *Thomas's restoration of defective plate in Sinclair's Hydrostaticks 1672.*

# CIVIL ENGINEER

AND

# ARCHITECT'S

# JOURNAL.

[70] *Civil Engineer & Architect's Journal with Thomas's annotations of authorship 1839.*

on an engineering career, no doubt to provide some relief from the relentless rigour of his apprenticeship. Robert however considered this distraction of his nineteen-year-old son sufficiently unwelcome to put pen to paper and urge him *to give up such nonsense and mind your business.*[58]

Thomas complied, and managed this situation by combining his interests in natural history, natural philosophy, writing and old books, even to restoring them, with civil engineering. [69] Fortunately, he had both the ability and, through his work, the opportunity. He was studious by nature, proficient at mathematics, although not arithmetical calculation, and eventually produced more publications than any other member of the family. Through these and his practice he made significant contributions to the development of lighthouse illumination and harbour engineering, producing valuable reference works.

Thomas's earliest known published combinations of his writing and engineering talents were anonymous articles in the leading engineering periodical of its day *The Civil Engineer and Architect's Journal* from December 1837 to 1841. Holograph annotations of his own copies [70] attest to his authorship of articles and correspondence on such divers subjects as the method of removal of a 40-50 ton stone from the River Tay near Perth during river deepening, descriptions of three 17th century suspension bridges over the River Charente, the use of blasting to demolish ruinous buildings, restoring rather than replacing ruinous historic buildings, river bank profiles and the repair of breaches, and an improved levelling staff and 'quick-set' level made to his specification.

To what extent his father knew and approved of these writings is not known but, more than a century later, the family's historian D. Alan shed some light on their relationship at about this time:

*From time to time Robert sent him [Thomas] copies of professional papers and in October 1837 he suggested that Thomas should write a description of Cardiff harbour works [where he had been sent to gain experince]. Thomas however fobbed him off with a letter saying that such a detailed account 'would weary both you and me'. Instead he described the arrangement of several notebooks which he was keeping. 'When I mention that each entry contained perhaps on the average 20 or 30 pieces of information on the subject, you will readily admit that my book will in good time be a perfect digest of engineering knowledge. . . . I keep another book which I call my office book of rules, formulae, &c. and another book in which all operations of machinery are drawn. Then I have a book fit for the pocket bound in vellum - a digest of all my other books is entered here. I hope it will be of vast use to me in after life'.*

*He mentioned that as he wrote he was occupied making notes from a report of a House of Commons enquiry for providing drinking water througout the London area. In conclusion he said that a newspaper had reported that Lord Hopetoun was objecting to a proposed [Edinburgh to] Glasgow railway for which the Stevensons were the engineers and commented - 'I think it would be of great consequence that Alan or you call on Hope the agent at 31 Moray Place [Edinburgh] and explain the advantages of our line. It is possible he might support it.' Thomas expected that these descriptions of his notebooks would please his father greatly, but it is doubtful if Robert welcomed the advice from his nineteen year old son on how to deal with the Earl's solicitor.'* [59]

In 1845 Thomas furnished the *Civil Engineer & Architect's Journal* with an abstract of his paper to the Royal Society of

[72] *Portable cofferdam, 1848. From Thomas's article in Edin. New Phil. J. 1848. XLV*

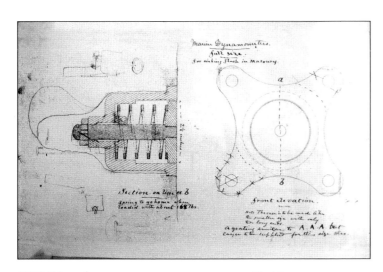

[71] Wave dynamometer. Drawing annotated by Thomas.

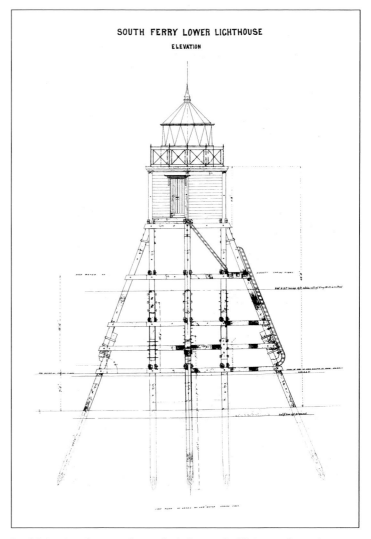

SOUTH FERRY LOWER LIGHTHOUSE
ELEVATION

[73] Tay South Ferry lower lighthouse [off Tayport], 1848.
Drawing signed by Thomas.

Edinburgh on forces exerted by sea-waves, the first significant practical work on this subject. His findings were based on data from an ingenious wave dynamometer of his own invention [71] with which, in 1845, he measured a wave pressure of nearly three tons per square foot at Skerryvore. These articles, together with others in *The Edinburgh New Philosophical Journal* on defects in rain gauges, the geology of Little Ross Island and other subjects, were the earliest of about a hundred publications by him in all. Many appeared in the *Transactions* of the Royal Scottish Society of Arts, the *Journal* of the Scottish Meteorological Society and *Nature*. Thomas's writings demonstrate his innate faculty for the quantitative investigation, particularly of natural phenomena, which enabled him to advance knowledge and practice by means of observation and experiment.

In 1843 when Alan succeeded Robert as Engineer to the Lighthouse Board, Thomas was appointed resident engineer to conclude the operations at Skerryvore, where he gained valuable experience on the installation of the light. For constructing a sloping masonry wall at Hynish [48], he developed a portable cofferdam, in which the piles were retained in place and guided during driving by an internal and external frame, an innovation which was assessed by civil engineer George Buchanan in 1848, as a *valuable auxiliary in the construction of marine works.*[60] [72] In the same year he let a contract for a timber lighthouse in the River Tay, a good example of its type, presumably to his design. [73]

On his father's retirement in 1846, Thomas became the firm's junior partner, which enabled him to engage

[75] *Anstruther Harbour 1991, D. & T. Stevenson were engineers for building the east pier, against which the North Carr Light Vessel can be seen*

effectively in research and development for many years. The fact that this work did not at first produce much income may have been a factor in David's delaying until 1872 the implementation an equal division of the firm's profits between them.

From 1855-84 Thomas, at David's instigation, acted jointly with him as Engineer to the Northern Lighthouse Board as part of the firm's business. Together they designed about 28 beacons and 30 lighthouses, including works of great difficulty on isolated rocks at Muckle Flugga 1857, Dhu Heartach 1872 and Chicken Rock, Isle of Man 1875. In 1881, when he took over the day-to-day management of the firm because of David's ill-health, Thomas found this duty taxing, combined with his existing work-load, and his health deteriorated. In 1885 David Alan was appointed with him as joint engineer to the Lighthouse Board, and increasingly carried out the lighthouse duties until Thomas's death.

Harbour work at Hynish, Lybster [74], Anstruther [75], Wick, Londonderry and elsewhere provided Thomas with opportunities to continue his practical investigations into the generation and force of waves. By 1852 he had formulated a tentative empirical relationship between the height and fetch [distance of open sea behind] of waves, which later became the formula, **H (feet) = 1.5 F$\sqrt{}$(miles)**.[61] The formula was still being used as an approximation by maritime engineers after the second world war. Other experiments led to formulae which enabled the effect of harbours and breakwaters in reducing the height of waves to be calculated. Thomas's valuable work in this field became widely known through his *Encyclopedia Britannica* article 'Harbour', separately published and enlarged as *Design and Construction of Harbours* in 1864, 1874 and 1886.

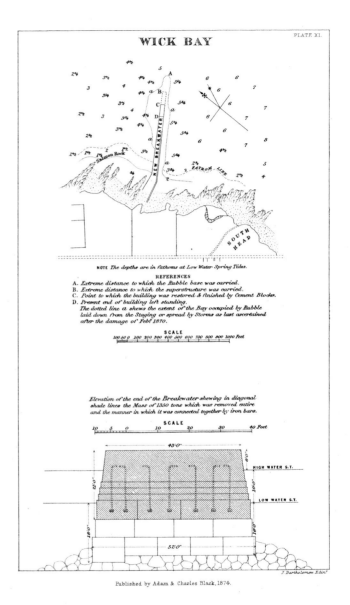

[76] *Wick breakwater plan and cross-section. Note the pierres perdues (rubble foundation) visited by Louis when diving. From Thomas's Design and construction of harbours, 1886.*

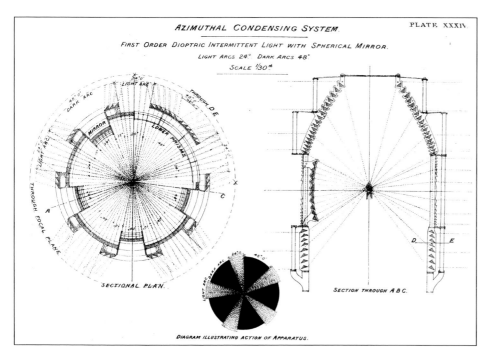

[77] *Azimuthal condensing system. From Thomas's Lighthouse construction and illumination, 1881*

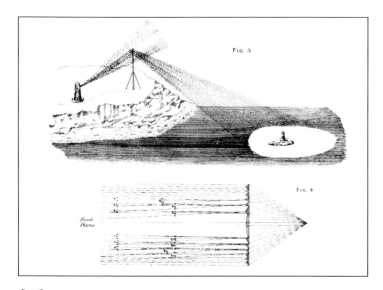

[78] *Indirect illumination and reflection at Stornoway. From Thomas's Lighthouse construction and illumination, 1881.*

The firm's harbour work was almost invariably successful, except for Wick breakwater for the British Fisheries Society which, as its construction progressed from 1863 into deeper water, by 1868 reaching out over 1,000 feet to a depth of 30 feet below low water, frequently experienced storm damage from waves up to 40 feet high. A major disaster occurred in 1870 when waves destroyed about one-third of the length of the breakwater. It was repaired but succumbed to destruction again in 1872 and yet again in 1877, when a composite mass of rubble concrete weighing about 2,600 tons was carried away by the sea. [62] [76] Following this disaster the project was abandoned as a costly, but most instructive failure. Meeting its expense was a factor in the demise of the Society by 1893.

A factor in the failure at Wick was that Thomas's formula under-estimated the height of the waves by at least 50 per cent because the conditions there were exceptionally beyond those upon which the formula was derived. In a modern evaluation Townson suggests that at Wick, because the fetch was more than 300 miles and the wind speed far above the 30 miles per hour at which the formula is now considered to provide a good approximation, its use would have indicated a wave height of 26 feet, only one-third to one-half of that now known to occur in the North Sea. In drawing attention to the failure in detail in his publications Thomas can be considered to have obviated similar situations occurring elsewhere. Townson commented that Thomas's advances in *meteorology were particularly frequent in the years following the Wick project and that he was the first to compare wind speed with barometric gradient. Not only does his*

PLATE XX.

HOLOPHOTAL AZIMUTHAL CONDENSING APPARATUS
FOR AN ARC OF 45° AS EMPLOYED
AT THE TAY LEADING LIGHTS FRONT VIEW

[79] *Holophotal azimuthal condensing apparatus for Tay lights. From Thomas's Lighthouse construction and illumination, 1881.*

*stature remain unimpaired by the shortcomings of his wave formula, but paradoxically science is the better for it.*[61]

Fortunately for Thomas his international reputation was broadly based. Details of his influential lighthouse practice are fully described in his *Lighthouse Illumination*, 1859 which was expanded into *Lighthouse Construction and Illumination* in 1881. In this field he developed the work of Augustin Fresnel and Alan and installed a catadioptric fixed holophote in the lighthouse at Peterhead North Harbour in 1849. This is believed to have been the first apparatus to combine the whole sphere of rays diverging from a light source into a single beam of parallel rays. In 1850 it was followed by the installation of the first dioptric holophotal revolving light at Horsburgh Rock, Singapore.

The holophotal system, which represented an important development in lighthouse illumination, was then adopted on a larger scale by the Northern Lighthouse Board at North Ronaldsay Lighthouse in 1851. The system subsequently came into universal use. Thomas also developed the concept of creating an *apparent* light on dangerous reefs by indirect illumination and reflection from a parent lighthouse and installed a *beautiful and ingenious contrivance* at Stornoway in 1851.[69] [77]

Thomas's crowning achievement was his azimuthal condensing system which reduced the available light in some sectors of azimuth and optimised it in others. [78,79] The system was introduced at Isle Oronsay lighthouse, Skye in 1857 to service Sleet Sound. He was assisted in some of the calculations required for his optical refinements by his cousin and life-long friend Professor W. Swan (1818-86) and Professor P. G. Tait (1831-1901). Abroad, his work included a dioptric floating light for the River Hoogly. [80]

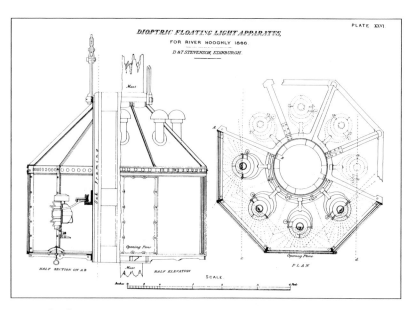

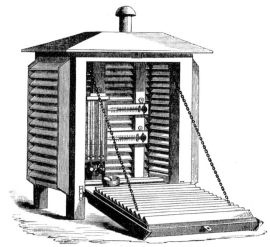

Fig. 13.

the *louvre-boarded box for thermometers*, constructed by Thomas Stevenson, C.E., Edinburgh, and now extensively used by the observers of the Scottish Meteorological Society, and other meteorologists. A figure of the box, fig. 13, is here given, with the

**[80]** *Dioptric floating light apparatus for River Hooghly, India. From Thomas's Lighthouse construction and illumination, 1881.*

**[81]** *Thomas's extensively used thermometer screen. The corner posts to be of sufficient length that the maximum thermometer was exactly 4ft. from the ground.*

Thomas was elected a Fellow of the Royal Society of Edinburgh in 1848 and became its President in November 1884. Unfortunately, because of ill-health, he was unable to complete his term of office and he resigned in September 1886. In 1864, sponsored by Thomas Bouch, later of Tay Bridge disaster notoriety, Thomas was elected a Member of the Institution of Civil Engineers in 1864. He was also a Fellow of the Geological Society of London from 1874-1887.

In furtherance of his profound interest in the weather and its effects Thomas became a founder member of the Scottish Meteorological Society in 1855 and its honorary secretary in 1871. Among the many and permanent contributions which he made to meteorology in addition to those already mentioned were, the Stevenson screen for the protection of thermometers, designed in c.1864 and which came into in universal use **[81]**; the introduction of the term 'barometric gradient'; and the

means of ascertaining, by high and low level observations at Ben Nevis and elsewhere, the vertical gradients for atmospheric pressure, temperature and humidity.

Thomas is best remembered today for his innovative development of maritime engineering and meteorology. Louis expressed this more narrowly and with filial pride in his dedication to *Familiar studies of men and books:*

*To*
*Thomas Stevenson*
*Civil Engineer*
*By whose devices the great sea lights in every quarter*
*of the world now shine more brightly*
*this volume is in love and gratitude*
*dedicated by his son*
*the author.*

**Family recollections**

Charles wrote,[92]

'Louis came along countless times to play with us' [at 25 Royal Terrace]. He had a passionate affection for his Aunt Elizabeth, and he wrote this of her to his cousin David:

'From La Solitude, Hyres-les Palmas, Var. Dec 31st.

[Louis was then 33 years old.]

My Dear Davie,

At the beginning of the end of this year, I had many thoughts of the past, many of yourself and many of your Mother who was the idol of my childhood. I had it in my mind to write to Uncle David but I thought it might be merely an importunate intrusion and decided to write rather to yourself. [Our father was entering into his last illness at North Berwick at that time.] The way in which life separates people is very painful. It is nearly a year since we had a New Year's walk; but I have not forgotten the past, and your Mother I shall never forget. I am profoundly a Stevenson in the matter of not giving presents. Once only that I can remember did I of my own notion, give a present; and that before '57 when I 'asked leave' to give a present to Aunt Elizabeth, and I do not suppose a greater testimony could be given to her extraordinary charm and kindness. I never saw anybody like her; a look from Aunt Elizabeth was like sunshine. Please accept this very blundering scrawl; understand what is unsaid, and accept for yourself and all the family, my most sincere good wishes,

Your affectionate cousin,

Robert Louis Stevenson.[64]

The back garden of our house in Royal Terrace was filled with sweet smelling gillyflowers, roses, honeysuckle, geranium, fox-gloves, cotoneaster and wisteria. Willow and elm trees found a place too. Louis with his bright most welcome presence invented endless games for the children. One he called 'The Rope of Good Hope', and he changed the rules every time! Flower pots were upturned on the seven steps and had to be negotiated on tip-toe, and a rope at the end had to be caught at a brisk run. Here too he taught us 'Inky, Tinky, Tetherly, Netherly, Bamfyl, Evil, Oval, Doval, La Ta Touche, Ding Ding Domino, Black Fish, White Trout, Eerie, Orie, You Are Out!!!'

At the top of the garden, well away from adult eyes, was a trellis arbour with unusual glazed *hollow* bricks for the path and these were ideal 'hidey holes' for our tobacco pipes when it was supposed we did not know anything about smoking! On the slopes of the semi-public garden of the Calton Hill we got superb views of Arthur's Seat, North Berwick Law and the Lomonds in Fife. The drawback for me to our house was the long distance to the Edinburgh Academy. Louis, from Heriot Row, was much closer.'[92]

Both Charles and David were at the Academy at the same time as Louis. Only a few hundred yards to the south of Royal Terrace lay the heart of Louis' Edinburgh playground in his adolescent years and he shared it often with these younger cousins. Every part of Holyrood and of Arthur's Seat they made their own. Charles' map gives a superb illustration of the ground they covered from the Haggis Knowe to Dunsappie Loch. Passing Dunsappie Louis always identified a non-existent cave and called it Dick Hatterick's Cave. [After the cave in Guy Mannering.] Probably he was also remembering the Grotto known to him in Italy, which he had visited with Bessy (oldest sister to David and Charles). She had arranged this whole trip in 1863 at the request of her Uncle Thomas. She went with a heavy heart because the Royal Archers Annual Ball was just coming up and she was hoping to get engaged to Alexander James Napier. She was very pretty and she need not have worried as he popped the question immediately on her return! Cummy's famous Diary of the continental trip had been given to her by Cashie. They were close friends all Cashie's life. Cashie, otherwise Catherine Doherty, later Fisher, died on March the 16th, 1899. Agnes ['Aggie'] Wilson, the other nurserymaid, ended her life at Marshall's Court, Edinburgh, where Cashie stayed with her for a while before her death in 1872.[5]

To explore Edinburgh the boys could turn either to the right or left at the end of the garden in Royal Terrace and following one of the many paths laid round the Calton Hill by their grandfather Robert after the soldiers had returned from the Napoleonic wars, they would arrive in a few minutes at Waterloo Place-the east end of Princes Street.

Many hundreds of thousands of people who *know* a great deal about Louis' life *know* that at least until he went to Samoa he had always expected to die and be buried in Scotland, either on the Pentlands or else in the 'gated cell' where his father already lay. Even in Samoa he was hoping to die in his native country. However it was not to be. When he realised he could never return he requested his family to have him buried on the top of Mount Vaea.

Blows the wind today, and the sun and the rain are flying,
Blows the wind on the moors today and now,
Where about the graves of the martyrs the whaups are crying,
My heart remembers how!
Grey recumbent tombs of the dead in desert places,
Standing-stones on the vacant wine-red moor,
Hills of sheep, and the howes of the silent vanished races,
And winds, austere and pure.
Be it granted me to behold you again in dying,
Hills of home! and to hear again the call;
Hear about the graves of the martyrs the peewees crying,
And hear no more at all.[65]

The three boys often visited the Old or New Calton Cemeteries, Louis on several occasions flirted with a maid who waved from one of the windows of the Waterloo Hotel, and David and Charles stopped always to admire their grandfather Robert's 'Panoramic Improvement' as Charles called it.

*North Berwick*
Here is what Louis writes in his 'Essay on the Lantern Bearers':

'. . . and say that I came upon such business as that of my Lantern bearers on the links; and described the boys as very cold, spat upon by flurries of rain, and drearily surrounded, all of which they were; and their talk as silly and indecent, which it certainly was. I might upon these lines, had I Zola's genius, turn out a page or so, a gem of literary art, render the lantern light with the touch of a master, and lay on the indecency with the ungrudging hand of love; and when all was done, what a triumph would my picture be of shallowness and dullness! How it would have missed the point! How it would have belied the boys! To the ear of the stenographer, the talk is merely silly and indecent; but ask the boys themselves and they are discussing (as it is proper they should) the possibilities of existence. To the eye of the observer they are wet and cold and drearily surrounded; but ask themselves, and they are in the heaven of a recondite pleasure, the ground of which is an ill-smelling lantern.'[67]

Anchor House was one of the venues where the boys gathered as 'Lantern Bearers' met.

Louis was helping David at the camera on the day a photograph was taken. It shows Thomas standing next Elizabeth, my mother, Bessie, Jane, Georgina and Mary, and Gina, David and Charles and an *unknown* boy are there- Thomas holding tight to 'Coolin' whose arrival into the household at 17 Heriot Row altered the life of all its occupants.[5]

Louis states:

'Four or five would sometimes climb into the belly of a ten man lugger, with nothing but the thwarts above them-for the cabin was usually locked, or choose out some hollow of the links where the wind might whistle overhead. There the coats would be unbuttoned and the bull's eyes discovered; and in the chequering glimmer, under the huge windy hall of the night, and cheered by a rich stream of toasting tinware these fortunate young gentlemen would crouch together in the cold sand of the links or on the scaly bilges of the fishing-boat, and delight themselves with inappropriate talk. Woe is me that I may not give some specimens-some of their

foresights of life, or deep inquiries into the rudiments of man and nature, these were so fiery and innocent, they were so richly silly, so romantically young. But the talk at any rate, was but a condiment; and these gatherings themselves only accidents in the career of the lantern-bearer. The essence of the bliss was to walk by yourself in the black night; the slide shut, the top-coat buttoned; not a ray escaping, whether to conduct your footsteps or to make your glory public; a mere pillar of darkness in the dark; and all the while, deep down in the privacy of your fool's heart, to know you had a bull's-eye at your belt, and to sing and exult over the knowledge.'[67]

In his essay called 'The Character of Dogs', Louis writes of 'Coolin':

'I knew another little Skye, somewhat plain in appearance, but a creature compact of amiability and solid wisdom. His family going abroad for a winter, he was received for that period by an uncle in the same city. The winter over, his own family home again, and his own house (of which he was very proud) reopened, he found himself in a dilemma between two conflicting duties of loyalty and gratitude. His old friends were not to be neglected, but it seemed hardly decent to desert the new. This was how he solved the problem. Every morning, as soon as the door was opened, off posted Coolin to his uncles, visited the children in the nursery, saluted the whole family, and was back at home in time for breakfast and his bit of fish. Nor was this done without a sacrifice on his part sharply felt; for he had to forego the particular honour and jewel of his day-his morning's walk with my father. And perhaps from this cause, he gradually wearied of and relaxed the practice, and at length returned to his ancient habits. But

Seal of William de Douglas 1332. Found at North Berwick 1788. R.P.Phillimore.

Covrt Y Tantallon North Berwic

[82] *Tantallon Castle, before restoration by James Richardson.*

Charles continued, 'Louis had his little grey friend, called after the range of hills in Skye with serrated peaks of great grandeur, for about 12 years. He is buried with his own tombstone in Swanston. Louis was to own many other dogs and he and his father always had a special relationship to their canine friends but to 'The Davids', as Louis always called the whole family, and to him Coolin was always very special and quite irreplaceable. It was to the nursery at 25 Royal Terrace that this little grey bundle would arrive at breakfast time when Louis was abroad escorted by David's eldest daughter Bessie".

The photographs of Tantallon Castle, that proud fortress of the Red Douglases, show the building as it was in the days when Louis and his gang of cousins would spend a whole day there armed with sandwiches for lunch. [82] With the tide out they could walk along the beach from North Berwick and on the rocky foreshore right beneath the towering ruin could still find arrow-heads made from flint and also occasional coins from the Stuart period. It was very unsafe and unstable and much was still slipping into the sea until the restoration by the 'Office of Works' in this century. One memorable day a yell from Louis brought Charles running to his side in one of the small chambers. 'Look, Chug', he said, 'at these feudal remains in the corner!' Remains indeed, but not very feudal! He was always in a state of great excitement with his imagination running very high. Tantallon has a deep well which was of brackish water brought in wooden piping from Auldhame, 130 feet above the castle. Years later, near the end of his life, and thousands of miles away in the tropic island of Samoa, Louis in his novel Catriona brought his hero David Balfour into the castle of Tantallon. [92]

the same decision served him in another and more distressing case of divided duty, which happened not long after. He was not at all a kitchen dog but the cook had nursed him with unusual kindness during the distemper; and though he did not adore her as he adored my father-although (born snob) he was critically conscious of her position as 'only a servant'- he still cherished for a special gratitude. Well the cook left, and retired some streets away to lodgings of her own; and there was Coolin in precisely the same situation as any young gentleman who has had the inestimable benefit of a faithful nurse. The canine conscience did not solve the problem with a pound of tea for Christmas. No longer content to pay a flying visit, it was the whole forenoon that he dedicated to comfort her solitude until (for some reason which I could never understand and cannot approve) he was kept locked up to break him of the graceful habit ... There are not many dogs like this good Coolin, and not many people.' [68]

'At last we came again within the sound of the sea. There was moonlight, though not much; and by this I could see the three huge towers and broken battlements of Tantallon, that old chief place of the red Douglasses. The horse was picketed at the bottom of the ditch to graze, and I was led within, and forth into the court, and thence into a tumbledown stone hall. Here my conductors built a brisk fire in the midst of the pavement, for there was a chill in the night. My hands were loosened, I was set by the wall in the inner end, and (the Lowlander having produced provisions) I was given oatmeal bread and a pitcher of French brandy. This done, I was left once more alone with my three Highlandmen. They sat close by the fire drinking and talking; the wind blew in by the breaches, cast about the smoke and flames, and sang in the tops of the towers; I could hear the sea under the cliffs, and my mind being reassured as to my life, and my body and spirits wearied with the day's employment, I turned upon one side and slumbered.

I had no means of guessing at what hour I was wakened, only the moon was down and the fire low. My feet were now loosed, and I was carried through the ruins and down the cliff-side by a precipitous path to where I found a fisher's boat in a haven of the rocks. This I was had on board of, and we began to put forth from the shore in a fine starlight.' [69]

Louis' incredible smile, and bright happy temperament meant that he was always given a very warm welcome when he visited Anchor House. It was summer holidays and the teen-age girls usually had their various friends to stay. On the dark or moonlit warm September evenings they would go down to the sands and march up and down singing 'catches' which were topical and amusing ... Many happy hours these girls had. Louis took it into his head that he would give the young ladies some fun, so one very still dark night with just the soft sound of the ripples of the sea on the sand, he got unseen between them and the water and a voice was heard, 'Blud'. Funny did you hear that? Again, 'Blud-a-Blud, Blud-a-Blud' in tragic tones and spacing. One girl dashed off in a panic and then another fled, and another, terrified-off to Anchor House for safety! The more hardy remained to learn in a few seconds that it was only Louis, who appeared petrified and dismayed at the end result of his practical joke. [5]

In North Berwick Louis attended the old parish church of North Berwick on the rising ground just behind the High Street. He wrote the 23 verses of 'A Lowden Sabbath Morn' about this church.

The prentit stanes that mark the deid,
Wi' lengthened lip, the sarious read;
Syne wag a moraleesin' heid,
   An' then an' there
Their hirplin' practice an' their creed
   Try hard to square.

It's here our Merren lang has lain,
A wee bewast the table-stane;
An' yon's the grave o' Sandy Blane;
   An' further ower,
The mither's brithers, dacent men!
   Lie a' the fower. [70]

Charles continued, 'The two ministers he sat under were the Rev. Peter McMoyland and the Rev. Dr Sprott. Of the first Louis in a note says, 'I have a special reason to speak well of him', and of the second, 'I have often met him in private and long (in the due phrase) sat under in his church and neither here nor there have I heard an unkind or ugly word upon his lips'. The preacher in the poem's verses has thus no original in the North Berwick parish church. Louis sometimes sat in the loft which was allocated to Sir Hew Dalrymple of Leuchie opposite the pulpit. A smaller loft was given over to Sir George Grant-Suttie of Balgone whose family, sons and daughters, attended regularly for many years. The pews of the church were mostly long benches with doors, but some of them were formed into squares, also with their own door, and these were allocated mostly to the owners of large farms in the parish such as Wamphray, Congalton, Bonnington, etc. The name of the farm was painted on the box. These boxes were a much more friendly method for a family attending church than the long bench of seats.'

Louis, David and Charles generally sat in the panelled loft of the darkest oak, and they came into the churchyard by the small wicket gate in the 'lang loan benorth the Kirkyard'. It is a dark bogle-infested lane within hand clutch I would say of the dead over the low wall and besides that the church itself had always an ill name since the days of James VI. According to Louis 'the devil's cantrips played therein when the queen was on the seas'.

The minister was opposite this dismal den with the precentor, and David, below him. The minister was adorned on each side by marble tablets to the dead. The sermons and prayers were all long and terribly dreary, the singing uninspired. The only redeeming feature was that the den was free from the admixture of peppermints, and humanity dressed in their 'Sunday best'. Also fixed in Charles' mind's eye forever was the beautiful and smiling face of Sir George Grant-Suttie's younger daughter, many years older than himself, sitting in the gallery nearly opposite the den.

There is no doubt at all that Louis got the bone structure of his nose from his mother my Aunt Maggie, but his long fingered delicate hands are identical with those in the portrait of our grandmother Jane. His eyes were absolutely unique in our family. When he looked directly at you and spoke to you it seemed possible to see directly into his soul. Many people have asked me to describe Louis down the years since his death. No photographs have been able to show his graceful movement and living expression. Perhaps today [1940] with the modern moving camera techniques if it could catch him completely unaware that he was 'on camera' a true likeness could be recorded. He did not come across from the stage as I have said as a particularly good actor.

The best representation that I know of him is certainly the two portraits that the famous painter John Singer Sargent did of him walking up and down in the drawing room in Bournemouth, and also the one where he is sitting down cross-legged that his wife Fanny is said to have destroyed. In my memory he is always happy and alive and indeed perfectly well. Our family have resented that he has so often been referred to as a more or less permanent invalid. He certainly had all the childhood illnesses that we all got some time or other and also a chest weakness that was greatly aggravated by the Edinburgh climate. His mother had this too, and both of them did well to escape the winter and head for the South of France. It is generally accepted today that Louis had bronchiectasis which did eventually cause severe haemhorrages but he made a good recovery from all the attacks. His death I think was an isolated stroke. He walked many miles on a daily basis and on some walking tours notched up 30 miles without undue fatigue. He had a very strong constitution indeed to withstand all the physical blows life dealt him.'[5]

All the Stevenson family worked hard at their vocation but none harder than Louis in the 44 years he had in life.

When the family was first torn apart by the struggle for shares in the business in 1872 Louis was only 22. The second struggle boiled up in 1887 he was 37 and now showed that he had a shrewd grasp of the situation. Letters which he wrote to James Dick of 10th and 12th April reveal that his legal training was employed on behalf of his father and mother. In a letter to his lawyer friend Charles Baxter of the 29th of April he says:

'My dear Charles,

Thank you for yours, the first decently supportable communication I have had in this matter. My idea is first of all, to compromise: secondly, to compromise as fairly as we are able. I don't think my father should be worried, nor my mother, nor yet me: and I don't think we fight for anything important, as I think ill of my father's health. This gives you a free hand, I think; I will back up almost anything. ...'[71]

**A professional aspect**

Although Louis never became a civil engineer, until he reached the age of 21, his parents hoped that he would follow in this family tradition and he was educated accordingly. In November 1867 he took a tentative step in this direction by enrolling as a student in the Arts faculty at Edinburgh University. It was not however until 1869/70 that he studied any engineering related subjects, namely mathematics and natural philosophy, continuing with these in 1870-71 together with the engineering classes of Professor Fleeming Jenkin (1833-85) which, being unable to follow, he refrained from attending.

By April 1871 after some three and a half years of dutifully, if increasingly half-heartedly, pursuing this career he felt unable to continue and announced his decision to give up engineering. This outcome was accepted with disappointment but also with *wonderful resignation*[72] by his father, no doubt recalling similar youthful tussles, on the understanding that Louis read for the bar, instead of writing literature, which he considered no profession! Engineering's loss proved outstandingly to be literature's gain, but Louis's writings benefited immeasurably from his maritime engineering experience both in context and detail.

Some of Louis's published writings even related directly to engineering such as his paper on *A new form of intermittent light for lighthouses*, his *Memoir of Fleeming Jenkin, Records of a family of engineers* and an essay, *The education of an engineer*. Louis and his father enjoyed corresponding on literary matters, each claiming to have improved some of the other's writings. Louis considered that he had *materially helped to polish the diamond* of his father's presidential address to the Royal Society of Edinburgh in 1885 and *ended by feeling quite proud of the paper as if it had been mine; the next time you have as good a one, I will overhaul it for the wages of feeling as clever as I did when I had managed to understand and helped to set it clear.*[73]

Louis's intermittent light paper, read to the Royal Scottish Society of Arts on 27 March 1871, was a creditable effort and earned him a silver medal of the Society. It also prompted his jaunty farewell *To the Commissioners of Northern Lights*, which concluded with the thought that as a future advocate he might one day be a commissioner himself!

> I send to you, commissioners,
> A paper that may please ye, sirs,
> (For troth they say it micht be worse
>     An' I believe't)
> And on your business lay my curse
>     Before I leav't
>
> I thocht I'd serve wi' you, sirs, yince,
> But I've thocht better of it since'
> The matter I will nowise mince,
>     But tell ye true:
> I'll  service wi' some ither prince,
>     An' no' wi' you.
>
> I've no been very deep, ye'll think,
> Cam' delicately to the brink
> An' when the water gart me shrink
>     Straucht took the rue,
> An' didna stoop my fill to drink-
>     I own it true.
>
> I kennt on cape and isle, a light
> Burnt fair an' clearly ilka night;
> But at the service I took fright,
>     As sune's I saw,
> An' being still a neophite
>     Gaed straucht awa'.
>
> Anither course I now begin,
> The weeg I'll cairry for my sin,
> The court my voice shall echo in,
>     An' - wha can tell ? -
> Some ither day I may be yin
>     O' you mysel'[74]

Louis's engineering education at Edinburgh University seems to have been characterised more by truancy and a very tolerant Professor Fleeming Jenkin than any serious acquisition of knowledge. Professor Jenkin, against his better judgement after much pleading by Louis for a class attendance certificate and after having at first told him *It is quite useless for you to come to me, Mr. Stevenson. There may be doubtful cases, there is no doubt about yours. You have simply not attended my class,*[75] provided him with one containing a form of words for his father's eyes indicative of his having satisfactorily completed the class-work in engineering.

Louis wrote, *I am still ashamed when I think of his shame in giving me that paper. He made no reproach in his speech, but his manner was the more eloquent; it told me plainly what dirty business we were on; and I went from his presence, with my certificate indeed in my possession, but with no answerable sense of triumph.*[75] There seems to have been no question of Louis graduating. This was the *bitter beginning* of his great friendship with Jenkin of whom he wrote in 1885 *'I never knew a better man'*[76] and on whom he bestowed to posterity a remarkable if not very comprehensive biography.

During the long summer vacations Louis gained practical experience of harbour and lighthouse engineering operations, particularly of pier construction at Anstruther and Wick in

[83] *Wick breakwater c.1865. Note the travellers and jennies at end.*

1868. He was fascinated by the experience of sea diving but, in general, found the site work physically demanding and uncongenial. He wrote to his father from Anstruther on 2 July 1868, *bring also my paint box. . . I am going to try the travellers and Jennies, and have made a sketch of them and begun the drawing. After that I'll do the staging.* The *travellers* were timber gantries that moved along the pier and ahead of its temporary end, on rails supported on piles at each side of the pier. The *Jennies* were cranes, which moved backwards and forwards transversely on top of the travellers, used for lifting and lowering stones into position.

*Tomorrow I will watch the masons at work at the pier foot and see how long they take to work that Fifeness stone you ask about: they get sixpence an hour; so that is the only datum required . . . It is awful how slowly I draw and how ill: I am not nearly done with the travellers and have not thought of the Jennies yet. When I'm drawing I find out something I have not measured, or, having measured, have not noted, or, having noted, cannot find; and so I have to trudge to the pier again, ere I can go further with my noble design.*[77] **[75]**

Of his experience at Anstruther Louis wrote, *What I gleaned, I am sure I do not know; but indeed I had already my own private determination to be an author; I loved the art of words and the appearances of life; and travellers and headers, and rubble, and polished ashlar* [squared masonry], *and pierres perdues* [rubble stone], *and even the thrilling question of string course* [of masonry set out by string line], *interested me only (if they interested me at all) as properties of some possible romance or as words to add to my vocabulary . . . though I haunted the breakwater by day, and even loved the place for the sake of the sunshine, the thrilling sea-side air, the wash of waves on the sea-face, the green glimmer of the divers helmets far below, and the musical chinking of the masons, my one genuine pre-occupation lay elsewhere, and my only industry was in the hours when I was not on duty.*

Then northwards. *Into the bay of Wick stretched the dark length of the unfinished breakwater, in its cage of open staging; the travellers (like frames of churches) over-plumbing all* **[83]**; *and away at the extreme end, the divers toiling unseen on the foundation. On a platform of loose planks, the assistants turned their air mills; a stone might be swinging between wind and water; underneath the swell ran gayly; and from time to time a mailed dragon with a window glass snout came dripping up the ladder . . . To go down in the dress, that was my absorbing fancy; and with the countenance of a certain handsome scamp of a diver, Bob Bain by name, I gratified the whim . . . Some twenty rounds below the platform, twilight fell. Looking up I saw a low green heaven* *mottled with vanishing bells of white; looking around, except for the weedy spokes and shaft of the ladder, nothing but a green gloaming.*

*Thirty rounds lower* [at a depth of about 30 ft], *I stepped off on the pierres perdues of the foundation;*[76] *a dumb helmeted figure took me by the hand, and made a gesture (as I read it) of encouragement; and looking in at the creature's window, I beheld the face of Bain . . . how a man's weight, so far from being an encumbrance, is the very ground of his agility, was the chief lesson of my submarine experience . . . As I began to go forward with the hand of my estranged companion, a world of tumbled stones was visible, pillared with the weedy uprights of the staging: overhead, a flat roof of green: a little in front, the sea-wall, like an unfinished rampart.*

*And presently, in our upward progress, Bob motioned me to leap upon a stone . . . Now the block stood six feet high; it would have been quite a leap to me unencumbered; with the breast and back weights, and the twenty pounds upon each foot, and the staggering load of the helmet, the thing was out of reason. I laughed aloud in my tomb; and to prove to Bob how far he was astray, I gave a little impulse from my toes. Up I soared like a bird, my companion soaring at my side. As high as to the stone and then higher, I pursued my impotent and empty flight. Even when the strong arm of Bob had checked my shoulders, my heels continued their ascent; so that I blew out sideways like an autumn leaf, and must be hauled in hand over hand, as sailors haul in the slack of a sail, and propped upon my feet again like an intoxicated sparrow . . . Bain brought me back to the ladder and signed me to mount . . . Of a sudden, my ascending head passed into the trough of a swell. Out of the green I shot at once into a glory of rosy, almost of sanguine light - the multitudinous seas incarnadined, the heaven above a vault of crimson. And then the glory faded into the hard, ugly daylight of a Caithness autumn, with a low sky, a gray sea, and a whistling wind.*

*Diving was one of the best things I got from my education as an engineer: of which however, as a way of life, I wish to speak with sympathy. It takes a man into the open air; it keeps him hanging about harbor-sides, which is the richest form of idling; it carries him to wide islands; it gives him a taste of the genial dangers of the sea; it supplies him with dexterities to exercise; it makes demands upon his ingenuity; it will go far to cure him of any taste (if ever he had one) for the miserable life of cities. And when it has done so, it carries him back and shuts him in an office! From the roaring skerry and the wet thwart of the tossing boat, he passes to the stool and desk; and with a memory full of ships, and seas, and perilous headlands, and the shining pharos, he must apply his long-sighted eyes to the petty niceties of drawing, or measure his inaccurate mind with several pages of consecutive figures. He is a wise youth, to be sure, who can balance one part of genuine life against two parts of drudgery between four walls, and for the sake of the one, manfully accept the other.*[78]

In a letter to his mother on 20-21 September, Louis wrote, *I was awakened by Mrs S. at the door* [of the New Harbour Hotel, Pultneytown - now a Customs office] *There's a ship ashore at Shaltigoe! I got up, dressed and went out. The mizzled sky and rain blinded you . . . Some of the waves were twenty feet high. The spray rose eighty feet at the new pier . . . The thunder at the wall when it first struck - the rush along ever growing higher - the great jet of snow-white spray some forty feet above you - and the 'noise of many waters', the roar, the hiss, the 'shrieking' amongst the shingle as it fell head over heels at your feet. I watched if it threw the big stones at the wall; but it never moved them.*

[next day] *The end of the* [breakwater] *work displays gaps, cairns of ten ton blocks, stones torn from their places and turned*

*right round. The damage above water is comparatively little: what there may be below, on 'ne sait pas encore'. The roadway is torn away, cross-heads broken, planks tossed here and there, planks gnawn and mumbled as if a starved bear had been trying to eat them, planks with spales lifted from them as if they had been dressed with a ragged plane, one pile swaying to and fro clear of the bottom, the rails in one place sunk a foot at least. This was not a great storm, the waves were light and short. Yet when we are [were] standing at the office, I felt the ground beneath me quail as a huge roller thundered on the work at the last year's cross-wall . . . [To] appreciate a storm at Wick requires a little of the artistic temperament which Mr.T.S.C.E. [Thomas Stevenson Civil Engineer] possesses . . . I can't look at it practically however: that will come I suppose like gray hair or coffin nails . . . Our pole is snapped: a fortnight's work and the loss of the Norge schooner all for nothing! - except experience and dirty clothes.*[79]

When leaving Wick, Louis, in a letter to his cousin Bob Stevenson, paints an indelible picture of the mail coach journey by night to the most northerly railway terminus, then at Golspie about 50 miles to the south. [The railway did not reach Wick until 1874.] **[84]** *The Wick Mail then, my dear fellow, is the last Mail Coach within Great Britain, whence there comes a romantic interest that few could understand. To me, on whose imagination positively nothing took so strong a hold as the Dick Turpins and Claude Duvals of last century, a Mail was an object of religious awe. I pictured the long dark highways, the guard's blunderbuss, the passengers with three-cornered hats above a mummery of great-coat and cravat; and the sudden 'Stand and deliver!' - the stop, the glimmer of the coach lamp upon the horseman - Ah! we shall never get back to Wick.*

*All round that northern capital of stink and storm there stretches a succession of flat and dreary moors absolutely treeless, with the exception of above a hundred bour-trees [elders] beside Wick, and a stunted plantation at Stirkoke, for the distance of nearly twenty miles south. When we left to cross this tract, it was cloudy and dark. A very cold and pertinacious wind blew with unchecked violence, across these moorlands. I was sick sleepy, and drawing my cloak over my face set myself to doze. Mine was the box-seat, desirable for the apron and the company of the coachman, a person in this instance enveloped in that holy and tender interest that hangs about the 'Last of the Mohicans' or the 'Derniers Bretons'.*

*And as this example of the loquacious genus coachman was more than ordinarily loquacious I put down my hood again and talked with him. He had a philosophy of his own, I found, and a philosophy eminently suited to the needs of his position. The most fundamental and original doctrine of this, was as to what constitutes a gentleman. It was in speaking of Lockyer of Wenbury that I found it out. This man is an audacious quack and charlatan,* destined for aught, I know, to be the Cagliostro [Italian charlatan] of the British Revolution; and, as such, Mr Lockyer is no favourite of mine: I hate quacks, not personally (for they are not men of imagination like ourselves?) but because of their influence; so I was rather struck on hearing the following. 'Well sir', said the coachman, 'Mr Lockyer has always shown himself a perfect gentleman to me, sir - his hand as open as you'll see, sir!' In other words, half-a-crown to the coachman!

As the pleasures of such philosophical talk rather diminished and the slumber increased, I buried my face again. The coach swayed to and fro. The wind battled and roared about us. I observed the difference in sounds - the rhythmic and regular beat of the hoofs as the horses cantered up some incline, and the ringing, merry, irregular clatter as they slung forward, at a merry trot, along the level.

First stage: Lybster. A Roman catholic priest travelling within, knowing that I was delicate, made me take his seat inside for the next stage. I dozed. When I woke, the moon was shining brightly. We were off the moors and up among the high grounds near the Ord of Caithness. I remember seeing a curious thing: the moon shone on the ocean, and on a river swollen to a great pool and between stretched a great black mass of rock: I wondered dimly how the river got out and then to doze again. When next I wake, we have passed the low church of Berridale, standing sentinel on the heathery plateau northward of the valley, and are descending the steep road past the Manse: I think it was about one: the moon was frosty but gloriously clear. In another minute -

Second stage: Berridale. And of all lovely places, one of the loveliest. Two rivers run from the inner hills, at the bottom of two deep, Killiecrankie-like gorges, to meet in a narrow bare valley close to the grey North Ocean. The high Peninsula between and the banks, on either hand until they meet, are thickly wooded - birch and fir. On one side is the bleak plateau with the lonesome little church, on the other the  bleaker, wilder mountain of the Ord. When I and the priest had lit our pipes, we crossed the streams, now speckled with the moonlight that filtered through the trees, and walked to the top of the Ord. There the coach overtook us and away we went for a stage, over great, bleak mountains, with here and there a hanging wood of silver birches and here and there a long look of the moonlit sea, the white ribbon of the road marked far in front by the newly erected telegraph posts. We were all broad awake with our walk, and made very merry outside, proffering 'fills' of tobacco and pinches of snuff and dipping surreptitiously into aristocratic flasks and plebeian pint bottles.

Third stage: Helmsdale. Round a great promontory with the gleaming sea far away in front, and rattling through some sleeping streets that shone strangely white in the moonlight, and then we pull up beside the Helmsdale posting-house, with a great mountain valley behind. Here I went in to get a glass of whiskey and water. A very broad, dark commercial said: 'Ha! do you remember me? Anstruther?' I had met him five years before in the Anstruther commercial room, when my father was conversing with an infidel and put me out of the room to be away from contamination; whereupon I listened outside and heard the man say he had not sinned for seven years, and declare that he was better than his maker. I did not remember him; nor did he my face, only my voice. He insisted on 'standing me the whiskey "for auld lang syne"; and he being a bagman, it was useless to refuse. Then away again. The coachman very communicative at this stage, telling us about the winter before, when the mails had to be carried through on

**[85]** *Louis's sketch of Muckle Flugga, 1869.*[81]

*horseback and how they left one of their number sticking in the snow, bag and all I suppose. The country here was softer; low, wooded hills running along beside the shore and all inexpressibly delightful to me after my six months of Wick barrenness and storm.*

*Fourth stage: name unknown. O sweet little spot, how often I have longed to be back to you! A lone farm-house on the sea-shore, shut in on three sides by the same, low, wooded hills. Men were waiting for us by the roadside, with the horses - sleepy, yawning men. What a peaceful place it was! Everything steeped in the moonlight, and the gentle plash of the waves coming to us from the beach. On again. Through Brora, where we stopped at the Post-Office and exchanged letter-bags through a practicable window-pane, as they say in stage directions. Then on again. Near Golspie now, and breakfast, and the roaring railway. Passed Dunrobin, the dew-steeped, tree-dotted park, the princely cluster of its towers, rising from bosky plantations and standing out against the moon-shimmering sea - all this sylvan and idyllic beauty so sweet and new to me! Then the Golspie Inn, and breakfast and another pipe, as the morning dawned, standing in the verandah. And then round to the station to fall asleep in the train . . .'*[80]

In June 1869 Louis accompanied his father on a voyage of inspection of lighthouses in Orkney and Shetland in the

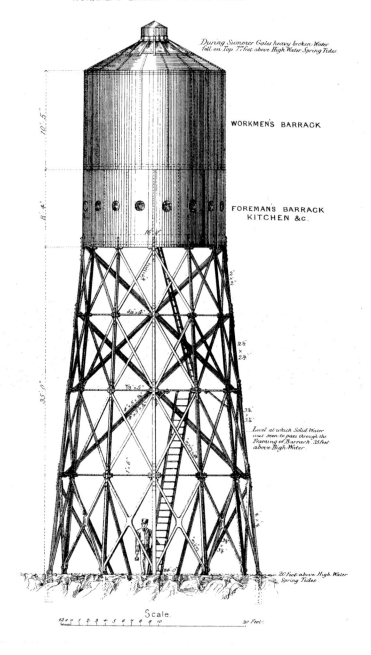

DHUHEARTACH

WORKMENS BARRACK ON THE ROCK.

PLATE V

*During Summer Gales heavy broken Water fell on Top 77 feet above High Water Spring Tides.*

WORKMEN'S BARRACK

FOREMANS BARRACK
KITCHEN &c.

*Level at which Solid Water was seen to pass through the Framing of Barrack 35 feet above High Water.*

*20 Feet above High Water Spring Tides.*

Scale.

20 Feet.

lighthouse steamer and provided his mother with a detailed account of his *sore journeying and perilous peregrination.* For example, *we sighted North Unst Lighthouse, the most northerly dwelling house in Her Majesty's dominion. The mainland rises higher, with great seams and landslips; and from the norwestern corner runs out a string of shelving ledges, with a streak of green and purple seaweed and a boil of white foam about their feet. The lighthouse stands on the highest - 190 feet above the sea; . . . the reefs looked somewhat thus . . .* [sketch **85,63**]. *We were pulled into the creek shown in the picture between the Lighthouse and the other rock, down the centre of which runs a line of reef . . . This is very narrow, little broader than a knife edge; but its ridge has been cut into stone steps and laid with iron grating and railed with an iron railing. It was here that we landed, making a leap between the swells at a rusted ladder laid slant-wise against the raking side* [of] *the ridge. Before us a flight of stone steps led up the two hundred feet to the lighthouse in its high yard-walls across whose foot the sea had cast a boulder weighing twenty tons. On one side is a slippery face of clear sound rock and on the other a chaos of pendulous boulder and rotten stone. On either side there was no vegetation save tufts of sea-pink in the crevices and a little white lichen on the lee faces.*[81]

During his summer vacation of 1870 Louis spent three weeks on the isle of Erraid [off Mull], from which he visited Dhu Heartach Lighthouse then under construction 15 miles to the south-west. **[62]** Two years later, although then pursuing his law classes at University, he managed in the summer to produce a lively account of the project. *Even before the work was sanctioned, he wrote, Dhu Heartach had given the engineers a taste of its difficulties. Although the weather was fine, Messrs Stevenson failed to effect a landing and had to send in their preliminary report based merely upon what they could see from the deck of the vessel. But even this had not prepared them for the continual difficulty and danger which accompanied every landing from the beginning to the end of the work. Favoured by the smooth egg-shaped outline of the rock, which is about [130] feet broad, [240] feet long and 35 feet above high water at its summit, the swell breaks at the one end, runs cumulating round each side, and meets and breaks again at the opposite end, so that the whole rock is girdled with broken water. There is no sheltered bight. If there be anything to aggravate the swell, and it is wonderful what a little thing it takes to excite these giant waters, landing becomes impossible . . . The probability is that the very height of Dhu Heartach rock, by causing the waves to rise, is what makes them so dangerous at a considerable elevation; in short the destructive character of a wave as regards level depends upon the relation between the height of the wave, the height and contour of the obstacle and the depth of water in which it acts.*

*The first object of the Messrs. Stevenson was to erect a temporary barrack for the residence of the workmen . . . it was decided that the structure - a framework thirty-five feet high, supporting a plated cylinder or drum twenty feet high and divided into two stories - should consist entirely of malleable iron.* **[86]** *The shore station was placed on Isle Erraid . . . On the twenty-fifth of June . . . they first took possession of the rock and disturbed the seals, who had been its former undisputed tenants. The work during this first season was much interrupted. Even when a landing was effected, the sea rose so suddenly and there was such a want of appliances upon the Rock itself, that the men had sometimes hard enough ado to get off again. The season which began so late closed finally on the third of September, and the first tier of the barrack framework was left unfinished.*

*All the winter of 1867-68, a band of resident workmen were carrying on at the shore station with its bothies, cottages, quarry and the workyard where every stone was to be cut, dressed, fitted and numbered before being sent out to the rock to be finally built into the tower; and on the fourteenth of April, the 'Dhu Heartach' steamer came back to her moorings in Earraid Sound. The result proved that she was too early; for there was no landing at all in April; only two in May, giving between them a grand total of two hours and a half upon the rock; and only two once again in June. In July there were thirteen, in August ten, in September eleven: in all, thirty-eight landings in five months . . . On the twentieth of August, the malleable iron barrack was so far advanced and the weather gave such promise of continuing fine, that Mr Alan Brebner C.E. (of Edinburgh) and thirteen workmen landed on the rock and took up their abode in the drum . . . A sudden gale however sprung up and they could not be communicated with till the 26th [August 1868] during the greater part of which time the sea broke so heavily over the rock as to prevent all work and during the height of the storm the spray rose far above the barrack and the sea struck very heavily on the flooring of the lower compartment which is 35 feet above the rock and 56 feet above high water mark.*

*The third season, that of 1869, saw the work properly commenced. The barrack had come scatheless through the winter,* and the master-builder Mr Goodwillie with between twenty and thirty workmen took up his abode there, on the twenty-sixth of April. On Isle Earraid, there was a good quarry of granite, two rows of sheds, two travelling cranes, railways to carry the stones, a stage on which, course after course, the lighthouse was put experimentally together and then taken down again to be sent piece-meal out to the rock, a pier for the lighters [stone carrying boats], and a look out place furnished with a powerful telescope by which it could be observed whether the weather was clear [and] how high the sea was running on Dhu Heartach as so judge whether it were worthwhile to steam out on the chance of landing. In a word, there was a stirring village of some [fifty] souls, on this island which, four years before, had been tenanted by one fisherman's family and a herd of sheep.

The life in this little community was highly characteristic. On Sundays only, the continual clink of tools from quarry and workyard came to an end, perfect quiet then ranged throughout the settlement, and you saw workmen leisurely smoking their pipes about the green enclosure, and they and their wives wearing their Sunday clothes (from association of ideas, I fancy) just as if they were going to take their accustomed seats in the crowded church at home. As for the services at Earraid, they were held in one of the wooden bothies, the audience perched about the double tier of box beds or gathered round the table. Mr Brebner [The Engineer] read a sermon and the eloquent prayer which was written specially for the Scottish Lighthouse service, and a voluntary band and precentor led the psalms. Occasionally a regular minister came to the station, and then worship was held in the joiner's shop.

On fine weather, before the sun had risen behind Ben-More, the Dhu Heartach steamed out of the bay towing a couple of heavy, strong built lighters laden with the dressed and numbered stones. It was no easy or pleasant duty to be steersman in these lighters, for what with the deck-cargo and the long heavy swell, they rolled so violently that few sailors were able to stand it. Dhu Heartach itself on some such calm, warm summer day presented a strange spectacle. This small black, almost out of sight of land in the fretful, easily irritated sea, was a centre of indefatigable energy. The whole small space was occupied by men coming and going between the lighters or the barrack and the slowly-lengthening tower. A steam winch and inclined plane raised the stones from the water's edge to the foot of the building; and it was a matter of no little address and nicety, to whip one of these great two-ton blocks out of the lighter, as it knocked about and rolled gunwale-under in the swell, and bring it safely up to the tower, without breaking it or chipping off some corner that would spoil the joint. Then, there would come the dinner hour; and the noise was incontinently quieted, there was no more puffing of the steam engine or clink of mallets on the building; the men sat scattered in groups over their junk [salt meat] and potatoes and beer.

By the end of this season, the tower had reached the height of eight feet four inches . . . But the heaviest end of the work was now over. In the fourth season, 1870, there were sixty-two landing days, and the white tower soon began to top its older brother the iron barrack. By the end of the season it was forty-eight feet high, the last stone was laid next summer, and during the present summer, the lantern and internal fittings have also been brought to completion. Before the end of 1872, the light will have been exhibited. For the tower . . . Messrs Stevenson adopted the form of a parabolic frustrum, to a hundred and seven and a half feet high, 36 feet in diameter at the base and 16 feet at the top all built of granite . . .

*The entire weight of masonry is 3,115 tons . . . The light will be fixed dioptric with a range of eighteen miles in addition to which there is machinery which rings during fogs a hundredweight bell.*

Anticipating possible future discomforts arising from the difficulty of landing supplies, he concludes: *Shortly before the light was first exhibited* [at nearby Skerryvore Lighthouse] *. . . a long track of storms extending over seven weeks prevented the tender from getting near the reef; and before the weather had moderated, the stock of tobacco in the tower was quite exhausted. On the morning of this catastrophe, the [workmen] ceremoniously broke their pipes and put up a chalk inscription over the mantle shelf in the kitchen: 'Such-and-such a date, Tobacco done - Pipes Broken.' Let us hope that no such 'memor querela' may ever be read over the chimney of Dhu Heartach.*[82]

It is doubtful whether Louis's delicate health would have allowed him to become a successful engineer even if he had had the inclination and had persevered with his engineering education. Fortunately for posterity he gave reign to what was undoubtedly his greater talent, but it was not to prove a decision which was to bring him complete peace of mind. At the age of 43, in the last year of his life, he wrote to W. H. Low in a fit of depression, that his literary achievements had been inadequate for *'the top flower of a man's life . . . Small is the word; it is a small age and I am of it. I could have wished to be otherwise busy in this world. I ought to have been able to build lighthouses and write 'David Balfours' too. Hinc illae lacrymae* [hence these tears]'.[83]

# Chapter Seven

## David A. Stevenson 1854-1938 - Extender of the coastal lights

**Family recollections**

David Alan, eldest son of David Stevenson, was born at 8 Forth Street. His younger brother, Charles, arrived less than a year and a half later. Both boys went to Scott's Preparatory School in Picardy Place and then on to Edinburgh Academy. **[87]** Much of their childhood held shared experiences but it is from Charles that we have an account of the houses they lived in and the times they spent with their first cousin Louis.

In 'Memoirs of Himself', written in San Francisco in 1880, Louis referred to his cousin:

'I learned to read when I was seven, looking over the pictures in illustrated papers while recovering from a gastric fever. It was thus done at a blow; all previous efforts to teach me having been defeated by my active idleness and remarkable inconsequence of mind. The same fever is remarkable to me for another reason; one of my little cousins (D.A.S.) having sent me a letter every day. This was a kindness I shall never forget till the day of my death; though I see little of him now, and cannot think he much affects me, I have an incredible smothered warmth of affection towards him in my heart. As he will probably outlive me, I hope he may see these words and take the thanks I have been always too shy to renew to him in person.'[84]

In 1870 David Stevenson wrote an account of his life and the various works for which he was responsible for the information of his children. This was done at the urgent request of Elizabeth. He had it privately printed and called it *Records of a mother.*

She had caught diphtheria when nursing Charles in 1871. Davie was not at home at the time; he was helping with the construction of Dhu Heartach. She died on the 7th of July, aged 55, and was a terrible loss, to David and his children. In later years Charles could never speak of his mother to anyone. Possibly he felt guilt of some sort that she had caught this illness while nursing him. David wrote that her last words were a request to him that none of the children were to see her as she was in death as she wanted them to remember her as she had been in life.

In the same year Davie captured the imagination of his uncle Alan:

'In 1861 when I was 7 years old my Uncle Alan presented me with the large picture of the Bell Rock in progress which hangs in our dining room. I don't know how he came to do this as he had a son R. A. M. Stevenson who was 3 or 4 years older than I was who however as it turned out did not become an engineer. The following is a copy of the letter Alan wrote to my father and of the inscription that was pasted on the back of the picture but which when it was cleaned some years ago the stupid people removed it.

Portobello
15th July 1861.
My Dear David,
I enclose a Latin inscription for the back of the picture which you can paste on when you get it. I hope dear D.A. may some day be able to read it and perhaps to point out some unclassicalism therein.

Ever your affectionate brother
Alan Stevenson

Davidi Alano Stevensono

carissimo nepote meo
hanc phari apud tintinnabuli rupen imaginem
(Patro mei carrique sui Roberti Stevensoni
laborum difficilliorum periculossimorum umque digni fructus)
dico imaginem amaris nei erga Davidulum meum patruus
dedi Alanus Stevensonus Portusbelli Idilis quinctil. A.D. 1861

The translation, by himself, reads:

To David Alan Stevenson
my dearest nephew,
this Picture of the Lighthouse on the Bell Rock
(the worthy fruit of the most arduous and perilous labours of
Robert Stevenson my father and his grandfather)
This picture I say I his Uncle have given
as a pledge of my love towards my dear little David.
Alan Stevenson, Portobello, July 1861.'[5]

His father took Davie with him in 1868 on board the *Pharos* as she sailed with the Commissioners of Northern Lights on their annual inspection voyage. Here are some extracts from the diary Robert insisted that he should write:

'Tuesday 7 [July 1868]
We also shipped at Port St Mary a Manx cat without a tail which on coming on board at once became perfectly intimate with Milo [the ship's dog] who was glad to get him for a companian.

Monday 13 [July 1868]
Then on to Isle Ornsay where we anchored for the night. ... here we put ashore our tailless Manx cat which the captain did not wish to keep on board. Milo missed it very much. Milo has been getting famous walks ashore. he is an extrordinary animal and if by any chance he be left ashore he waits patiently till he hears them weighing the anchor and then he jumps into the sea to swim to the ship no matter how far off she is.'[85]

Davie went again with the Pharos in 1869 and 1870. Now aged 16 he makes these shrewd observations:

*July 6th Wedensday.* We left Edin. at 2 o'clock and arr. in Glasgow at + past 3 and drove to the Greenock station where we got a train at 4 which brought us to Greenock at 5. We went to the Ton Tine Hotel where we took rooms and dined. After dinner we got a waggonette and drove along the esplanade to Gourock where it was once proposed to make a harbour and a fine harbour it would have been if there had been money enough to carry it out. We walked home through the town and along the quays, the former swarmed with shows and drunk people and on enquiry learned that the next 3 days were the fair. From the latter we saw several fine steamers starting, the Dacian for New York, the Wolf for Belfast and the Camel for Derry.'[85]

1870 also saw the 'Davids' as Louis called them move again, this time to the fashionable west end and 45 Melville Street. Bessie [Elizabeth] had married Alexander J. Napier, W.S., in 1867. Jane's husband was William Mackintosh, later Lord Kyllachy. [109] They married in 1869.

There is a far from flattering account of the great 19th century scientists written by Davie when recalling his university education:

'In 1869 I left the Academy and in 1870 went to the Edinburgh University and took the degree of B.Sc. in Engineering in April 1875. The Professor's lectures I attended were Kelland mathematics, Crum Brown chemistry, Tait natural philosophy, Geikie geology, Fleeming Jenkin engineering. I had as fellow students Sir John Murray of Challenger expedition fame, principal Ewing, Professor Laing of St Andrews. In Tait's laboratory, which I attended, I saw a good deal of the above, afterwards well known men, while Sir William Thompson, afterwards Lord Kelvin, and Sir James Dewar were frequent visitors of Tait and carrying on experiments there in the laboratory in which we assisted. In this connection I was a regular attender of the evening meetings of the Edinburgh Royal Society and the Society of Arts where we had papers from Kelvin, Tait, Laing and many other well known scientists. The only thing I would say now is that these gentlemen lectured us as if they had arrived at the root of all natural physics, which has proved not to be the case and I am glad that scientific men in similar walks in life today realise not only that what was put forward then, as being the last word, was not so, but that the advances made since are still far from being final.'[86]

Davie was in due course apprenticed to his father and Uncle Thomas. During university vacations, David took him on inspection or business journeys in Scotland and England. After Charles graduated the two young men visited engineering works in the eastern part of the United States of America and Canada during six weeks of a very hot summer, details of which follow later. They followed much the same route as David had taken forty years before. It took them only ten days in the *California*

and the same time back in the *Anchoria*. On their return they took their places in the family firm as full-time assistants and their talent and the result of their careful training was now obvious to others, including their Uncle Thomas.

Six years after his sons had returned from America David had to retire. Fortunately several years earlier the firm had taken on as assistant Alan Brebner (1826-90). He was the son of a mason who had worked on the Bell Rock. A gifted and well-educated man whom, having qualified as a civil engineer in 1878, the family firm had the great foresight to make a salaried partner. His experience and stability were essential during the 1880s. New contracts had to be negotiated to let Brebner and the young men have anything like a reasonable share in the profits and Thomas was quite unable to appreciate that his health was also failing. He was absent for months on end but was very proud to be the head of the firm and he would return at intervals and accomplish a great burst of work before disappearing again to be nursed by his family. With great patience and restraint from Davie and Charles, new contracts were drawn up but only Thomas's death in 1887 gave them and Alan Brebner the chance for a fair financial deal. Louis, as he said, had never paid any attention to these matters and he was angry with Davie when he got a long letter in Bournemouth asking for his help.

'19th April, 1887.
My Dear Louis,

Mr. Dick tells me that he has had some correspondence with you in reference to our office arrangements. He also says that you propose an interview with me on the subject. I am afraid that such an interview would be very painful & not likely to result in good. As however from your proposing an interview I conclude you are desirous of an interchange of views on the subject & are now acting for your father, I will frankly give you mine, little as I relish the job. From what Mr. Dick tells me I do not think you realise the position. When the present contract was made as perhaps you don't know my father was so ill that he never knew that an arrangement was going on, there was a great deal of discussion, Charlie & I it is needless to say were not satisfied but we were ultimately told, take what is offered or clear out altogether. Against my will but on the advice of friends we agreed to go into the business on the understanding that there should be a revision of the division of profits in 3 years & arbitration if necessary. This time has now come & if Uncle Tom had been well & doing his share of the work up to date this revision would have taken place as between Charlie & myself and we should certainly have been entitled to more favourable terms. But not only has the time for revision come but a very different state of matters has arisen my uncle has not been able to do a hands turn of work for more than 18 months & as this is the case not only are we entitled to still further consideration but Mr. Brebner also has his claim. His view I may say has been from the first that your father should retire on the £500 provided for that purpose in the contract at least till he was able to resume work again. I suppose you have no hope of his ever being able to resume work again & I fear from what Dr. Balfour says there is none. If that is so then the only fair & honest thing to do is for him to retire on his £500.

The ground on which the last contract was drawn so much to our disadvantage was stated to be that my father had drawn more from the business than your father. This was raised when my father was unable to enlighten us on the subject & we had to fight with our hands tied as we knew nothing about it & had not access to his papers. But since his death I have of course seen his papers & I now know where we are.

In drawing that contract it was ignored that my father was a member of the firm 8 years before your father entered the office & that the business was practically his, his share of the profits the year before your father was taken in was over £2000. Consequently my father as senior partner & managing partner was entitled to a larger share of the profits & I say managing partner advisedly as he did by far the larger share of the work even up to recent times as the books and those who knew the business can testify. If such argument as that is to be used & with much more reason (for he came into the office only 1 year after me & joined the firm only 3 years later) Charlie will come down on me in years to come because I am drawing more than he is at present.

It was further ignored that my father gave up the individual appointments of engineer to the N.L.C. & the Fishery Board & got your father conjoined with him thereby giving up 2 retiring allowances and yet after being only 6 months out of the office he was ejected from the business without a sixpence of retiring allowance whereas a retiring allowance of £500 was secured to your father: & not only so, but in the event of his death, this sum is to be paid to his heirs to the end of the contract!

To come now to the more personal matter, even supposing your father was foolish enough not to get his fair share of the profits during the former contracts, I fail to see why we are to suffer for that. and suffer some we have. Summing the 11 years I worked in the office under the previous contract, for the first 6 I got nothing, & for the last 5 the princely sum of £100 per annum, Charlie was 10 years & never got a sixpence!! During that time our time was charged as assistants, & we worked hard I can tell you. I don't know how it looks to you but if I had been a member of the firm during that time I should be ashamed to treat anyone in such a way. I have already detailed how we were treated when the present contract was being arranged & the figures which Mr. Dick has put I understand before you speak for themselves, & it is needless to say I am not satisfied with the present arrangement.

Now the point is simply this, is my uncle to continue to draw from the business money for which he is not working. During the existence of present contract he has drawn half of the whole profits of the business leaving the other half for division between Brebner, Charlie & myself & has done nothing since August 1885 & was really unfit for business some time before that. An Engineer's business is a personal matter & is not like a grocer's business, & to treat it as a *family possession* is absurd. We derive no benefit from your father's being in the firm unless he were here & able to take up remits made to him (which do not come as he is not here) & the business would then be much more prosperous than it is. The family argument is really too much; you tried engineering & did not like it & took to literature. I stick to Engineering & work at it & as I understand it you think you have a claim on my exertions, are you prepared to share the profits of your work with me?

I think the terms we prepared were extremely liberal an income of £1200 a year for doing nothing for 2 years & at the end of that time which would be 3 years of idleness surely if still unable for business it would not be too much to ask a man to retire on the £500 provided in the contract for the purpose. I am not so sure now as I was at the time when this proposal was made 4 months ago of getting the matter so satisfactorily settled as it is now only too evident that a rest has done your father no good.

I would only say that if you could send someone like Charles Baxter to talk to Cheyne on your father's behalf (instead of Mowbray who is like a bear) Cheyne says matters might yet be arranged. If not I hope one of the three arbiters we named may be at once selected as time presses & arrangements should be made to have Brebner's claim also settled under it. Now you will perhaps think I have just spoken my mind too openly but I thought it best to let you see the bottom at once & I regret at once if I have pained you in any way but I would remind you of what I endured when the present contract was being drawn.

I hope that you are keeping well & that Mrs. Louis is also well. I have been reading your pessimistic politics with interest. I hear your father is to be home this week which I hope means that he is better.

Yours sincerely,
D. A. Stevenson.'[87]

Louis replied by return:
'Skerryvore  Bournemouth  April 21st. 1887
Dear Davie
It would be impossible for you and me (of all people in the world) to discuss the conduct of our respective fathers; and it was far from that that I ventured to propose. Just this much

I will say since you have referred to it: that to all human affairs there are two sides: I am sure there is something on your side; be you sure, too, there is something on ours.

But what I wish explained, and had hoped we might discuss, was very different.

Mr Dick's last statement was to all of us here a mere amazement. My father, my mother – and seemingly Mr Dick himself, until he restudied the matter, had understood the contract one way; and now we hear it is to be understood in quite another, of which we can no more approve than you would do yourself. That this ambiguity should ever have existed, that it should still exist – for neither Mr Dick nor you have said one word about it – is enough to stop further negotiation. For you must see for yourself that my mother and I can come to no decision as to a contract when we do not know what that contract is; and that it would be absurd to lay a case before arbiters till it has first been laid before the partners. Besides when I perceived the possibility of so great an error on our side, I thought it not improbable there might be some on both sides, & that a meeting might have cleared up all. You think the meeting impossible; doubtless you are right; and yet it is necessary for us to get the facts. I have therefore, so far as I am able, decided to adopt your alternative, and to ask Charles Baxter to see Mr Cheyne upon the matter. I trust he may see his way to act.

I must say one word in conclusion as to what you say of me. I have not put myself forward, except to spare my mother some pains, and to avert if possible a family difference; but you have referred to me so pointedly that I find that I must make at least this much of an answer. I have indeed no claim on the business; I have made none; if I thought I had one, I should be the last man to advance it. That you may have heard something which sounds the contrary of this, I think possible; nor can I explain that now: the explanation indeed might occur to you yourself; and it is sufficient for me —- it is all I am able to do —- at present, to set you right as to the fact. I am not quite indifferent to the result; for supposing my father to live, I may have to help him. Outside of that, it touches me not; nor shall that amount of self-interest make me at all ashamed to continue to help my mother in this correspondence. And I am sure of this: that no one who knows me, however slightly, will suppose me to think once of my own pocket.

My father has gone North today; he is very far from being well indeed.

Yours sincerely,
Robert Louis Stevenson.'[88]

Thomas and Louis had both been too ill to come north to attend to matters, and it was Maggie who arrived in Edinburgh as battle raged between the lawyers. When Thomas did go north it was in a private railway carriage taking him home for the last time. Louis could not believe that the firm would be able to carry on at all without his father; however, his cousins' partnership was to last for fifty years. Brebner died suddenly of a stroke in 1890, aged 63, but David and Charles combined their mutual talents and held the business together.

Marriage for Davie was to come three years after Charles. At his wedding he had met one of the bridesmaids called Dorothy Roberts, daughter of William Roberts of Beckenham in Kent, a cousin of Field Marshall Lord Roberts. David and Dorothy were married at St Paul's Church in Beckenham. The honeymoon was a splendid tour of the continent starting and ending in Paris.

'Among the many presents we received I valued two especially. One was the clock with Neptune on the top presented by nine Inspectors of Works who had all done good work for me at the various lighthouses and harbours I was engaged on and a silver bowl from my co-directors of the Scottish Equitable Insurance Company.'[5]

Davie and Dorothy returned to 45 Melville Street where he had lived with his sisters since his father's death, and they moved out into lodgings. Their first child Dorothy Emily Stevenson was born in November the same year and another daughter Kathleen was to be their last child. They moved to No. 14 Eglinton Crescent.

Davie was a member of the Royal Company of Archers, the Royal Scottish Society of Arts, the Highland and Agricultural Society and the Royal Meteorological Society. In succession to his father he was a Director of the Scottish Equitable Assurance Company for fifty-four years.

He was unlucky that he did not enjoy the excellent health that Charles had all his life. He had to stop work in 1888, only a year after his Uncle Thomas had died, and then again in 1889 and also after his marriage in 1885. He had a wide circle of friends in all walks of life. An extrovert by nature, he was easily depressed and worried when the workload increased. The personal historical notes written by himself show the astounding amount of work he did for the Northern Lighthouse Board but even a supportive wife and family did not save him from what today would be recognised as excessive stress leading to nervous breakdowns. Charles stood firm for his brother and coped with both the lighthouse work and the family firm during his absences. Both men were outstanding engineers and their combined achievements in that field are as remarkable as anything from their forebears. David worked amicably for over fifty years with his brother.

He was an excellent husband to Dorothy Roberts, and extremely proud of his two daughters.

Dorothy Roberts came from a family superior in social status to the Stevensons. She was an old school friend of Meta's and remained close to her for many years while their children grew up. She probably did not know that Meta was jealous of her in petty ways such as owning her own carriage to make her weekly social calls. [88,89]

Davie died, at his home, Troqueer, in Colinton, in 1938 only a few months after he retired.

**A professional aspect**

David A. was thoroughly trained in the traditional engineering mould as an entry from his diary for 11 July 1870 for landing stones at Dhu Heartach lighthouse works, when he was 15 years old, amply demonstrates, . . . *if a heavy sea is seen coming round the rock [rope] B is slackened and A is tightened and the lighter glides off from the rock allowing the sea to pass. Whenever the lighter comes alongside the Rock a steam crane on the landing place raises the stone out of the lighter to the rock* [sketch 'process of landing' - **90, 62**] *Another crane lifts the stone on to a truck which running on rails is pulled up to the top of the rock by a steam winch. Another crane lifts the stone on to the top of the lighthouse and the 5th crane places the stone in its place. When we landed the 14th course was being laid.*[85]

The most authoritative outline of David A.'s career and the firm's work before the first world war is to be found in his

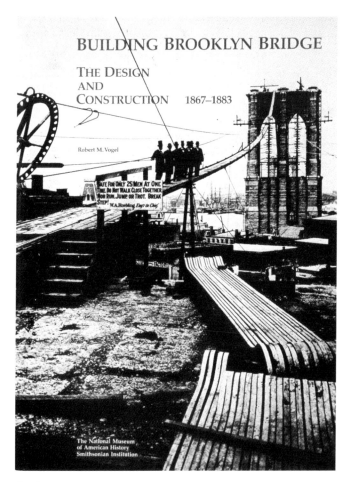

*te rock allowing the seas pass*
*mes*
*am*
*rane*
*raises the stone out of the light*
*ne lifts the stone on to truck*

[90] *Davie's sketch of landing stones at Dhu Heartach, 1870.*

**BUILDING BROOKLYN BRIDGE**

THE DESIGN AND CONSTRUCTION 1867–1883

Robert M. Vogel

The National Museum of American History Smithsonian Institution

[91] *Brooklyn Bridge similar to as seen by Davie and Charles, 1877.*

holograph *Personal Historical Notes* covering the period 1871-1914.[86] *In 1875, having got my degree,* he wrote, *I formally entered the office of my father and uncle Thomas Stevenson as a apprentice. In 1877 I was awarded a Manby Premium of the Institution of Civil Engineers for an account read before them of Dhu Heartach Lighthouse. In 1877* [with Charles] *I visited the United States and Canada for the purpose of studying the principal engineering works of their countries. I went out to New York . . . There I crossed the Hudson* [he means the East River] *on the temporary gangway of the suspension bridge then building* [Brooklyn Bridge - the four feet wide, swaying, lofty, gangway provided for the workmen during stringing of the main cables - **91**]. *I was accorded a warm welcome from all the engineers to whom I had letters of introduction and made a tour going south first to Boston then to Washington, then to St. Louis, north to Chicago, then east to Niagara, Toronto, Montreal, Quebec, and back to New York and home. When in New York I attended a lecture given by Bell the inventor of the telephone and was greatly interested in hearing a band which he said was playing in Boston. This I could hardly believe at the time was true. On my return home I was engaged in making surveys and plans for harbour works at Port Seton, Boddam, St Monance, Burnmouth and the construction of a small lighthouse on Holy Island* [Arran] *at the entrance to Lamlash harbour.*

*In 1878 . . . I now became a partner in the firm and had great difficulty in getting reasonable terms. My uncle took into the firm Mr Alan Brebner who had been for many years an assistant in the firm and a very able one, but he declined to take in my brother Charles. There was a long controversy on the subject . . . declined to join the firm unless Charles was also taken in. This was ultimately* agreed to but the terms he got were very meagre . . . The firm was much engaged at this time with the Clyde Lighthouse Trustees Bill for the deepening and improvement of the Clyde from Port Glasgow down to the sea, considerable opposition coming from the Greenock and even the Clyde Trustees the interests of Glasgow and Greenock being somewhat antagonistic. I was also engaged in the construction of a bridge at Hutton[89] and with designs for a proposed harbour at Gourock.

In 1879 I was principally engaged with the Clyde Bill, with improvements on Anstruther harbour and a proposal to erect a lighthouse on the South Carr Rock near Seacliff. The main question whether the light should not be on the Bass instead, this being our view and was ultimately adopted. In 1880 the Clyde Lighthouse Trustees Bill providing for the deepening of the Clyde to 18 feet at low water was passed. I was further engaged in designing and carrying out a scheme for purifying the Dunse Sewerage before it passed into the stream, on harbour works at Burnmouth, Port Seton, Boddam and Findochtie, on reporting for the Board of Supervision on schemes of water supply for a large number of towns. For the Northern Lighthouse service I was engaged on the introduction of the Courtenay Whistling buoy, the survey for a light on Langness in the Isle of Man and an important report on the better lighting of the coasts specially in Orkney and Shetland which I visited for the purpose.

In 1881 the first Pintsch lighted gas buoy was laid down on the Gannet Rock near Inch Keith. I was much engaged with work in connection with a committee on the power of the various sources and apparatus that was in use in lighthouses. Also with meeting a proposal by the French Lighthouses Authority to introduce electric light in all the important lights on their coasts which we considered unnecessary to adopt in this country and as a matter of fact was not

carried out even in France. Considerable damage was caused to several lighthouse stations on the west coast by an exceptionally severe winter gale and the carrying out of the necessary repairs occupied a considerable part of my time. I also was appointed to value the water power of the mills on the North Esk, to form the basis of an assessment to raise money to maintain the North Esk reservoir [in the Pentland Hills near Carlops]. In 1882 the strengthening of the Skervuile lighthouse tower in the Sound of Jura and attending a conference on buoyage at the Trinity House presided over by the Duke of Edinburgh were the most important work I was engaged in. While an exhaustive report on the state of the Haddington Fishery harbours, and harbour works at Lossiemouth, Bruichladich (Islay) and quays at Londonderry occupied my attention. The opposition to the Forth Bridge by the Caledonian Railway Company to secure that it was made such a height as not to interfere with navigation involved some interesting surveying of the tidal currents in the neighbourhood which we carried out with theodolites fixing the position of floats.

In 1883 Mr Joseph Chamberlain, then president of the Board of Trade, was taking a great interest in the discussion that was going on as to whether oil, gas or electricity was the best illuminant for lighthouses. The Trinity House were in favour of oil, the Irish Board of gas and the French of electricity. Our view in Scotland was that it depended on the circumstances which it was best to adopt. He came down to Granton in the Trinity House yacht 'Galatea' and as my uncle [Thomas] was unwell I met him . . . he expressed himself as very desirous that we should . . . give a trial of putting in a powerful electric light and chose ultimately the Isle of May. This was subsequently done. I was engaged during this year with work on the illuminants committee with the construction of the Ailsa Craig light and fog signals and also with the preparation of an important report

on the necessity of several lights on the coasts of Orkney and
Shetland for which purpose I visited and surveyed the several sites
proposed.

In 1884 I was admitted a member of the Institution of Civil
Engineers [A.M.I.C.E., becoming M.I.C.E. in December 1886].
I visited and surveyed Mulroy Bay in the north of Ireland and
advised Lord Leitrim on the improvement of the navigation . . . I
also was very busy in preparing information for my uncle to give
evidence on behalf of the Mersey Harbour Board against the
original Manchester Ship Canal scheme. The Bill had been passed
the previous year by one committee of Parliament and thrown out
by another, and was again put forward this year. We were called in
to assist Mr Lyster the Liverpool harbour engineer and there is no
doubt that the evidence given by my uncle threw out the Bill. The
proposal was to form the canal by river walls constructed in the
estuary. Our view was that such walls would result in silting up
the estuary and so diminish the amount of tidal water that
would flow into it at every tide and thus reduce the scour over
and hence the depth of the bar beyond Liverpool, a very serious
matter. I made investigations at the Dee, the Nith, the Lune
where such effects had resulted and was long in London
watching the case and coaching my uncle who was far from
well. The Bill was thrown out and next year a scheme was
brought forward, that was actually constructed, under which
the estuary was not interfered with. It was opposed again but we
declined to support the opposition as our objections were
removed, and the Bill passed.

In 1885 my uncle being unwell, I was appointed joint
Engineer with him to the Commissioners of Northern
Lighthouses. Indeed I had for some years being doing most of the
work. I was a good deal engaged this year with experiments

[92] *Ailsa Craig Lighthouse and foghorn, 1886. Plan from David's prize-
winning paper in Min. Proc. I.C.E., 1887.* [89]

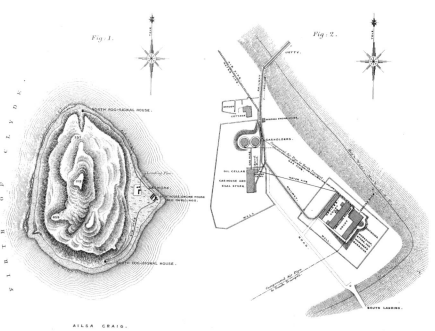

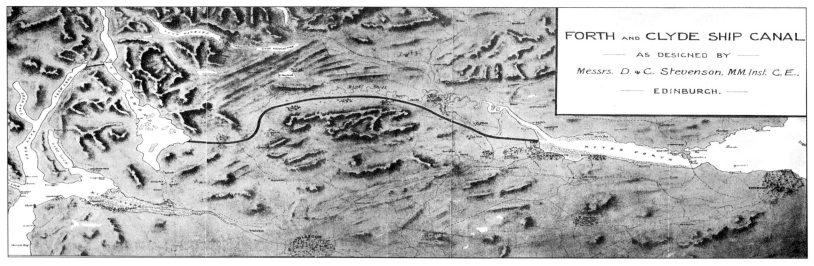

**[93]** *D. & C. Stevenson's Forth & Clyde Canal plan, c. 1913. Proposed to be level between sea locks, 100ft. wide at bottom and 31ft. deep. Not executed.*

*carried out at the South Foreland lighthouse by the Trinity House on the power of various forms of illuminants and apparatus for lighthouses. Sir James Douglas and S. Mathews being respectively the chief and assistant engineers of the Trinity House. I saw a good deal of them. I also was engaged in the construction of a station at Port St Mary for the Chickens Rock lightkeepers and their families, a harbour at Coldingham, now called St Abbs, and Reports on the state of a number of harbours on the Irish coast. In 1886 my father died . . . my brother and I revised, brought up to date. and published a 3rd edition of our father's book on 'Canal and river engineering'. I was also engaged in the introduction of the electric light into the Isle of May lighthouse, designing various pieces of apparatus for it, also on the completion of Ailsa Craig light and fog signal station* **[92]** *and the design and erection of the Oxcar light in the Firth of Forth.*

*In 1887 I read a paper before the Institution of Mechanical Engineers giving an account of the installation of electric light at the Isle of May. Also a paper on the Ailsa Craig light and fog signal station before the Institution of Civil Engineers for which I received*

*the Telford premium. In this year also my uncle died and I was appointed sole Engineer to the Commissioners of Northern Lighthouses. I was principally engaged in the design and construction of the North Carr light vessel laid down off Fifeness. It had several novelties including the introduction of steam engines on such vessels for actuating the fog horn. In 1888 I was engaged in the construction of a pier at Broadford [Skye] for the Scottish Fishery Board, also a new outfall for the Water of Leith sewer at Leith. In 1889 we were asked by a committee of Edinburgh gentlemen interested in trade to design a ship canal on the line of the present Forth and Clyde barge canal. We looked into the matter and recommended that a ship canal on that line was not feasible and recommended a route through Loch Lomond into Loch Long. It was approved of but made no progress.* **[93]**

*In 1890 Mr Alan Brebner died and my brother and I were left sole partners and altered the name of the firm to D. & C. Stevenson, my uncle having altered it in [1883] to T. & D. Stevenson. In this year the Clyde Lighthouses Trustees got an Act to deepen the Clyde within their jurisdiction to 23 feet at low water.* **[113]** *There was* strong opposition but we overcame it, in fact it tailed out and I gave the necessary evidence before the Committee of the House of Lords. I also read a paper before the International Conference on Inland Navigation held at Manchester on our proposed Forth and Clyde ship canal scheme. We also originated and put forward a scheme for a railway from Longniddry to Gullane which in conjunction with Blyth & Cunningham was put forward by the North British Railway Company as a Bill and ultimately was carried out. Beacon lights of a temporary character were also erected on Stroma in the Pentland Firth and Grey Rocks [Glas Eileanan?] in the Sound of Mull.

In 1891 I was principally engaged in designing and carrying out schemes of improvement of the River Lune by river walls and new quays, also in designing an important new lighthouse on Sule Skerry, a low rock 40 miles north of the Butt of Lewis and the same distance from the west coast of Orkney. Also with the erection of beacon lights at Weaver Point, Castle Bay and Culavary [Calvay], all Uist. In 1892 . . . the lighthouses on Fair Isle, one at each end were completed. I was also engaged with constructing oil gas works at Oban for making oil gas for lighting buoys and beacons on the west coast. Beacon lights at Kyle Rhea, Carloway [North Lewis], Beamer Beacon [Fife], Croulin [Applecross], Risantru [Jura], Dul Sgeir [Kerrera] were also in progress. 1893 . . .the lighthouse on Helliar Holm near Kirkwall was completed. I was much employed in designs for piers to accommodate the lighthouse tenders at Stromness and Oban. Also with a report on the places on the coast that needed lights and fog signals, the intensity of the lights on the coasts and beacon lights at Foula Ness [Shetland], Heston [Kirkcudbrightshire], Dunvegan, Eyre Point.

1894. In this year the important light on Stroma in the Pentland Firth was begun, trials of the Courtenay Whistling Buoy were carried out, a trial was made of a wireless signalling scheme proposed by my brother for use at remote lighthouse stations, beacon lights at Vaila and Loch Eribol [Sutherland] were proceeded with, a further Report on the lights needed in Orkney and Shetland was prepared . . . Oxcar lighthouse was up to this time lighted with an oil burner and attended by keepers, but to save expense of maintenance I suggested it should be lighted with gas and unattended except at intervals of 2 or 3 months. This scheme was carried out with success. Apart from lighthouse work I was engaged on a scheme for improving the navigation of the Forth up to Stirling and on a pier at Lamlash in Arran.

1895. Rattray head lights and Sule Skerry were completed.[98,99] An attack having been made on the Commissioners, by shipowners who pay the dues, at the Departmental Enquiry as to the cost of the works carried out by them and various other matters I prepared a defence which was adopted by the Commissioners and this was lodged with the Board of Trade. It is an important document and goes very fully into the various points raised and I think is a complete answer to the complaints made. Skerry of Ness [Orkney], Balta Sound and Hillswick beacon lights were erected. Several less important lights were converted to be lit with gas and the keepers withdrawn with the exception of one attendant. Surveys were made for new lighthouses at Noup head in Orkney and Flanan Islands. An important scheme for further deepening the Clyde under the jurisdiction of the Clyde Lighthouses Trustees so as to provide 27 feet at low water up to Glasgow was gone into and reported on.

1896. The lighthouse on Stroma was completed. Oban and Stromness piers to accommodate the lighthouse tenders were proceeded with. I introduced a motor driven siren and established the first of them at Butt of Lewis and this was found to be a great improvement. I also reported this year on the advantage of reducing the length of the periods of fog signals. A complaint was made of the Mull of Kintyre fog signal not being properly heard and Admiral Nares of the Board of Trade came to investigate the matter. I accompanied him to the station along with Sheriff afterwards Lord Johnston and Sheriff afterwards Lord Dundas. The Admiral was quite satisfied. Experiments were carried out as to the use of acetylene gas for lighthouse purposes and beacon lights were established at Muckle Roe, Scarnish and Noness [Shetland].

1897. Tod Head lighthouse was completed. An unattended lightship was designed and laid down to mark the Otter Rock in the Sound of Jura. Loch Ryan lighthouse was converted to gas. The French lighthouse authorities declared their intention to reduce the length of the flash of light shown by their lights to be one tenth of a second as being quite long enough for full visibility. I was asked to report on this and came to the conclusion that this length of flash was too short and that the flash should not be less than one second, and this is now generally accepted as being necessary. In this year also group flashing buoy lights were proposed, now generally adopted. A report on the necessity for several lighted buoys on the west coast was prepared. On behalf of the Town of Oban I was employed and gave evidence against the proposed extension of their quay in Oban Bay. I objected to the effect the vertical walls they proposed would have on the tranquillity of the anchorage in the bay and succeeded in the company coming under an obligation to make the quay of open timber work with a sloping [battered stone] talus beneath.

1898. Noup head lighthouse was completed and was the first light in the service to have the lens carried on a mercury float, a system introduced in France. Lighthouses at Tiumpan Head in Lewis, Killantringan in Wigtownshire and Barns Ness near Dunbar were begun. Experiments on the use of acetylene gas were continued, Corran [Argyll], Kyle Akin [Skye], **[64]** and Oronsay lighthouses were converted to oil gas with only one keeper in charge. Incandescent oil gas burners were introduced.

1899. The lighthouse on Flannan Island was completed. This was a most difficult work. The island lies 15 miles off the west side of Lewis. Although it is 280 feet above high water heavy water passes over it. It is very steep and until we made the concrete step and paths up to it, almost inaccessible. When making the survey we had to take off our boots and clamber up on all fours. It was at this station in [1900] after a severe gale that the three keepers disappeared and were never heard of. The building of Bass Rock lighthouse was begun. This was a difficult work as the foundations had to be incorporated in the ruins [of the castle] and the laying of the air piping for the fog horn from the station over the top to the north side of the island was a troublesome operation. A new and powerful dioptric apparatus of novel design was made for the Bell rock, also an enlarged lantern to hold it. The apparatus was exhibited at the Exhibition being held in Glasgow in 1901 before being erected at the lighthouse. Beacon light were erected at Bunessan, Haxa. Clett Tower and Breasclete [Lewis]. I was asked by the proprietors of fishings on the Teith and Forth to advise them in opposing a Glasgow Bill for taking more water from the tributaries of their rivers without providing any extra compensation. In this year the Advisory Committee of Ship Owners was instituted by the Board of Trade who promised not to sanction any expenditure on new works without bringing it before this committee. This committee has opposed practically every proposal for lights on the Scottish coast.

*1900. The erection of the lighthouses at Tiumpan head and Killantringan were completed. Also the new lantern and apparatus for the Bell Rock were proceeded with. The Bass Rock lighthouse was begun. Another Report on the needs of the coast for additional lights was prepared. Surveys were made for a light on Hyskeir and additional beacon lights in Shetland, further experiments on the use of acetylene gas were carried out, the use of carbon tipped burners for beacons introduced and the subject of intensities of lighthouse apparatus further dealt with.*

*In 1901 Barns ness lighthouse was begun. Acetylene lighted gas beacons were established for the first time. An important trial of the effectiveness of the various forms of fog signal were carried out at St Catherines by the Trinity House and the siren signal sent by the Northern Lighthouse Board proved its superiority. I attended the trials, but in many respects they were badly arranged and the results in several instances were therefore inconclusive as I pointed out in a Report to the Commissioners. Unattended beacon lights were established at Haxa, Clett Tower in Orkney, Bunessan, Breaslete and the Black memorial light on the west coast and the Otter unattended light vessel of the south end of Islay. In 1902 the Bass Rock [lighthouse **94**] was completed, as also Barns ness and in consequence of the claims made by the contractor in the latter case a lawsuit became necessary. I gave evidence on the subject and won our case on all points . . .*

*In 1903 the town council of Oban asked us to report on the best means of dealing with the sewage of Oban which was run into the bay from numerous small sewers and made the state of the foreshore at low water a nuisance. I after careful consideration designed a scheme of carrying out the whole of the sewage along the spit . . . that runs out into the Bay. The scheme was bitterly opposed by several large proprietors and an Enquiry had to be held before the Sheriff. The scheme was sanctioned however and when carried out has proved a great success. It was a work of considerable difficulty the sewage being collected in a main drain that was run along the front streets of the town at a level just above that of high water . . .*

*In this year [1903] Sir John Jackson the contractor was induced to take an interest in our Forth and Clyde ship canal scheme and in conjunction with [name missing] and the Duke of Sutherland found the necessary money to make a complete survey of the ground from end to end and prepare parliamentary plans with a view to going for an Act of Parliament to carry out the work. This of course involved a great deal of work. The plans were completed and ready for deposit but at the last moment it was decided to delay proceeding with the Bill in the meantime. The principal reason for this delay was that the large sum that had to be deposited on a bill involving an expenditure of £20,000,000 and had to lie in the hands of the government till the Bill is disposed of, without interest. Lloyds wished to establish stations for signalling to passing vessels at Dunnet head, Cape Wrath, St Abb's head and Butt of Lewis and they came to us to design and carry out the work of establishing them. They each involved the provision of offices and accommodation for 4 families and owing to the remote positions were works of considerable difficulty, but were successfully carried out. In this year I introduced the use of incandescent oil burners. I adopted that known as the Chance burner and it was gradually introduced at all the lighthouse stations in the service, greatly increasing the power of the lights. Additional beacon lights were established at Lady Isle, Sgur Buidhe and Isles of the Sea.*

*1904. Hyskeir lighthouse was completed and beacon lights established at Barra Head, Mull of Eomick, Symbister, Southerness,*

*Whitehills and Craigton. I introduced a fusible plug to prevent the oil burners in unattended lights from getting too hot and causing fires of which there had been one or two cases. At this time I saw some prospect of being able to use wireless as a fog signal which I had for a long time considered might be attained. With this view I had been in communication with the Marconi Company without result so far . . .*

*1905. Holy Island Lighthouse was completed and unattended beacons established at Dul Sgeir, Cath Sgeir [Gigha], Roseness [Orkney], & Arnish.*

*1906. In this year I appeared before the Royal Commission on Canals and gave evidence in support of our Forth and Clyde ship canal scheme. Beacon lights were established at Swana, Eigg, Green Island, Rhuad Sgeir, an unattended lightship of large size and with a powerful light laid down at Sker..[?], a dangerous rock in the Minch, as also a boat lightship at the Whitestone Bank in the Isle of Man.* [Also, Group flashing lights installed at Mull of Kintyre Lighthouse. **95,96**]

*1907. A trial of the Diaphone fog signal was made at Inch Keith but it was not found to be better than the powerful sirens we had in use. Beacon lights were established at Swana, Milmore [Campbelltown], Lachy Rock, Canna and Churin.*

*1908. A Royal Commission on Lighthouses sat this year and I was much engaged in preparing to give evidence before it which I did. Mr Gerald Balfour was the chairman and the result was favourable to the way in which the work of the Northern Lighthouse Board was conducted in all departments. Beacon lights were erected at Elieness, Cairns of Coll, Trodday. I was also engaged in an investigation of the river that runs into Loch Ailort in connection with fishing rights. In fixing the boundaries of fishing at Carnoustie, in a remit from the Court of Session with reference to*

[**97**] *Lother beacon, 1910. A standardised design, note the similarity with Covesea Skerries beacon, 1844.* [**46**]

tar from the Edinburgh Gas Works polluting a brewery well at the foot of the Calton Hill and with an important an interesting case between the town of Aberdeen and the Forbes family as to the true position of the Mouth of the Don. I was successful before the courts of proving the contention of the Aberdeen Town Council being the correct view.

*1909. Neist Point light was completed, and beacon lights established at Calf of Eday, Firths Voe, Sound of Ness and Rilff Reef. I again appeared before the Royal Commission on Canals and gave evidence in support of the Forth and Clyde ship canal. And the committee's finding was that our scheme for the canal was the best and the only one the government would assist which was satisfactory as far as it went. I also was asked to appear before the committee of Imperial Defence as also was Sir John Jackson which we did in support of the canal scheme.*

*1910. Beacon lights were erected at Lother Rock* [Pentland Skerries - **97**] *and Sandaig. We were consulted by the authorities of Guernsey as to providing a fog signal for the entrance to that harbour. We designed a scheme which was unique and which when carried out was a great success. We installed on the shore electric plant* [at Doyle Fort], *we carried out to a tower erected on the* [Platte Fougère, near the entrance to St. Peter Port] *rock a* [1 mile long submarine] *cable to carry the power to work the air compressors and siren fog horn and the light and also fog signal machinery ashore that could be brought into use in case anything happened to the signal on the rock, it being unattended.* [This ingenious and novel sea-mark was designed by Charles] *I carried out some experiments at Inch Keith and using a rod for submarine fog signalling. The principle was to lay a rod from the shore out into deep water and to hammer the end on shore with the view of making it ring like a bell and the sound would then travel in water*

to considerable distances. As sound travels better in water than air this promised to be a good thing and would take the place of the submarine bell fog signal which could not be used efficiently off headlands, though very satisfactory on lightships. The results were fairly satisfactory but have not been introduced in practice. I was also engaged in opposing the order for the bringing water to East Lothian from [name missing] on behalf of the Mills on the Tyne, as it was not prepared to give a proper amount of compensation water to the Mills. This however I succeeded in securing. James Fleming was the Commissioner. Macmillan was counsel for the promoters and our counsel was Robert Home who afterwards was Chancellor of the Exchequer.

*1911. At this time I was engaged in advocating the quick starting of fog signals immediately on the appearance of fog. I was also engaged in sending out the machinery for an up-to-date fog signal to China . . . Also a boat shelter for Lossiemouth, the introduction of wireless control to turn on an acetylene gun fog signal on Roseneath patch on the Clyde of the appearance of fog. I was also engaged on an Enquiry as to the effect of works proposed by the Railway Company off Bo'ness harbour on the effect on the foreshore and other harbours in the neighbourhood.*

*1912. The lighthouse on Rhuad Rhea* [Ross & Cromarty] *was completed. An acetylene fog gun was established at Dhu Heartach lighthouse and an unattended beacon erected at Milaid* [Lewis]. *I was engaged with plans for still further deepening the Clyde from Port Glasgow to Greenock, the proposal being to make the channel 27 feet deep at low water. I was also asked by the Manchester Ship Canal Company to advise them as to the effect of works the Mersey Docks & Harbour Board were proposing to carry out near the bar, and in company with a committee of other three engineers reported on the subject.*

*1913. I was engaged in enlarging the buoy and other lighthouse stores at Granton. Also with designing a plan for erecting a lighthouse on the outmost reef at Cape Wrath to take the place of the old light which was too high and frequently obscured by fog. This involved some new features in lighthouse construction, the sinking of a vertical shaft down to the level of the reef with a lift in it, the construction of a covered way over the reef, the construction of 2 bridges, and the erection of a tower and fog horn house on the extreme end of the reef. The work was begun, but the contractor deserted the work, and on account of the Great War coming on it was found impossible to get a contractor to finish the work nor to carry it on by days wages. It is still (1927) uncompleted.*

*1914. Maughold head lighthouse in the Isle of Man was completed and an unattended beacon was erected on Mackintosh Rock near Rosyth.'* [ends, written in 1927][86]

Much of the foregoing also relates to Charles's work. David A. was at pains to point out to the Commissioners of the Northern Lighthouse Board that his reports to them were *drawn up jointly by my brother and myself.* An indication of the division of their responsibility is given in D. Alan's unpublished notes, *Except where clients asked for him David restricted his horizon to the Northern Lighthouse Service while Charles dealt with the other work, but all matters were debated between them before reporting. David should perhaps have been a lawyer as were most of his friends, or, as he had a command of words and wrote well, he could have become an author . . . New ideas came from Charles, called forth by the needs of the occasion. His views were basic and convincing in their simplicity and reasonableness' His writing ability was not so good as his brother's, his paragraphs tended to length and his sentences fitted together like a puzzle; dissection destroyed the natural sequence of his reasoning. Adjustment and polishing of Charles's reports was one direction in which David proved the benefit of their partnership.*[90] This combination of talents and David A.'s evident management ability, somewhat similar to that which existed between his father and Thomas a generation earlier, worked well and ensured the success of the firm until its dissolution in 1936.

For the Board, David A., with the assistance of Charles, was responsible for the design and construction of 24 lighthouses, 48 fog-signals, 5 light-ships, 75 minor lights and many beacons and buoys. Of these lighthouses, according to J. D. Gardner, Engineer to the Board from 1946-55, Sule Skerry **[98]** - Britain's remotest lighthouse 45 miles north-west of Dunnet Head, Flannan Islands, Bass Rock, and Oigh Sgeir were works of particular difficulty *requiring the exercise of sound judgement and engineering skill.*[91] To these can be added Rattray Head **[99]**, which was novel in that the lower part of the tower contained an engine room and foghorn. It was the first first-class siren to be installed in a rock lighthouse.

During David A.'s period of office with the Board the brightness of lights increased greatly. In 1875 the most powerful light on the Scottish coast was 44,500 candle-power. By 1901 there were several lights over 100,000 candle-power and the Isle of May electric light of 3,000,000 candle-power. This increase in power was achieved by long focal distance apparatus designed by David A. and Charles and the introduction of Charles's equiangular prisms.

Although only five lighthouses were constructed by the Northern Lighthouse Board after 1914, during David A.'s last 24 years in office, the firm kept very busy not only modernising the Board's by now very substantial amount of equipment, but also on its general business of river improvement, harbour, sewerage and water supply work.

In addition to the Board's work David A. and Charles acted jointly as Engineers to the Clyde Lighthouses Trust and the Fishery Board and as consulting engineers to several colonial and foreign lighthouse authorities. Notable work included successive deepenings of the Clyde from 18 to 30 feet west of Port Glasgow for the Clyde Lighthouses Trust, and the £20m. Forth & Clyde Ship Canal project, more or less on the proposed, but not adopted, northern line recommended by Smeaton in 1764. This canal project, which was undoubtedly feasible, but for which funding was not forthcoming, formed the subject of at least three of David A.'s characteristically well-written publications. He was elected a Fellow of the Royal Society of Edinburgh in 1884 and served on its Council from 1928-31.

When David A. retired from his Northern Lighthouse Board post on 31 March 1938 at the advanced age of 83, after a remarkable 52 years in service as their Engineer, the Board recorded its appreciation of his *invaluable services.* The Corporation of Trinity House, London also wrote expressing thanks *for his ready help and co-operation in solving the many lighthouse problems which had arisen in his day and congratulated him on the advances he made and helped to make in lighthouse techniques.*[91] These advances undoubtedly included his advocacy of economic illuminants and the successful introduction in 1903 of Chance's incandescent oil burners which were subsequently adopted universally. David A. is remembered today as an effective and outstanding engineer. With his retirement the Board severed its 130-year connection with the Stevenson engineers and appointed John Oswald (d. 1946) as Engineer.

# Chapter Eight

## Charles Alexander Stevenson 1855-1950 - Inventor, electrical and radio engineer

### Family recollections

When Charles was born the family of five girls and two boys moved to 25 Royal Terrace, a large four-storied house of Craigleith sandstone. Near the end of his life he wrote about his very happy childhood in an unpublished book.[92] [100]

'The quiet management of the family by my father and mother and the absence of bullying words, voices raised in anger or sulking children must have been one of the reasons why our cousin Louis visited us often. There was always someone at home to give him time and attention. There was much song and music. Here too he could enjoy the superb model theatre, as well as the magic lantern, built by my father, his Uncle David. There was nothing for sale in Edinburgh, anything like it, complete with drop curtain, trap doors, side boxes and scene changing devices. We also had a "peep show" with 8 inch diameter lens and mirror.

We were at the Edinburgh Academy [101] at the same time as Louis. Only a few hundred yards to the south of Royal Terrace lay the heart of Louis' playground in his adolescent years and he shared it often with us. Every part of Holyrood and of Arthur's Seat we made our own. A map illustrates the ground we covered from the Haggis Knowe to Dunsappie Loch. Passing Dunsappie Louis always identified a non-existent cave and called it Dick Hatterick's Cave. [After the cave in Guy Mannering.] Probably he was also remembering the Grotto known to him in Italy, which he had visited with Bessy (my sister). She had arranged this whole trip in 1863 at the request of our Uncle Thomas. She went with a heavy heart because the Royal Archers Ball was just coming up and she was hoping to get engaged to Alexander James Napier.

She was very pretty and she need not have worried as he popped the question immediately on her return! These Balls given by the Royal Company of Archers were few and far between and invitations were much prized.

We could turn either to the right or left at the end of the garden in Royal Terrace and following one of the many paths laid round the Calton Hill by our grandfather Robert after the soldiers had returned from the Napoleonic wars, we would arrive in a few minutes at Waterloo Place-the east end of Princes Street. Years later Louis was to write in Samoa, remembering the family graves at the New Calton Cemetery in Edinburgh:

The tropics vanish, and meseems that I,
From Halkerside, from topmost Allermuir,
Or steep Caerketton, dreaming gaze again.
Far set in fields and woods, the town I see
Spring gallant from the shallows of her smoke,
Cragged, spired, and turreted, her virgin fort
Beflagged. About, on seaward-drooping hills,
New folds of city glitter. Last, the Forth
Wheels ample waters set with sacred isles,
And populous Fife smokes with a score of towns.

There, on the sunny frontage of a hill,
Hard by the house of kings, repose the dead,
My dead, the ready and the strong of word.
Their works, the salt-encrusted, still survive;
The sea bombards their founded towers; the night
Thrills pierced with their strong lamps. The artificers,
One after one, here in this grated cell,
Where the rain erases and the rust consumes,

Fell upon lasting silence. Continents
And continental oceans intervene;
A sea uncharted, on a lampless isle,
Environs and confines their wandering child
In vain. The voice of generations dead
Summons me, sitting distant, to arise,
My numerous footsteps nimbly to retrace,
And, all mutation over, stretch me down
In that denoted city of the dead.'[66]

The gated cell is the only one in the cemetery to retain its original roof. Robert used the same method in its construction of 'dove-tailing' the stones into each other that he had employed in the building of the Bell Rock Lighthouse.

'In our young days the Castle would sound out the Bugle call at six o'clock in the morning and this could be clearly heard by Louis from Heriot Row. The sight of soldiers marching with their band playing swinging down from the castle to Jock's Lodge always affected us deeply and we stopped to watch them go by. With a Highland regiment the kilts would swing almost imperceptibly and on a recruiting march the music would be to some light air such as 'The girl I left behind me . . .' This would set Louis off marching alongside them admiring the action of the drummer and the strong muscles of the men.'

A railway line ran from Edinburgh to North Berwick from 1848 and the 'David Stevensons' took a house down the coast there for two or three of the summer months in the West Bay. Uncle Tom and Aunt Maggie were there also in various villas and Maggie names most of them in her diaries. Even after they took Swanston on a long lease when he was 17 years old, Louis would turn up to his much loved old playground.

'The sands below Dirleton had the unenviable but still commonly accepted story attached to them that a man, horse and cart had been swallowd up in a quicksand. Many times I explored this territory with Louis but we never found anything but a softness due to entrapped seaweed. Louis never let slip an opportunity to impress me with a very grave face on the advisability of keeping well up onto the dry sand. Walking there with him I flicked with my walking stick a stranded sheep's jaw against his cheek. No serious damage was done but he gave me a well deserved 'round of the guns'! The only other occasion that I remember being in his really bad books took place on the banks of the Forth at Stirling where he and I were examining a beech tree on which my father, years and years before, had cut his initials D.S. and those of my mother his beloved fiancée E.M. deeply into the bark. Very stupidly I picked the centre out of the letter D. and Louis to his horror realised what I had done. It was a heinous sin in his eyes and again I was treated to some well chosen words!

The home-made 'land' boat made by my brother and myself when we were very small children is particularly successful. The hull is made out of tea-chests, etc.; the mast a clothes drying pole, two toy guns are on deck, thole pins, sails, bladders, anchor (a stone one) were got off the beach. In Louis' words 'I am a-steering of the boat', and David is at the helm. The year is 1860 and the setting the back of Anchor House , North Berwick. [102] A few years later in 1865 my father took the photo of the three of us-David, Louis and myself blowing soap bells with an ordinary cutty clay pipe.

The mouth piece was always carefully covered with red sealing wax by my mother to prevent damage to our lips. [103] The table, used to rest the soap mixture on, was the steps the maids used to hang up 'the washing' in the garden. The washing was a very large affair in our household with such a number of young girls with their spotless and bright summer dresses. Rafts, model boats, bicycles and kites were all home-made-the latter had messages sent along the string and the adjustment of the right number of bows on the tail was a special skill. On many days a joyous lot of boys would proceed along the Longskelly Beach to the Eel Burn-referred to by Louis in Catriona as a 'cressy burn' about a mile west of the end of North Berwick Links in the days of our boyhood. It was the ideal place to build a dam with plenty of water from a large drainage area round about Dirleton, an abundance of sand and no rocks or stones, and certainly no people anywhere in sight to disturb us. We built by heavy digging high and broad embankments and felt sure we could make a permanent diversion of the burn. Always a hopeless task as a high tide with an on-shore wind left the sand smooth and level and no sign that we had ever been there!

...We learnt to play golf from the earliest possible age and always loved the game. Davie came to championship standard with a handicap of just 4. We were members down at North Berwick and, in later years, the Old Luffness, Gullane, The Royal and Ancient at St Andrews and the Honourable Company of Edinburgh Golfers at Muirfield. Louis always despised this activity and games of robbers and pirates or just simply exploring along the coast or deep into the Lammermuirs meant much more to him. It was quite a tough little climb for him to the top of North Berwick Law but Louis did it often and there was a memorable bright moon-light night he remembered when he wrote this poem in Underwoods in 1887:

A MILE AND A BITTOCK
A mile an' a bittock, a mile or twa,
Abüne the burn, ayont the law,
Davie an' Donal' an' Cherlie an' a',
    An' the müne was shinin' clearly!

Ane went hame wi' the ither, an' then
The ither went hame wi' the ither twa men,
An' baith wad return him the service again,
    An' the müne was shinin' clearly!

The clocks were chappin' in house an' ha',
Eleeven, twal an' ane an' twa;
An' the guidman's face was turnt to the wa',
    An' the müne was shinin' clearly!

A wind got up frae affa the sea,
It blew the stars as clear's could be,
It blew in the een of a' o' the three,
    An' the müne was shinin' clearly!

Noo, Davie was first to get sleep in his head,
'The best o' frien's maun twine,' he said;
'I'm weariet, an' here I'm awa' to my bed.'
    An' the müne was shinin' clearly!

Twa o' them walkin' an' crackin' their lane,
The mornin' licht cam gray an' plain,
An' the birds they yammert on stick an' stane,
   An' the müne was shinin' clearly!

O years ayont, O years awa',
My lads, ye'll mind whate'er befa'-
My lads, ye'll mind on the bield o' the law,
   When the müne was shinin' clearly.

Donald was my pony. **[104]**

Fidra, the Lamb, Craigleith and the Bass were all left behind after the ice-age had passed by, going from west to east, and grinding and scraping away the softer material, leaving the hard rocks sticking up with precipices on their eastern and sheltered sides. The very small scratches of the ice are still visible in spite of the weathering. Louis described Fidra as 'a strange grey islet of two humps, made the more conspicuous by a piece of ruin and I mind that (as we drew close to it) the sea peeped through like a man's eye.' The eye is a hole through the main hump of the island about 29 feet in height. In Louis' day (and mine of course) the Eye used to be a marked and lovely feature of Fidra on the road leading out of Dirleton towards North Berwick and with the sea behind, it looked like a great waterfall but grown trees have now shut off this unique angle [1940]. There was of course no lighthouse in those days. At the end of the sandy Longskelly Beach away past the Eel Burn, Louis would still press on over the rocks to where there stood a small villa-right down by the sea but lost in the woods a mile below the big house known as Archerfield. It was always of great interest to him whether the villa was shuttered or not and I had no interest in

this. We crept along, heads well down right by the margin of the sea.

To the East of North Berwick Harbour lies the Black Rock. Just up from it there is still a house called Rockend that was taken for the Summer of 1860 by Louis' father and mother, my Uncle Tom and Aunt Maggie. The Rock was the scene for nursery-maids sewing, knitting and chatting while their charges played around with wooden spade and pail. To climb to the top was endlessly absorbing. Released from nursery strings a few years later we were with a crowd of boys in 'The Ladies Walk' or simply 'The Glen'. This sunless dingle of elder trees was massed over with damp dead leaves and patches of grass. A strong stream ran down the middle of it and dotted here and there were the ruins with roofless walls-the cold homes of Anchorites. To fit ourselves for life and with a special eye to acquire the art of smoking many happy hours were spent there. Here we came to 'particulars' as our mutual grandparents used to call it!

Along the East Bay still further was 'Campbell's cave' at Point Garry. This was one of the meeting places of the 'Lantern Bearers', the story of which has often been told in biographies of Louis. David and I were old enough to join in. The gulley is 7 feet deep and luckily has a stone wedge in between its sides at the top. We could with some difficulty climb across to get access to the cave. At night the passage would be impassible without the aid of our 'lanterns'.

Croquet was very fashionable, but like golf it was hated by Louis. Later, with Frances Sitwell in England, he came to love the game and was an expert at it. Croquet was often played on North Berwick Links but Louis seldom joined in.

I once played croquet on the Bass! My families and Cheynes

from Shetland going on a picnic expedition-about the year 1901!

Our new home in Melville Street, where we moved in 1870, had the usual large double drawing room found in New Town houses and the sun streamed in from early morning until late afternoon. The whole house was lighted by gas chandeliers and sidelights and except for the blazing coal fire in the drawing room it was heated by stoves and gas fires, a very up-to-date invention in those days, and a great saving of heavy labour for the servants.

At the top of the house I had a laboratory and workshop combined. A turning lathe which also worked an electric machine of my own design, a home-made spectroscope giving absolutely perfect lines, chemical apparatus for making gunpowder and fireworks, gas for explosives and lead to make bullets for catapults, and a home-invented seismograph for showing tremors in gales and earthquakes. I collected the lead from the neighbour's roof flashings that seemed to me to be unnecessarily deep! Invitations from myself to Louis when he was in the house to come upstairs to enjoy the delights of my laboratory met with a very definite negative! Nothing at all of an engineering nature was of real interest to him. My enthusiastic youthful engineering was also called into use by my sisters after 1870 when the enormous crinolines that had been fashionable were diminished by half the diameter. By cutting the steel rings and splicing them I was able to prevent unequal bulging.

Louis would come along to 45 Melville Street either alone or with our cousin Bob, Alan's son. They always walked in unannounced by the servants. Robert Alan Moubray Stevenson was only three years older and from the day he first came into Louis' life when Bob was nine years old and Louis seven the two had been the closest possible friends. Bob and his three sisters, who included Katherine (later Katherine de Mattos), were educated largely abroad and Bob was, like Louis, remarkably free of the strict Edinburgh social conventions of the day. He was a most lovable man and shared the same love of laughter and life as Louis. There were three beautiful paintings of his, one done when he was in Fontainbleau, another of the Bridge at Grez, and the third a river scene on the upper Thames hanging in our house.

My father had collected pictures and prints for many years both in this country and abroad and we had the superb watercolour by Turner of the Bell Rock Lighthouse, also Sam Bough's watercolour of North Unst, a lovely skating scene by Klein and many fine engravings. A marvel to Louis and Bob was a very rare engraving in silver and gold that had the picture frame on pivots so that it could be slewed up or down to produce the effect of night or day. It was by Zeuder and probably of Amsterdam, showing houses, boats and sails, people, a drawbridge and Town Hall clock in silver and gold lettering with the hands engraved in extraordinary detail.

The arrival of Bob and Louis always meant a call from them both for music. Bob had a superb tenor voice and could play the piano with a delicate touch that could really move the hearts of his audience, and my sister Mary played the harp as a perfect accompaniment to him. [105] Georgie could replace Bob on the piano and we all could sing to excellent effect. I remember the day when the clash of cymbals was heard on the street and to our delight we found two men dressed in blue with a stout pole and a dancing bear on a leash. Bob and Louis were in ecstasy over the bear and themselves danced in the window recesses in the same lumbering manner as the bear to the clash of the cymbals. Money was sent down with a servant which was evidently appreciated as the men gave a second performance which we had asked for.

Immediately after Louis's book *Inland Voyage* was published he walked along from Heriot Row to Melville Street and with much amusing formality presented it to his Uncle David with his name on it. Both of them were remembering the 'History of Moses and the march of the Israelites out of Egypt'. His uncle had offered a prize to one of the cousins for the best essay on the subject. Louis was only six years old and my father had given him the first prize for his superb effort dictated to his mother and illustrated by himself. David Stevenson had written *The principles and practice of canals and river engineering* and they could joke together of plagiarism as both had been travelling in 'narrow waters'!

Fleeming Jenkin was Professor of Engineering at Edinburgh University from 1868 to 1885 and this meant that Louis in 1867, next David in 1871, and then myself in 1872 were all members of his university class in different years. The theatricals held by the professor and his wife were a great pleasure for Louis because all his life he loved 'dressing up' in any way that was unusual. The essay he was eventually to write about Fleeming Jenkin showed how important the special friendship they had for Louis was to be in shaping a large part of his life. I attended the theatricals held in Great Stuart Street many times and I was always there if I knew that Louis was in the cast. I really had no idea how well he was acting the part, but I could never take my eyes off him. Socially it was a great pleasure to meet the audience, so many of them were family friends.

Fleeming Jenkin and James Simpson were splendid ice-skaters and members of the old Edinburgh Skating Club. I passed all the very difficult club tests when I was 24 years old in 1879 and my brother David the same year. Later I wrote a pamphlet on the 'Statistics and dynamics of ice skating' that incorporated the club rules, usually forgotten between one generation and another. My father had it privately printed for me and it sold well. Before the turn of the century I was one of only two British skaters qualified to judge the gold medallists of that day. Skating had been a big part of our lives since my grandfather Robert's day. He had skated on bone skates, but fifty or so years later we were using hollow grounded steel blades and the Old Edinburgh Skating Club had adopted the English style of skating. The menbers skated in tall hats and morning tailcoat, waistcoat and trousers, and proudly wore the club medal with the Prince of Wales feathers on it. 'Good Form' was imperative, and onlookers were astonished to see perhaps eight fine skaters keeping perfect time with each other and following a complicated pattern of figures without any apparent effort. One of the compulsory tests for admission to the club was the ability to jump over a row of twelve tall hats with their own on top! The motto on our medal was 'OCIOR EURO', Swifter than the wind. The officer of the club was a splendid fellow wearing a long dark blue great coat or 'Ulster' with a red collar and brass buttons. A ring of snow was all that was required to mark off a portion of the ice for the members to practise their acrobatic feats, and a tent was pitched on the south side of Duddingston for our exclusive use. [106]

In winter when the ice was bearing for skaters the flag on the City Chambers was hoisted, Louis would appear at our house to borrow my steel skates and a merry party would set off. Louis could skate gracefully and well, doing little twists and twirls within a two foot compass, and this seemed to give him great pleasure, skating always backwards until in the Adirondacks in the U.S.A. after his marriage. He never could be persuaded however to practise sufficiently to become a member of the club. As he said so often to us he had 'better things to do'. Indeed he had! I read with so much pleasure now his superb poem called 'Duddingston'. The second part goes thus:

Now fancy paints that bygone day
   When you were here, my fair-
The whole lake rang with rapid skates
   In the windless, winter air.

You leaned to me, I leaned to you,
   Our course was smooth as flight-
We steered-a heel-touch to the left,
   A heel-touch to the right.

We swung our way through flying men,
   Your hand lay fast in mine,
We saw the shifting crowd dispart,
   The level ice-reach shine.

I swear by yon swan-travelled lake,
   By yon calm hill above,
I swear had we been drowned that day
   We had been drowned in love.

We had frost every year between 1879 and 1889 lasting for almost six weeks. The Secretary printed slips to members telling us if the loch at Linlithgow was bearing, and Bathgate also had a good skating loch. Louis skated at these places also on the tiny pond in the gardens outside Heriot Row; here he could practise his personal technique. The following letter went to Bob on 14th February 1877:

"A fortnights frost and I have skated every afternoon-I can't skate more; I make some progress and do some back things smaller and faster than my fellow contrymen generally, but as what they hanker after is bigness, and slowness, and ever a greater protraction of the leg, that is perhaps not much to boast of."

Duddingston Loch has the church on the north side without the manse that is there today. The pavilion has long since gone but presumably it was a refuge for skaters in winter and for boats in summer. This lovely loch lying at the foot of Arthur's Seat is a bird sanctuary, and the nesting place in the reeds for countless migrating birds. Cars can pause and people get out and refresh their city minds with the beauty of the hill and the water. For a couple of hundred years now, since the forest that grew over part of the hill and provided a close hunting ground for the kings and queens who occupied Holyrood has all vanished away, the south and east slopes of our Arthur's Seat has been covered in whin or broom and for many weeks in late spring and summer the brilliant yellow flowers can be seen for many miles down the coast. They were there in Louis' day and have spread threefold now.

With the advent of a direct railway route from Edinburgh

and before the middle of the century the Stevenson family had discovered the delights and health-giving properties of Bridge of Allan and its spa in Stirlingshire.

Maggie, Tom's wife, was writing the dates of all their visits in her diary that she kept from the time she ended Louis' *Baby Book*. A careful search by the late David Angus throughout the district has revealed the visits the other members of the family were making at the same time to various hotels and boarding houses.

'David and Thomas and their families were frequently there together. Charles and Louis travelled back to Edinburgh in April 1879.

FROM A RAILWAY CARRIAGE

Faster than fairies, faster than witches,
Bridges and houses, hedges and ditches;
And charging along like troops in a battle,
All through the meadows the horses and cattle:
All of the sights of the hill and the plain
Fly as thick as driving rain;
And ever again, in the wink of an eye,
Painted stations whistle by.

Here is a child who clambers and scrambles,
All by himself and gathering brambles;
Here is a tramp who stands and gazes;
And there is the green for stringing the daisies!
Here is a cart run away in the road
Lumping along with man and load;
And here is a mill and there is a river:
Each a glimpse and gone for ever!
R.L.S.

As the train rushed on a new sight would catch Louis' interest. Everything that was seen for a few moments was photographed on Louis' mind and written down as he and I sat at the window seats of the railway carriage while we were whisked along. We were travelling between Bridge of Allan and Edinburgh. The train whistled as we went through a station. Sitting opposite me Louis would ask now and then, 'Can you get anything to rhyme with cart, Chug? Try Horse, Lump, and Screech!'

The green meadow, horses and cattle – the child alone gathering brambles – the mills and rivers and the shimmer of rain, etc, are all burned into my memory. I was with Louis hundeds of times, many of them very clear in my mind, but this journey with Louis composing and writing all the time has a special significance because of his superb combination of sight and sound turned into verse.

Louis was always very enthusiastic on the subject of the inheritance of the 'genes'.

"For that is the mark of the Scot of all classes: that he stands in an attitude towards the past unthinkable to Englishmen, and remembers and cherishes the memory of his forebears, good or bad; and there burns alive in him a sense of identity with the dead even to the twentieth generation. ... The power of ancestry on the character is not limited to the inheritance of cells. ... some Barbarossa, some old Adam of our ancestors, sleeps in all of us till the fit circumstance shall call it into action; ..."
[*Weir of Hermiston*, London, 1896, V, 3.]

He was under no misapprehension that the 'genes' and inherited characteristic all came from the male side.

MATER TRIUMPHANS

Son of my woman's body, you go, to the drum and fife,

To taste the colour of love and the other side of life-

From out of the dainty the rude, the strong from out of the
frail,

Eternally through the ages from the female comes the male.


The ten fingers and toes, and the shell-like nail on each,

The eyes blind as gems and the tongue attempting speech;

Impotent hands in my bosom, and yet they shall yield the
sword!

Drugged with slumber and milk, you wait the day of the
Lord.


Infant bridegroom, uncrowned king, unanointed priest,

Soldier, lover, explorer, I see you nuzzle the breast,

You that grope in my bosom shall load the ladies with rings,

You, that came forth through the doors, shall burst the doors
of kings.'


Charles as a child found it difficult to write easily or to express himself well. A close friendship developed between Davie and Louis who probably never knew how much Charles idolised him. Louis's ignorance of Thomas's financial dealings at the Northern Lighthouse Board and the miserable wages paid to his nephews was a serious matter for Charles whose hatred of rows of any sort was an outstanding part of his character. For the last few years of Thomas's life Charles, acting still as a paid assistant, was giving his uncle new technical innovative ideas for which he himself was never given any credit. Fortunately for the two young men Thomas's death came before his nephews'

patience had come to an end. Alan (Skerryvore) and Charles were probably the two members of the Stevenson dynasty who had a really close 'grass roots' affinity with nature, that provided the power-house for much that went into the inspiration in their work.

*Marriage*

Charles married Margaret Sherriff on January 19th, 1889, in St Paul's Episcopal church in York Place. **[107,108]** She was the daughter of Lieut.-General John Pringle Sherriff. They moved at once into 28 Douglas Crescent, facing north over the Belford Bridge, Dean Cemetery and to the sea and far shore of Fife. The house was a large double fronted stone villa with all the main rooms facing onto the cold north side of Edinburgh. It was a splendid commodious home for the family of three they were to have. Charles was a very mature young man and with absolute confidence in his own talents he started his married life in a style he meant to continue. Meta had been sent home as a child from India where her father John Sherriff served as a general in the Indian Army. She lived with her grandmother at Bairnkin, Southdean, Roxburghshire on the Scottish Borders. Presumably she was educated at a private school. She was intelligent, vivacious, loved gossip and enjoyed a gay social life after her marriage. Maggie Stevenson wrote in her Diary on 13th June 1889, when she had returned from Samoa to clear up 17 Heriot Row, that she found Meta 'pretty and pleasant.' Charles loved and spoilt her all their married life. She in turn spoilt and indulged their only son David Alan who was born on the 7th February 1891.

Frances Margaret, was born on the 21st May 1892 and five years later Evelyn Mary completed their family.

Charles was nearly 80 years old before he started to dictate to his youngest daughter May Yeoman the memories he held of his first cousin Robert Louis Stevenson. With bad eyesight but very bright mentally, and entirely in his right mind, he could still see the photographs for his book. He made several pencilled amendments to the script as it went along. Blindness or near blindness was a terrible blow to him and his daughter suggested this venture to relieve the boredom for his very active mind. She wrote exactly as he dictated it without any alteration whatever. He laid it aside several years before his death with a note that he wished it to be brought to publication standard by a younger member of the family. It is from this book that excerpts are quoted by the present author.[92] **[110]** Charles died at 28 Douglas Crescent, Edinburgh, aged 96.

### A professional aspect

At Edinburgh University Charles followed closely in the footsteps of David A., graduating with a B.Sc. degree in 1877. He too kept the customary journal, for no less than six lighthouse inspection voyages before his 25th birthday. An entry in August 1873 describes the cast iron diving bell in use at Anstruther harbour . . . *It is 6 feet long, 4 feet broad, 5 feet high, about 2 in thick but it is 3 in thick at the bottom to make it stand steady, and weighs 5 tons and displaces 3.5 tons of water when quite filled with air that is it is less than a half its weight in the water. There are eight strong convex lenses sunk into the top of the bell each 6.5 inches in diameter, but sometimes these dont give sufficient light when the sea is discoloured and the sky dark. The air is supplied by a force pump with two cylinders 8 in diameter with a one foot stroke. Four men work the pump and gave while there were 2 men it and a few feet under water . . .*[93] **[111]**

Charles's avid interest in recording enginering operations even extended to a sketch and description of the operation of Oakbank shale oilworks near Ormiston, Kirknewton, West Lothian in April 1874. **[112]**  He wrote, *The shale, which is brought to the works straight from the pit, is in pieces about 1 ft. square x 2 in. On arriving it is put between rollers which break it up to about 3 in. sq[uare] x 1 in. It is then raised to the same level & put into small carts by a series of revolving buckets like a dredge[r]. It is then rolled in the carts to the top of the furnaces where it is shot down. On being treated the oil passes off in vapour and the vapour is easily condensed (by being passed through pipes exposed to the air) on account of its latent heat being very small. It is then purified with sulphuric acid and caustic soda. Then it is put into shallow vessels where it is allowed to settle. The fineness of the oil depends on the length of time it is allowed to settle. If they wish to use it for making candles they freeze it - put it in cloth bags and squeeze with hydraulic presses so as to make it into cakes.*[93]

In 1875 Charles and David A. visited London to attend an Enquiry where their father successfully opposed Sir John Coode's proposal for Peterhead harbour.  On returning, they visited sewage farms at Leamington and Coventry and Charles was amazed *that the dried sludge made good manure and that the water passes out of the basins into the river colourless, tasteless and inodourous and it is said with .04% of organic matter, which is less than ordinary drinking water. I don't understand how such a simple process can make sewage water fit to drink.*[93]

By 1888, two years after Charles had been taken into partnership, his publication with David A. of an enlarged edition of their father's book on canal and river engineering helped to establish the new partnership's authority nationally in this discipline. Its reviewer in *Nature* on 23 December 1886

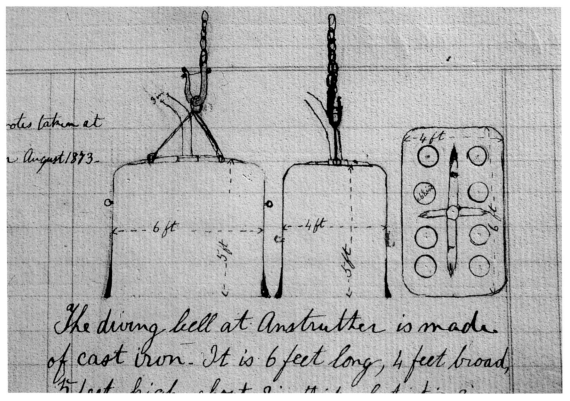

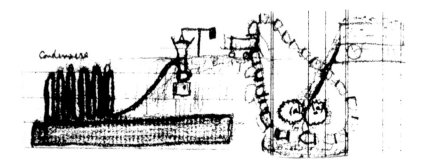

**[111]** *Charles's Sketch of diving bell at Anstruther, 1873.*

**[112]** *Charles's Sketch of oil shale extraction at Kirknewton 1874.*

considered it . . . *an excellent account of the principles and practice of river engineering, to the successful practice of which its able authors have so largely contributed.* During the next half century the firm, as Engineers to the Clyde Lighthouses Trust, was responsible for deepening the lower Clyde from about 16 ft. at low water to 29 ft. Charles took a particular interest in this work **[113,114]** and later with D. Alan devised and directed river deepening measures which enabled the largest ships to go to sea.

R W Johnstone, Charles's Royal Society of Edinburgh biographer who knew him very well, stated that, *Charles Stevenson was a man of great intellectual acumen, but for work of this sort he had a very special natural aptitude - a sort of instinctive grasp of how nature would work in the waves and winds and tides.*[94] His journals abound with evidence of this, for example, his entries relating to the Tay Bridge disaster:

[Undated entry, but very soon after the collapse on 28th December 1879]

***Tay Bridge.*** *Left Edinburgh at 9.30 with General Robertson arriving in Dundee at 12. Got on board the Tay steamer "Misty" which was taking out to the Tay Bridge some men to assist in the operations of raising the girders from the bed of the river. In about a quarter of an hour we reached the bridge & got the men on board*

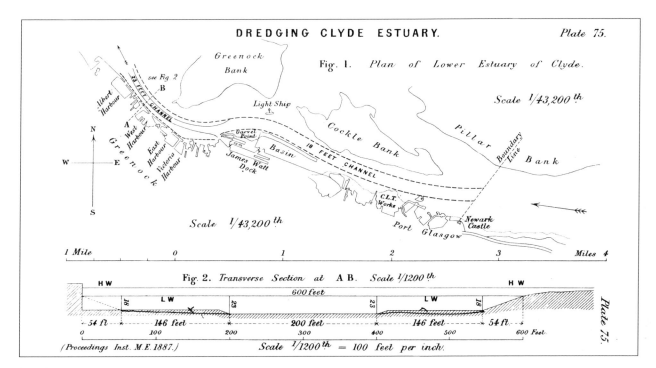

DREDGING CLYDE ESTUARY. *Plate 75.*

Fig. 1. *Plan of Lower Estuary of Clyde.*

*Scale 1/43,200th*

Fig. 2. *Transverse Section at A B. Scale 1/1200th*

(*Proceedings Inst. M.E. 1887.*)

*Scale 1/1200th = 100 feet per inch.*

**[113]** *Dredging Clyde Estuary. Plan and section from Charles's IMechE paper, 1887.*

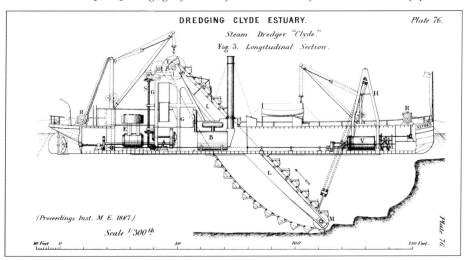

DREDGING CLYDE ESTUARY. *Plate 76.*

*Steam Dredger "Clyde."*

Fig. 3. *Longitudinal Section.*

(*Proceedings Inst. M.E. 1887.*)

*Scale 1/300th*

**[114]** *Steam Dredger Clyde. From Charles's IMechE paper, 1887.*

the barges which are used by the divers who are at present making chains fast to the ends of the Southmost girder of the fallen ones & otherwise preparing them for being lifted which operation of lifting is to be commenced tomorrow by raising them by means of two sets of pontoon barges, each set consisting of two joined together by very strong bracing. The bracing in the one being iron girders (with hydraulic lifting apparatus) and in the other of 6 strong wooden trusses with 6 lifting screws to be worked by means of nuts and worked by hand. There will be thus 4 fixtures at the one end of girders & 4 at the other, eight in all. (The nuts and screws dont look strong enough for their work.) **[115,116]**

*There seemed to be about 8 divers at the bridge. I landed on No.[blank] pier ie the [blank] from the south end & one in which part of the coping of the pier had been turned up on the windward side.* **[117]** *Inspected it thoroughly. The details of the iron columns appeared to me to be very defective, details which I think should have been made substantially. At any rate - It appears to me that the bridge gave way through* **not having sufficient base** *to withstand the pressure of the wind, the whole fabric thus wanting to come down the bracing (which by the way appeared to me to be monstrously too weak & perfectly incapable of withstanding any* **thrust***) gave way & consequently at the same time the fixtures of the columns to the sockets etc, the bridge falling over thus -* **[115]**

*The greatest damage to the stonework of the piers is at the N. end which fact together with the fact that the least damage done to the* **iron piers** *is towards the S. end show - 1st. that the N. end was forced over by a steady push such as would be caused by the the wind & 2nd. that the S end was pulled over by a quicker force a kind of jerk in fact which points to this end having been destroyed by the fall of the more Northern portion.*[93]

Charles's conclusions that the bridge did not have sufficient base to withstand the pressure of the wind and that the weak bracing gave way and consequently at the same time, the fixtures of the columns to the sockets, the bridge falling as indicated, accords with Martin and MacLeod's

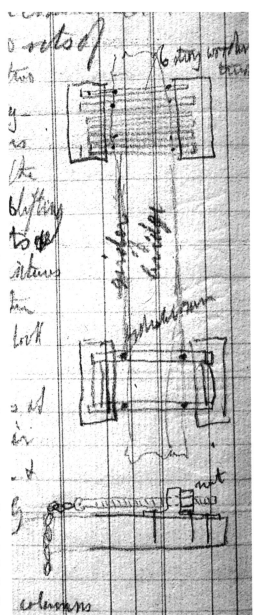

**[115]** *Tay Bridge - Charles's sketches, 1880. Pontoon for lifting girders, and pier overturning.*

[116] *Tay Bridge - A fallen girder beached on its side after retrieval. Note lifting chains.*

recent computer analysis of the failure[95] and Shipway's conclusions.[96] However these authorities are unconvinced by his arguments that the northern end of the navigation spans failed first, believing that the failure mechanism probably began at or close to the point where the train fell. At this point the bridge was taller and the overturning wind force would have been more likely to induce a greater uplift force on the base holding down bolts. Whilst this is a reasonable hypothesis it cannot be considered conclusive as it is based on surmise about the uniformity of wind pressure, pier bracing strength and the resistance of the base to uplift.

An indication of Charles's work during the early years of the new partnership, from 1887-1891, is provided in the statement which accompanied his application to become a Member of the Institution of Civil Engineers in 1891. It read, *he has (along with his brother) been Engineer to the following harbour works, viz.:- Coldingham, Port Knockie, Baltinore, Broadford, Ness, Lossiemouth and Loch Ranza, which are either in progress or completed; quays at Lancaster, and the improvement of the river Lune, and dock-gates at Glasson; also the following lighthouse apparatus, etc., for Girdleness, Inchkeith, Point of Ayre and Corsewall worked by oil engines. He is also engaged in large dredging operations on the estuary of the Clyde. The aggregate expenditure on the*

[117] *Tay Bridge ruins, 1880. Note upturned coping on the windward side referred to by Charles.*

*above-named works will amount to about £180,000. His firm are Engineers to the projected Forth and Clyde Canal.*

In lighthouse illumination, Charles applied the equiangular prism to condense a beam of light into a narrower and therefore more brilliant beam than previously. **[118]** D. Alan wrote of this work in 1936, *all the important and most powerful maritime lights of Scotland utilise equiangular prisms of his design instead of Fresnel's prisms or utilize his combination apparatus [with existing first order lenses] . . . these two inventions making the lights of this country shine more brightly. These great maritime lights in Scotland on his design are twenty-four in number and range from 160,000 candlepower to 1,000,000 candlepower . . . obtained from a single paraffin oil mantel burner without having recourse to the electric light which is so much more costly . . . Charles's design increased the power of the light beam by about 10% over Fresnel's prisms and his uncle Alan's alterations and did not require so large a lantern.*[97] He also improved the distinctiveness of buoy and beacon lights, at first on the lower Clyde, by utilising a small gas meter and bypass with each light to make them flash.

Charles was a pioneer of the development of wireless communication. In 1892 he conducted experiments in electrical induction by means of a telephone transmitter from which he received speech over a distance of two miles without wires. He is believed to have pre-dated Marconi, Heaviside, Preece and others in becoming the world's first wireless broadcaster. His apparatus did however have the drawbacks of being inconvenient to use because of the large diameter of the coil arrangements required and in having a limited range. **[119]**

Charles also invented the *Leader Cable* for guiding vessels by means of an electric submarine electric cable laid on the ocean bed.[98] Ships with appropriate receivers could be brought safely up channels and along dangerous coasts in safety during fog or at night. In 1893-94 both these innovations were the subject of papers read to the Royal Society of Edinburgh, to which Charles had been elected a Fellow in 1886. He did not however get much encouragement from Lord Kelvin, who wrote, *You might just as well boil the sea.*[97] Nevertheless, the leader cable system was developed and eventually installed at several large ports in Europe and the U.S.A., the first being at Heligoland. During the war the system was also used in the North Sea off Harwich to guide vessels through mine fields.

Apart from the invention of the *Talking Beacon* which is described in more detail in the next chapter, the firm also re-established parabolic mirror glass reflectors at Toward Lighthouse, in which an incandescent mantle from an oil light producing 1100 candlepower produced a beam out to sea of 340,000 candlepower. This improvement marked a return to the catoptric system, which forms the basis of present-day lighting with the very bright electrical sources now available. Other important lighthouse service innovations by Charles included radio controlled lights and fog signals.

Charles's numerous research and devlopment based contributions to engineering practice involving optics, electricity and radio, and their harnessing to works of maritime convenience, usefulness and safely, were in the finest tradition of his profession. Charles was the only Stevenson to become a member of the Institution of Electrical Engineers, being admitted as an Associate in 1893 and becoming a Companion in 1929. With the possible exception of Thomas, he was the most inventive member of the Stevenson engineers.

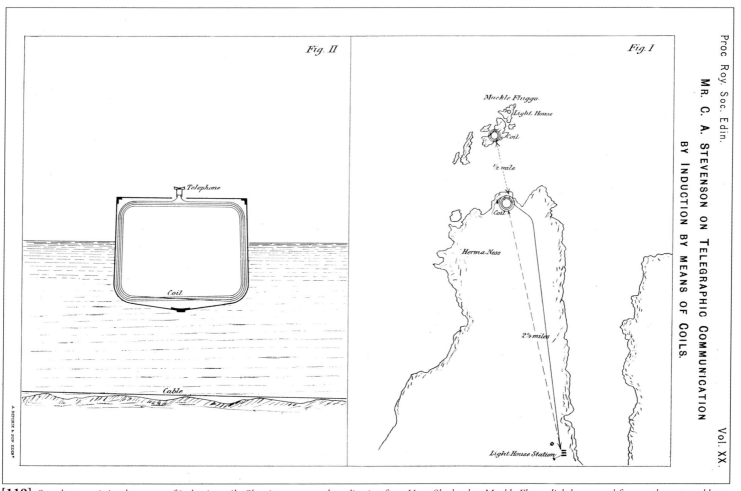

Proc. Roy. Soc. Edin.

MR. C. A. STEVENSON ON TELEGRAPHIC COMMUNICATION BY INDUCTION BY MEANS OF COILS.

Vol. XX.

**Fig. II**

Telephone

Coil

Cable

A. RITCHIE & SON EDIN^R

**Fig. I**

Muckle Flugga

Light House

Coil

½ mile

Coil

Herma Ness

2¾ miles

Light House Station

[119] *Speech transmission by means of inductive coils. Showing a proposed application from Unst, Shetland to Muckle Flugga lighthouse, and from underwater cable to a ship. From Charles's RSE paper 1895, XX, 196-200.*

## Chapter Nine

## D. Alan Stevenson 1891-1971 - Last of the line and lighthouse historian

**Family recollections**

David Alan Stevenson, or D. Alan as he was often called, was born on 7th February 1891, the eldest child and only son of Charles and Meta. He was born one year after the death of still-born twins.

Alan was a handsome child, but in early childhood he developed a stammer which he did not overcome until his mid twenties. The usual five years were spent at the Edinburgh Academy but like his cousin Louis he hated school games and his mother found excuses to let him off. His musical talents were obvious from his earliest years, and violin and piano lessons were substituted. He became a competent performer on both piano and violin, and an opera buff, attending the first performance in Edinburgh of Wagner's 'Ring' Cycle in 1910. While at University he enjoyed two 'Grand Tour' visits to Europe's capital cities, avidly seeking historic sites, concert halls, museums and art galleries. At home, he played golf and tennis with his father and his sister Frances.

At twelve years old he went on his first voyage on the *Pharos*. He visited the firm's office in George Street on a regular basis when, after shaking hands solemnly with the assistants, his father would set him to work on some useful educational task. His uncle David gave him every kind of assistance, and took him with him on many of his assignments, such as for the River Clyde, and also the River Ouse.

After school and Edinburgh University he passed the necessary exams to qualify as a B.Sc. Besides having a passionate interest in lighthouses this talented boy built up a unique collection of stamps, specialising in 'Cape Triangulars'. Later in life he wrote a book about stamps and then sold his entire collection for £10,000-a large sum of money in those days.

With the outbreak of the Great War in 1914 all the lighthouses ceased to show their lights unless they had been informed that British ships were in the vicinity and needed help. Foghorns were silent when fog rolled up the coast. Alan of course was eligible to be called up for the services but David and Charles put forward a case that he was needed by the Lighthouse Board as the lights were all still manned and much maintenance work had to be done. It was degrading and difficult for a young man to be seen still in 'mufti' in the middle of this horrendous war and many strangers were handing him 'white feathers' on the streets of Edinburgh.

The solution came in 1915 when he was required to go to the Dardanelles to place Charles's new invention-lightweight portable acetylene lights-round the coast in an effort to help the Royal Navy. A request had come from Admiral de Roebeck for somebody to be sent out. The Stevensons asked for a military rank to be given to Alan for this job and he was commissioned a Captain in the Royal Marines. When the task was finished he dispatched his mechanic assistant named Clark home by sea direct from Malta. He then decided to take a good holiday by himself and he travelled home through Italy and France taking several weeks en route. He was able to enjoy ten operas and in Paris he visited the Folies Bergère and the Pathé Gramophone Parlour.

He had been made an Associate Member of the Institution of Civil Engineers in 1916 and a year later, when he was 28, he completed his apprenticeship and joined the family firm on a salary of £100 a year. He was able to continue to wear his uniform for the duration of the war.

In 1923 Alan married Jessie MacLellan from Glasgow. Her father was an electrical engineer. They lived at 22 Glencairn Crescent. Rhoda Laura Helen was born in 1924 and Joyce Margaret Beryl in 1927. Robert Quentin Charles completed the family in 1932.

As his father and uncle David aged, Alan was able to help them both - by doing lighthouse inspection tours for David, and working together with Charles on the Clyde and other consulting business of the firm.

Alan was Honorary Secretary of the Royal Scottish Geographical Society and lectured for them. He was also an elected member of the Athenaeum in London. In his private life he belonged to six golf clubs, including Muirfield, and was Secretary to the Edinburgh Skating Club. He successfully broke the traditional Sunday Sabbath by creating a Sunday afternoon skating club at the Haymarket Skating Rink. It ran from 1926 to the start of the 1939 War. It showed his excellent organisational ability. It was strictly for the conventional closed society, still rigid in Edinburgh during the '20s and '30s. Following family tradition Alan was also a member of the Royal Company of Archers.

In 1929 Charles invented the 'Talking Beacon'. This enabled a ship to take its bearings from a radio signal-invaluable in thick fog. Charles gave half the credit for the idea to his son and indeed it was Alan who revealed the details at the first International Conference on Lighthouses held in London. The Talking Beacon attracted interest in the U.S.A., Canada and Scandinavia, and the Clyde Lighthouse Trustees took it on. As Engineers to the Clyde Lighthouses Trust, father and son were asked to deepen the channel of the Clyde for the launch of the Queen Mary and together they tackled this successfully. The ship negotiated the bends they had altered and sailed into the open sea in 1936.

The year 1936 was to end any possibility of the Stevenson dynasty continuing because Alan had grown impatient with the uncertainty of obtaining the post as Engineer to the Northern Lighthouse Board and he forced his uncle David to show his hand regarding this important matter. David, who of course did not have any children, seemed in good health although frail and showed no signs of retiring voluntarily. The only way David could resolve the situation was to break up the family firm by his own withdrawal from it.

David and his lawyer entered into legal battle with Charles and Alan. Telegrams flew from the offices of the firm, upstairs to downstairs, where the Nothern Lighthouse Board had its offices, and it was a panic situation for Charles and Alan with a 'NOTICE OF REMOVAL' hanging over their heads. Messrs Mackenzie and Kermack acted for Charles and Alan, and Messrs Tods Murray and Jamieson for David. By October there was a threat of actual eviction sent from the Secretary of the Northern Lighthouse Board, J. Glencourse Wakelin, and Charles and Alan had to pack their bags and remove to a few doors away at 90a George Street. The following letter was sent both to David and to Charles and Alan, as the tenants of the ground floor of 84 George Street:

'Northern Lighthouse Board,
84 George Street,
Edinburgh, 2, 15th October, 1936.
Dear Sir,

With reference to the enclosed official letter regarding your vacation of the premises, I have been asked by the Commissioners to say that they greatly regret to learn that it has become necessary to dissolve the firm of Messrs. D. & C. Stevenson with whom they have been associated for so many years, and that they trust that the action which they now take will be construed as being unavoidable in the peculiar circumstances of the case.

Yours faithfully,
J. Glencourse Wakelin' [99]

The new partnership of A. & C. Stevenson lasted until Charles's retirement in 1940. Alan continued in the post of Engineer to the Clyde Lighthouses Trust up to his retiral in 1952, to devote his time to lighthouse and family research. He had already published *The triangular stamps of Good Hope*, a work that gained for him the Crawford Medal of the Royal Philatelic Society. In 1959 the *World's lighthouses before 1920* was published and firmly established him as the foremost authority on the historical aspect of early lighthouses.

David died two years after the break-up of the family firm, but not before handing to his nephew all the historical documents dating back to the time of Thomas Smith and Robert Stevenson. He had great faith that Alan would be an excellent custodian for them and indeed he was. He added many relevant items to the collection and pursued his research with infinite care and patience, travelling all round the world. He died aged 80 with the work almost completed but not yet into the hands of a publisher. He liked to describe himself as a 'Technical Historian.'

David Alan died on the 22nd of December 1971. In 1993 all the valuable engineering papers, maps, &c. passed into the safe hands of the National Library of Scotland. The family Trustees named by Alan before his death accepted only a nominal sum for them.

**A professional aspect**

Alan was the last practising member of the Stevenson engineers. From 1908 he attended Prof. Sir Thomas Hudson Beare's engineering course at Edinburgh University. After graduating he was trained in the office of 'D. & C. Stevenson' until 1914. He then became an assistant engineer in the firm and a partner in 1919. In the same year he was elected a Fellow of the Royal Society of Edinburgh. The firm's work then, as before, was mainly concerned with river navigation improvements, harbours and piers, drainage and sewerage, water works, lighthouses and fog signals. Although the period of great development on harbours, lighthouses, and navigational river deepenings had passed and with it the greatest days of the dynasty, the firm still kept busy in these branches, for example on the River Clyde deepening, on sewerage and water supply projects, and more particularly on the modernisation of lighthouse and communications equipment.

In 1925 Alan with the support of his father, uncle, Prof. Beare and others became a Member of the Institution of Civil Engineers [M.I.C.E., a grade which changed to fellowship - F.I.C.E. in 1968]. His supporting statement read that *Mr Stevenson has devoted his life to engineering work, and has been specially engaged in optical and hydraulic science. His lighthouse experience extends to the erection of lights in this country and in the Eastern Mediterranean, and he has experience of ship-building and other marine engineering, such as harbours, and is specially versed in tidal phenomena and the action of works as affecting these*

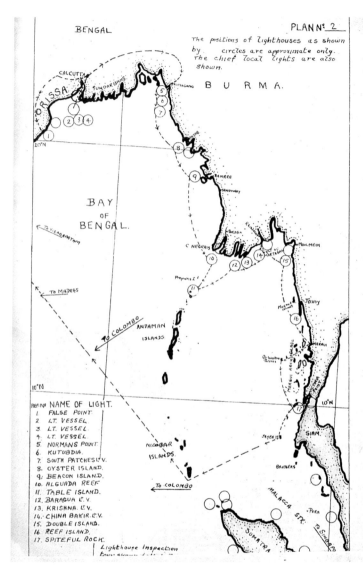

BENGAL

PLAN N° 2

The positions of lighthouses as shown by circles are approximate only. The chief local lights are also shown.

BURMA.

BAY
OF
BENGAL.

ANDAMAN
ISLANDS

NICOBAR
ISLANDS

SIAM.

SUMATRA

MALACCA STR.

REF N° NAME OF LIGHT.
1. FALSE POINT.
2. LT. VESSEL.
3. LT. VESSEL.
4. LT. VESSEL.
5. NORMANS POINT.
6. KUTUBDIA.
7. SOUTH PATCHES L.V.
8. OYSTER ISLAND.
9. BEACON ISLAND.
10. ALGUADA REEF.
11. TABLE ISLAND.
12. BARAGUA L.V.
13. KRISHNA. L.V.
14. CHINA BAKIR.L.V.
15. DOUBLE ISLAND.
16. REEF ISLAND.
17. SPITEFUL ROCK.

Lighthouse Inspection

**[120]** *Indian Lighthouses 1927. Plan 2 from Alan's report showing the site of Alguada Reef Lighthouse 1865 which was modelled on Skerryvore Lighthouse.*

*phenomena, especially their action on the flow of rivers. Has contributed numerous, reports, articles, etc., on the works enumerated above, and has done special research work, probably unique, on tides and their phenomena . . . the Rivers Ouse, Forth and Clyde have been the subject of special investigation.*

In 1926-1927, for the Government of India, Alan inspected and valued the lighthouses of India, Burma, Persian Gulf and Ceylon, more than a hundred in all, and advised on the organisation of a centralised lighthouse service. **[120]** In a comprehensive report he recommended the improvement of many existing lighthouses and the establishment of new ones.

In 1928 Charles and Alan, prompted by the earlier development of radio in navigation signals in the United States, developed and installed the first wireless telephone in Scotland between a lighthouse and the shore in their capacity as Engineers to The Clyde Lighthouses Trust. Their Talking Beacon invented soon afterwards and installed, at the Trust's Cumbrae and Cloch lighthouses, enabled the position of ships in the Clyde to be plotted from synchronised radio and foghorn signals. Alan in his unpublished presidential address in 1948 to The Watt Club[100] (now administered by Heriot-Watt University) *On the navigation of ships in fog*, commented that, *for the first time in navigation,* the new system gave *from one station alone the means of a ship obtaining her position from only one land station. The radio alone gives direction on any simple rotating radio receiver on board and distance is got by reading the time elapsed between hearing the same blast of air signal through a microphone by radio telephony and through the air.*

He continued, *The principle is that of thunder and lightning or of sound ranging. The lightning is transmitted instantaneously all round the horizon at practically all distances while the time of*

# THE WONDER OF THE NEW TALKING LIGHTHOUSE

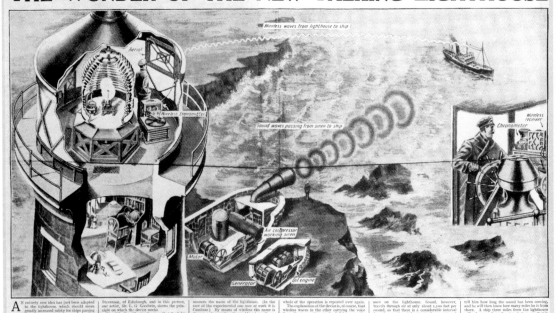

A N entirely new idea has just been adapted to the lighthouse, which should mean greatly increased safety for ships passing round our coasts in foggy weather. The difficulty of fog is, of course, that the light cannot be seen. Stevenson, of Edinburgh, and in this picture, our artist, Mr. L. G. Goodwin, shows the principle on which the device works. By means of wireless this name is thrown out upon the ether. Almost simultaneously the siren also throws out blasts and have travel measure the name of the lighthouse. (In the case of the experimental one now at work in Cumbrae.) By means of wireless this name is thrown out upon the ether. Almost simultaneously the siren also throws out blasts and have travel whole of the operation is repeated over again. The explanation of the device is, of course, that wireless waves in the other carrying the voice from the transmitter on the lighthouse to the ship, travel at a different rate from the sound once on the lighthouse. Sound, however, travels through air at only about 1,100 feet per second, so that there is a considerable interval from the sounding of the siren to the reception of its sound by the ship. tell him how long the sound has been coming, and he will then know how many miles he is from shore. A ship three miles from the lighthouse will, of course, hear the siren out that is four miles away. It is a very ingenious device.

**[121]** *The New Talking Lighthouse. Charles and Alan's invention as shown in This and That, 14 February 1931,10.*

*receiving the thunder through the air is in proportion to the distance of the observer from the source of the disturbance. The rate of travel of sound through the air is about 5.5 seconds per mile . . . Instead of the seaman requiring to measure the time lag by stop watch, a gramophone record is operated at the lighthouse at which the radio signal and air fog signal are operated. The radio signal even incorporates directions for its own use. At Cloch Point Lighthouse the record transmits the following signal by radio repeated every 50 seconds. "Cloch Point lighthouse speaking. At the instant when you hear through the air the commencement of the second blast of this fog signal your distance in cables from this lighthouse is stated on the radio". This is followed by counting in speech in cables from 1 to 30 or 3 sea miles.*

*The system has been long in advancing and there are still [after 20 years] only the two Clyde stations in service in Britain. The United States at once adopted the idea but they do not use the gramophone record and require that a ship's captain should use a stop watch and listen for a telegraphic impulse to represent the zero or moment of seeing the lightning. There are now 74 of these stations in U.S.A. and Canada and they are now being fitted in rapidly by the Scandinavian countries.*

The innovation attracted considerable press publicity. **[121]**

In a paper read to the Royal Society of Arts in 1931 Alan illustrated the system as installed at Cumbrae and gave a demonstration by gramophone of its talking beacon. The Society recognised this achievement by awarding Alan and Charles its prestigious *Thomas Gray Award*, including £100 each.

In 1936 the firm, again for the Clyde Lighthouses Trust, successfully advised on and superintended the skilfully engineered deepening of the existing curved channel of the river Clyde to about 30 ft. from Port Glasgow westwards for about 3 miles to enable the largest new ships to go to sea. **[113]** Most of this work fell to Alan as the most active member of the firm. The skill came in rejecting the alternative most certain to meet the objective, which was, straightening the channel at more than ten times the cost. By the time Alan retired as Engineer to the Clyde Lighthouses Trust in 1952, Stevenson engineers had served the Trust for a continuous period of more than one and a half centuries.

By the time of his retiral Alan had become increasingly involved in historical pursuits, an interest which can be traced back to an article 'Early Scottish Lighthouses' in *Chambers Journal* in 1917. His Royal Society of Arts lecture of 1931, which was subsequently repeated in Baltimore and elsewhere, also had an historical element. **[122]** However, it was not until 1949 that he published his first full-length book - an account of Robert's *English lighthouse tours 1801 1813 1818.* **[123]** In 1959, based on family records and seven years of intensive research and travel, Alan produced his authoritative, although referenceless, *magnum opus* on *The World's Lighthouses before 1820.* **[124]**

It was in March 1966, when Alan was working on a book which he did not live to complete, *Some Records of R.L.S.'s Family of Engineers,* that the author first met him at his Great Stuart St. office. On the first visit he was courteously received as a fellow civil engineer with an interest in engineering history, and tantalised by a glimpse of part of the family's wonderful engineering archive (now in the National Library of Scotland), but not allowed to look at anything! On another occasion the visit was terminated only minutes after it had begun after the author had suggested that it would be instructive to have known which books Robert had thought it worthwhile to include in his office library. On further visit in 1970, when Alan's office was being wound down, deep discussion ensued on the use of the office's eidograph made for Robert by Adie of Edinburgh for copying, reducing or enlarging plans, and also, on Lord Stuart de Rothesay's facilitation of Alan's visit to the lighthouses and

TWO SEPARATE LECTURES
BY
D. ALAN STEVENSON
B.Sc., M.Inst.C.E., F.R.S. (Edin.)
who has lectured to the Royal Scottish Geographical Society, the Scottish Society of Arts, British Literary Societies and also in Canada and U.S.A.

*on*

FROM PRIMITIVE LIGHTHOUSE
TO RADIO BEACON

*and*

PRESENT-DAY PORTUGAL

**[122]** *Prospectus for Alan's lectures c. 1932.*

workshops of France in 1835!

Alan's most important work was probably that for the Clyde Lighthouses Trust, but he deserves to be remembered not so much for his engineering achievements as his painstaking historical work which led to him becoming the nation's, if not the world's, foremost lighthouse historian of his day. **[125]**

[87] *David A., 'Davie', aged 15.*

[100] *Charles, aged 14.*

[109] *Janey MacKintosh, Lady Kyllachy.*

[105] *Charles's home at 45 Melville Street, Edinburgh with his sister Mary playing the harp c. 1873.*

**[89]** *David and Dorothy with daughters Dorothy [Peploe] and Kathleen [Chambers].*

**[88]** *Dorothy, née Roberts, David's wife.*

**[102]** *David and Charles's boat at Anchor House, North Berwick.*

**[101]** *Mr. Clyde's Class of 1865 at Edinburgh Academy Charles 6th from right back row.*

[3] *Thomas with the Royal Edinburgh Volunteers 1802. Believed to be the stout one!*

[18] *Old drawing of the Bell Rock Lighthouse kitchen as formerly decorated for visitor and library use.*

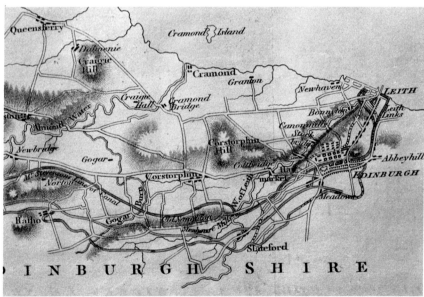

[25] *Part of Leith to Glasgow canal proposal, 1817. Note the routes through Edinburgh.*

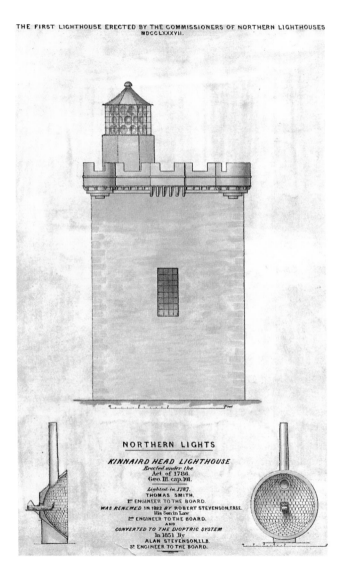

THE FIRST LIGHTHOUSE ERECTED BY THE COMMISSIONERS OF NORTHERN LIGHTHOUSES
MDCCLXXXVII.

NORTHERN LIGHTS

*KINNAIRD HEAD LIGHTHOUSE*
*Erected under the*
Act of 1786,
Geo. III. cap.101.

*Lighted in 1787,*
THOMAS SMITH,
1ST ENGINEER TO THE BOARD.
WAS RENEWED IN 1822 BY ROBERT STEVENSON, F.R.S.E.
His Son in Law
2ND ENGINEER TO THE BOARD.
AND
*CONVERTED TO THE DIOPTRIC SYSTEM*
In 1851 By
ALAN STEVENSON, LL.B.
3RD ENGINEER TO THE BOARD.

[5]   *Kinnaird Head Lighthouse and reflector lamp.*

[12]   *Jane, Robert's daughter in her early twenties.*

154

[**14**] *Jane, Mrs Warden with her daughters Jessie and Mary 1861.*

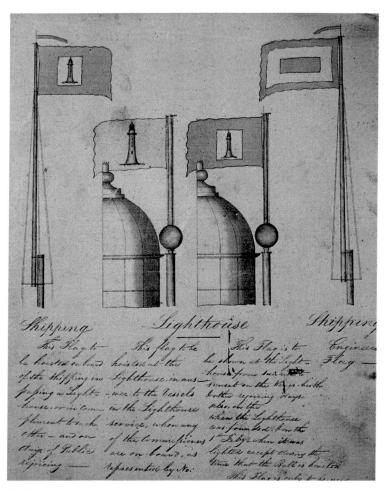

[**21**] *Northern Lighthouse Board shipping flags, Robert's on the right.*

[45] *Skerryvore Lighthouse, 1844. Photograph by courtesy of Mr. R.R.G. Kinnear, former Principal Civil Engineer, NLB who regards the lighthouse as one of the world's most beautifully engineered structures.*

[22] *Cape Wrath Lighthouse, 1828.*

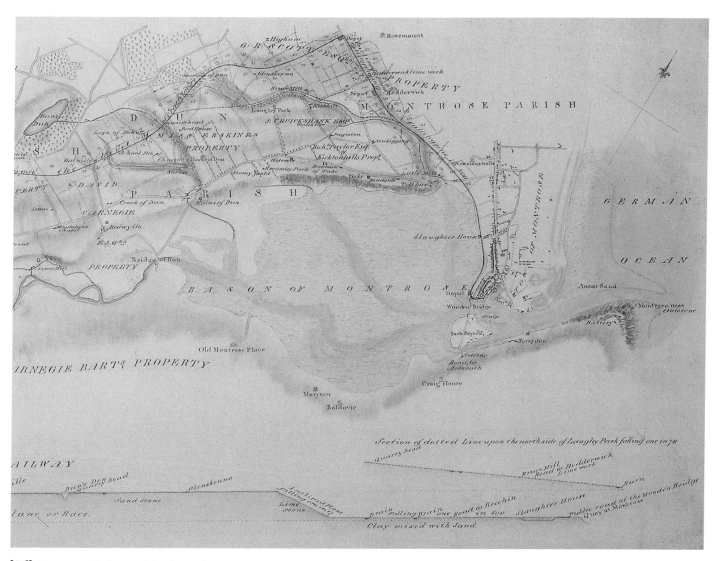

**[26]** *Montrose end of proposed Brechin Railway, 1819. Note the wooden bridge at Montrose and the Bridge of Dun reported on by Robert in 1811.*

**[30]** *Temporary bridge over r. Clyde at Portland Street, Glasgow, 1832-46.*

**[31]** *William IV, or New Bridge, over r. Forth, Stirling, 1829-32.*

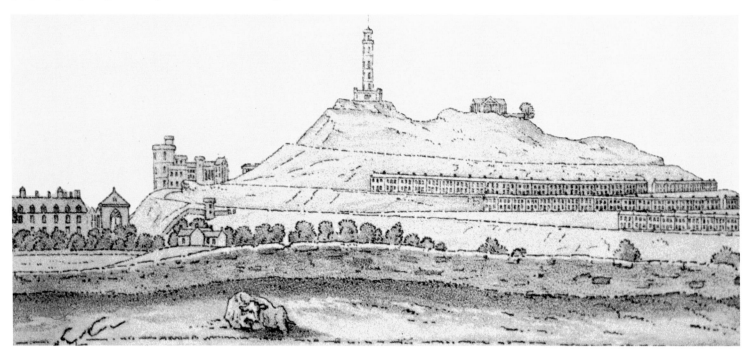

**[32]** *Design for building on the Calton Hill, 1815. Robert Stevenson FRSE Civil Engineer. Drawing by Robert's assistant G.C.Scott. Not executed as shown.*

[34] *Regent Road retaining wall c. 1818 and Burns' Monument, 1830.*

[36] *Kearvaig (Chearbhaig) Bridge, 1828 on 11-mile access to Cape Wrath Lighthouse.*

[95] *Mull of Kintyre Lighthouse, 1822. Plaque for lighting apparatus, 1906.*

[94] *Bass Rock Lighthouse, 1902. D. & C. Stevenson. Tantallon Castle and the Isle of May in distance.*

**[35]** *Marykirk Bridge, Kincardineshire, 1811. Robert's first major bridge. Note his use of hollow spandrels for lightness and strength.*

[41] *Alan surrounded by his family, c. at Anchor House, North Berwick c1860. Three generations: Alan centre front and R.A.M. his son behind. Davie leaning on his knee and Charles standing up to his right. Thomas at back with Maggie his wife and R.L.S. in front. David far right, "Cashie" the nanny holds baby James Thomas. Elizabeth, David's wife at back. All their children are there.*

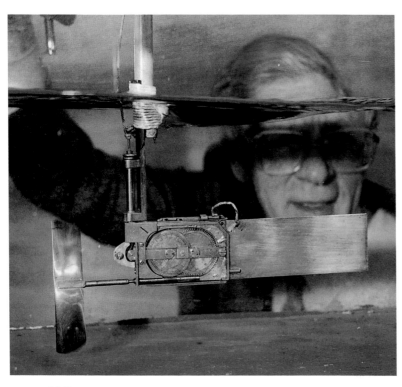

[61] *David's Adie & Son tachometer being used by the author to measure underwater current velocity at Heriot-Watt University. to be read off.*

[96] *Mull of Kintyre Lighthouse, 1822. Note the later adoption of Alan's inclined astragals, and continuing use of Charles's equiangular prisms.*

[55] *David and his son 'Bo' aged 4 years.*

[53] *Miniatures of David and Elizabeth, 1840.*

163

[54] *David and family, 1854. Elizabeth on left holds young Robert 'Bo', RLS's first playmate. Behind her is Elizabeth ['Bessie'] and, continuing right, Georgina Burke, Georgina, Mary Smith Stevenson and Jane.*

[56] *'Bessie', David's eldest daughter in later life.*

[62] *Dhu Heartach Lighthouse c. 1854.*

[64] *Kyleakin Lighthouse, [1857] of Gavin Maxwell fame and Skye Bridge nearing completion, 1995.*

[**63**] *Muckle Flugga Lighthouse, 1857.*

[98] *Sule Skerry Lighthouse, 1895. Believed to be Britain's remotest lighthouse 40 miles west of Orkney.*

[108] *'Meta' and George Sherriff, her brother, aged 6 and 4.*

[99] *Rattray Head Lighthouse, 1895. The first to be constructed with a fog-horn and signal room beneath its tower.*

[118] *Charles's equiangular spherical prism refractor for Fair Isle Lighthouse c. 1890.*

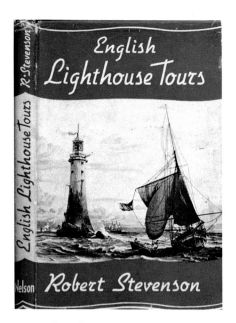

[123] *Alan's first book.*

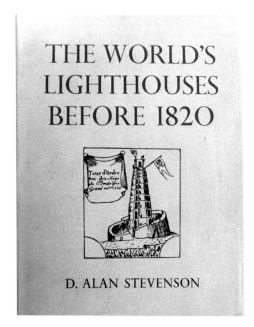

[124] *Alan's classic lighthouse work, 1959.*

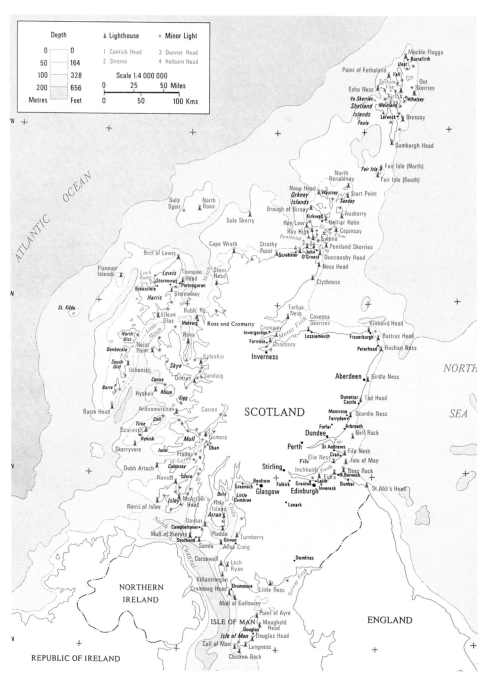

[126] *Map of Northern Lighthouse Board Lighthouses.*

**[104]** *Charles with pony.*

**[103]** *Louis blowing bubbles with Charles at North Berwick. Photograph by David 1865.*

**[106]** *Charles and George Scott-Moncrieff skating at Duddingston Loch.*

[110] *Charles at his desk at D. & C. Stevenson's office, 84 George Street, Edinburgh, c.1920.*

[107] *Margaret, 'Meta' Sheriff, Charles's wife.*

[125] *Stevensons at the Bell Rock in 1975. The author Jean Leslie in foreground and from left to right, Simon Leslie, Norma Stevenson, Sandy Leslie, Quentin Stevenson, his son Nikki, Richard and Archie Leslie.*

**Source notes**

[1]    Peter Williamson. *Edinburgh directory*. Edinburgh, 1781.

[2]    Peter Williamson. *Edinburgh directory*. Edinburgh, 1790.

[3]    *Edinburgh Evening Courant*, 17.4.1800, 4b.

[4]    R. L. Stevenson. *Records of a family of engineers.* Edinburgh, 1896.

[5]    Family papers.

[6]    Edinburgh City Archives: ED.005/1/1, 17-18.

[7]    National Library of Scotland: MS. Acc. 10706, 88.

[8]    Scottish Record Office: MS. Minute books of the Board of Manufactures, NG.1/125/208-9.

[9]    SRO: Northern Lighthouse Board minute books, 21.3.1787.

[10]   Glasgow Archives: Clyde Port Authority, T-CN 40.

[11]   SRO: NLB minute books, 26.12.1793.

[12]   'Reflector for a light-house.' *Ency. Brit. Suppl.*, 3rd ed., 1801; *Ency. Brit.*, 6th ed., 1823. Possibly written by the editor, Dr George Gleig. Attributed to either Thomas Smith or a friend of his by Sir David Brewster in the *North British Review*, 1859, XXXI.

[13]   R.L. Stevenson. *The manuscripts of Robert Louis Stevenson's Records of a family of engineers. The unfinished chapters, edited with an introduction by J. Christian Bay.* Chicago, 1929. NLS: X.170.a. The manuscripts are in the Beinecke Library: 6749-6782.

[14]   Robert Stevenson. 'Reminiscences of Sir Walter Scott, Baronet.' In: Scott, Sir W; Laughlan, W.F. (ed.). *Northern Lights, or A voyage in the Lighthouse Yacht to Nova Zembla and the Lord knows where in the summer of 1814.* Hawick, 1982, p. 155.

[15]   Robert Stevenson. J*ournal of a trip to Holland. Communicated during a short tour in the year 1817, in letters to his daughter.* Edinburgh, 1848.

[16]   Henry Cockburn. *Memorials of his time.* Edinburgh, 1856,p.241. NLS: R.251.e.

[17]   Robert Stevenson. 'Disposition and Settlement.' SRO: SC.70/4/12, 482-537.

[18]   Act, 46 Geo. III, c. 132.

[19]   SRO: NLB minute books. Dec. 1806.

[20]   Sir J. Rennie, *An . . Account of the Breakwater in Plymouth Sound*, 1848.

[21]   *Civil Engineer and Architect's Jrnl*, 1849. XII. 77-79,136- 142, 1 pl.

[22]   David Stevenson, *Life of Robert Stevenson,* Edinburgh,1878. 21-22 & Thomas Stevenson, *Lighthouse Construction and Illumination,* Edinburgh,1881. 17.

[23]   C. Mair, *A star for seamen*, 1978. 66-68.

[24]   D.Alan Stevenson. *The world's lighthouses before 1820,* 1959.  299-301

[25]   NLS: MS. Acc. 19806. Rennie papers.

[26]   *The Caledonian* [Journal], Dundee, 1821. I, 376-378. Based on data from David Logan, the Clerk of Works for building the lighthouse. See his letter of 21.10.1820 to John Rennie (NLS. MS. 19806). Although Logan and Robert later fell out, his information can probably be relied on, except regarding the base diameter of the

lighthouse which the author has measured at 42 ft. From 1815 Logan, who according to Robert in a letter of 22 June 1815 *was a very deserving artist. He conducted himself most faithfully and correctly in his charge at the Bell Rock and also as Inspector of the bridge works at Marykirk.* From 1815 Logan was employed as a resident engineer by Telford, Rennie and others on harbours at Dundee, Donhagadee, Port Patrick, Whitehaven, Port Rush, Belfast and finished his career as Engineer for the Clyde Navigation. According to Logan the patterns for the counterpoise crane were made wholly under Watt's directions and he superintended the casting of the crane at Calder Ironworks.

[27]   *The Caledonian* [Journal]. Op. cit. & *The Surveyor, Engineer, and Architect,* 1 July 1840, [Ed. R. Mudie].

[28]   S. Smiles *Lives of the Engineers,*1862. II, fifth thousand. 233-234.

[29]   *The Caledonian* [Journal], Op. cit. & *Mechanics Magazine,* 4 Sept. 1824 & *Dictionary of Mechanical Science,* 1828,  [Ed. A. Jamieson].

[30]   NLS: MS. Acc. 10706, Business Records of Robert Stevenson & Sons, Civil Engineers. 3.

[31]   *Min. Proc. ICE,* 1845. IV.

[32]   David Stevenson, *Life of Robert.* Op. cit., 181-182.

[33]   NLS: MS. Acc. 785, f. 9.

[34]   NLS: MS. Acc. 10706. 12.

[35]   NLS: MS. Acc. 10706. 96.

[36]   David Stevenson, *Life of Robert.* Op. cit., 111-129.

[37]   D. McNaughton, *The Elgin Charlestown Railway 1762-1863,* [1986].

[38]   Courtesy Robert Stephenson Trust. MS. Extract from letter of R. Stephenson to W. James. 8 Dec., 1822. Drawn to the author's attention by Mrs Vicky Howarth, Secretary to the Trust.

[39]   NLS: MS. Acc. 10706. 101.

[40]   NLS: MS. Acc. 10706, 82, no. X.

[41]   Alan Stevenson. *Account of the Skerryvore Lighthouse, with notes on the illumination of lighthouses.* Edinburgh, 1848.

[42]   Alan Stevenson. *The ten hymns of Synesius, Bishop of Cyrene, A.D. 410, in English verse, and some occasional pieces.* Edinburgh, 1865, 52. New College Library: E16/b.6.

[43]   James Wilson. *A voyage round the coasts of Scotland and the Isles.* Edinburgh, 1848.

[44]   Alan Stevenson. *The ten hymns of Synesius, . . .* Op.cit.

[45]   Alan Stevenson. *Account of the Skerryvore Lighthouse.* Op. cit. 61.

[46]   Ibid.  55-56.

[47]   Abridged from NLB Minutes 3 January 1866.

[48]   Family source - David Stevenson's holograph 'Life History' covering 1824-1855. Written in 1870 for private information.

[49]   Margaret Stevenson, née Balfour. 'Diary, 1853-1897.' Beinecke Library, Yale University: 7304.

[50]   R.L. Stevenson. *The letters of . . . edited by Bradford A. Booth and Ernest Mehew.* Newhaven and London, 1995, 5, 286.

[51]   Margaret Stevenson, née Balfour. Letter to R.L. Stevenson, 31.7.1886. Bancroft Library, University of California.

[52] NLS: MS. Acc. 10706. Diary of David Stevenson, 1830-1836.

[53] Family papers. D. Alan's notes on David Stevenson.

[54] *100 years of British glass making, 1824-1924*. Chance Brothers & Co., n.p., 1924.

[55] Richard Henry Brunton, *Building Japan* 1868-1876, Folkestone, 1991. 25.

[56] *Nature*, 26 June 1884.

[57] R.L. Stevenson. 'Thomas Stevenson, civil engineer.' In *Memories and portraits*. London, 1887.

[58] C. Mair. Op. cit., 143.

[59] Family papers. D.Alan's notes on Thomas Stevenson.

[60] Thomas Stevenson, *Description of a portable cofferdam*, Edinburgh, 1848.

[61] J. M. Townson, 'The Stevenson formula for predicting wave height', *Proc. I. C. E.,* Pt 2, 1981, 71, 907- 909. and, 'Pioneers in Coastal Studies: III. Thomas Stevenson', *Shore & Beach*, 1976, 44, No.2, 3-12.

[62] Thomas Stevenson, *The design and construction of harbours*, 3rd ed., 1886.

[63] 'Report of the committee appointed by the Royal Scottish Society of Arts on Thomas Stevenson's paper on dipping and apparent lights', *Trans. RSSA*, 4 (1846-55), 291.

[64] R.L. Stevenson. *The letters of . . . edited by Bradford A. Booth and Ernest Mehew.* Op. cit., 4, 228.

[65] R.L. Stevenson. *Poems volume one. The works of . . .* Tusitala ed. XXII. 168.

[66] Ibid., 155.

[67] R.L. Stevenson. *The works of . . . with biographical notes by Edmund Gosse*, 1907, XV, 223-236.

[68] R.L. Stevenson. *The works of . . . Memories and portraits and other fragments.* Tusitala ed. XXIX, 98-99.

[69] R.L. Stevenson. *The works of . . . Catriona.* Tusitala ed. VII, 116-117.

[70] R.L. Stevenson. *Poems volume one. The works of . . .* Tusitala ed. XXII. 108.

[71] R.L. Stevenson. *The letters of . . . edited by Bradford A. Booth and Ernest Mehew.* Op. cit., 5, 403.

[72] R.L. Stevenson. *The letters of . . . edited by Bradford A. Booth and Ernest Mehew.* Op. cit., 1, 209, Margaret Stevenson's diary 8 Apr. 1871.

[73] R.L. Stevenson. *The letters of . . . edited by Bradford A. Booth and Ernest Mehew.* Op. cit., 5, 68.

[74] R.L. Stevenson. *Poems volume two. The works of . . .* Tusitala. ed. XXIII. 101.

[75] R.L. Stevenson. *Memoir of Fleeming Jenkin*, 1912.

[76] R.L. Stevenson. *Poems volume three, ed. S. Colvin. The works of . . .* Tusitala ed. XXXIII. 47. Letter from Louis to Mrs Fleeming Jenkin 12 June 1885.

[77] R.L. Stevenson. *The letters of . . . edited by Bradford A. Booth and Ernest Mehew.* Op. cit., 1, 129.

[78] R.L. Stevenson, 'The Education of an Engineer - More random memories', *Scribner's Mag.*, New York, IV, Nov. 1888, 636-640.

[79] R.L. Stevenson. *The letters of . . . edited by Bradford A. Booth and Ernest Mehew.* Op. cit., I, 156-158.

[80] Ibid., 169-172.

[81] Ibid., 181.

[82] R.L. Stevenson, *The new lighthouse on the Dhu Heartach Rock, Argyllshire. Edited with an introduction by Roger G. Swearingen.* St. Helena; California, 1995.

[83] R.L. Stevenson. *The letters of . . . edited by Bradford A. Booth and Ernest Mehew.* Op. cit.,8, 235.

[84] R.L. Stevenson. *Memoirs of himself.* Philadelpia, 1912.

[85] Family papers - David A.'s 'Book of Travel' (1868-1870).

[86] Family papers - David A.'s 'Personal Historical Notes'. (1871-1914)

[87] Family papers - Letter from David. A. to Louis 19 April 1887.

[88] R.L. Stevenson. *The letters of . . . edited by Bradford A. Booth and Ernest Mehew.* Op. cit.,5, 397.

[89] The bridge over the r. Whitadder, Berwickshire, consisted of three iron lattice truss spans by Oliver & Arrol. Recently replaced. Its name-plate is preserved in the ICE Museum at the Civil and Offshore Engineering Department of Heriot-Watt University, Edinburgh.

[90] Family papers - D. Alan's notes on David and Charles.

[91] J.D. Gardner, 'David Alan Stevenson, B.Sc., M.Inst. C.E.', *PRSE*, LVIII, (1937-38), pt. III.

[92] All the excerpts are taken from Charles' 'R.L. Stevenson. Scraps from his life.' Originally taken down and arranged by E.M. Yeoman; edited, 1994-95, by Jean Leslie. Family papers.

[93] Family papers - Charles Stevenson's diary (1872-1883).

[94] R.W. Johnstone, 'Charles Alexander Stevenson, B.Sc., M.I.C.E.', *RSE Year Book*,1950-51, 61.

[95] T. Martin and I.A. Macleod, 'The Tay rail bridge disaster - a reappraisal based on modern analysis methods', *Proc. I.C.E.*, 1995, CVIII, 77-83.

[96] J.S. Shipway, *The Tay Railway Bridge, Dundee 1887-1987*, Edinburgh,1987.

[97] Family papers - D. Alan's notes on Charles.

[98] [Knott, C. G.] 'Notes on a correspondence between the French Academy of Sciences and the Royal Society of Edinburgh regarding the invention of the pilot cable (Cable guide), By the General Secretary.' *Proc. R.S.E.,* 1923, XLII, 348-51. Read 19.6.1922. Also issued separately on 16.10.1922. Relating to Charles's priority of invention of the leader cable over M. W. A. Loth, a Frenchman who had been awarded a prize of 6,000 francs in 1921 by the French Academy for a development of the same invention.

[99] SRO: NLB Letter Book, 1936.

[100] The Watt Club was instituted in 1854.

[101] Mike Chrimes, 'Bridges: a bibliography of articles published in scientific periodicals 1800-1829' *History of technology,* 1985. X, 217-257.

[102] Most details including grid references kindly supplied by Mr. W.T. Johnston. Courtesy NLB.

## Select Bibliography

Note: See Source notes and Appendix 1 for other works.

David Stevenson, *Life of Robert Stevenson*, Edinburgh, 1878. Contained previously unpublished material.

R.L. Stevenson, *Records of a family of engineers*, 1896.

*Dictionary of National Biography*, Oxford, 1885 et seq.

George Blake, *Clyde lighthouses,* Glasgow, 1956.

D. Alan Stevenson, The world's lighthouses before 1820, 1959.

J.M. Townson, 'Pioneers in coastal studies: III. Thomas Stevenson.', *Shore and Beach*, 1976, 44, No.2, 3-12. An authoritative modern assessment of Thomas's maritime work. See also J.M. Townson's 'Thomas Stevenson 1818-87.', *Trans. Newcomen Soc.*, 1980-81. 52, 15-29. Lists many of Thomas's published works not given in Appendix 1.

Craig Mair. *A star for seamen*, 1978.

Ronald M Birse, *Engineering at Edinburgh University*, Edinburgh, 1983.

Obituary notices:

'Thomas Smith'. *Edinburgh Advertiser*, 30.6.1815; *Edinburgh Evening Courant*, 1.7.1815; *Caledonian Mercury*, 1.7.1815.

Alan Stevenson, *Biographical sketch of the late Robert Stevenson*, 1851. Illustrated ed. 1861.

'Alan Stevenson', *PRSE*, 6 (1866-67), 23-25.

David Stevenson, *Memoir of Alan Stevenson, LL.B., M.Inst.C.E.,* 1867.

'David Stevenson.', *PRSE*, 14 (1886-87), 145-151.

'Thomas Stevenson'. *Min. Proc. I.C.E.,* 1888, XCI, 424-426. Mentions his last paper.

R.L. Stevenson, 'Thomas Stevenson, civil engineer.', *Contemporary Review*, June 1887. Reprinted in *Memories and portraits,* 1887 and in many subsequent editions.

W. Swan, 'Thomas Stevenson', *PRSE*, 1895, XX, lxi-lxxv, With David A. Stevenson's Supplementary Notice.

R.W. Johnstone, 'Charles Alexander Stevenson, B.Sc., M.I.C.E.', *RSE Year Book*, 1950-51, 61-63.

J.D. Gardner, 'David Alan Stevenson, B.Sc., M.Inst. C.E.', *PRSE*, LVIII, (1937-38), pt. III.

'David Alan Stevenson B.Sc.(Edin.), F.I.C.E., F.R.S.G.S.', *RSE Year Book*, 1972-73, 51.

[D. Alan]. A. Robertson (Gen.Man.,NLB), *International Lighthouse Authority Bulletin*, April 1972.

## Appendix 1 - Select list of publications with notes

Notes: Includes most of the publications known to the author. Entries broadly chronological. 'pl.' preceded by a number indicates the number of plates.

ROBERT STEVENSON

*Memorial and state relative to the light-houses erected on the northern part of Great Britain: and relative to a proposal for erecting a light-house upon the Bell or Cape Rock.* Edinburgh, 1803, 13-38. Dated 23 Dec. 1800. Reprinted in Robert's *Account of the Bell Rock Light-house,* 1824.

*Report relative to the harbour of Stonehaven.* By Mr. Stevenson, Civil Engineer. Aberdeen, 1812. 1 pl.

Articles in the *Edinburgh Encyclopedia.* Edinburgh, 1830:

'Bell Rock'. III, 441-443. First published c. 1810.

'Eddystone Rocks'. VIII, 328. First published 1814.

'Inchkeith'. XII, 9-12. First published Nov. 1817. Includes details of the lighthouse and its revolving light.

'Lighthouse'. XIII, (1)-18, 3 pl. [7, 9,] First published 1818. An authoritative account of lighthouses from the earliest times. Includes illustrations of Corduan, Eddystone, Kilwarlin, Corunna, Genoa, Naples, Ramsgate, Tay leading lights and Inchkeith. Reference is made to distinguishing lights and the application of gas to lighting.

'Roads and Highways'. XVII, 349-360, 1 pl. First published c. 1824. Includes a review of practice from Roman times. Advocates stone tracks on gradients, a practice implemented at Leith Walk and other locations in Edinburgh.

'Railway'. 1830, XVII, 303-310, 1 pl. First published c.1824. Relates to pre-locomotive railway practice. Also published as 'Notes on rail-ways, with a suggestion for a smooth and durable city road.' *Trans. Roy. Highland & Agric. Soc. Scot.*, 1824. VI.

*Report on the improvement of the harbour of Dundee.* [Dundee?], 1814. 2 pl.

[Engraved plan & elevation] *Reduced plan of the lands of Calton Hill and design for a new approach to the City of Edinburgh by a bridge over Calton Street, and elevation of the bridge and cellars under the roadway.* Edinburgh, 1814. Following a competition in 1815 the architect Archibald Elliot's design for the proposed buildings and what became known as the Regent's Bridge was adopted to Robert's basic line, level and concept.

[Engraved plan - with John Steedman] *Nautical survey of the Frith of Tay.* Dundee, 1816. An important Scottish maritime chart showing coastline, channels, sand banks, water depths, lights &c. Other editions 1819, 1855.

'Description of the bridge of Marykirk.' *Scots Mag.*, Dec. 1816, LXXVIII, 883-885,1 pl. Robert's first large bridge, completed 1814. View engraved by R. Scott from a drawing by Robert's assistant John Steedman.

'Observations upon the alveus or general bed of the German Ocean and British Channel.' *Memoirs of Wernerian Natural History Society*, Edinburgh. 1818. II, pt. ii, 464-490. Read 2nd March 1816. Separately published in 1816 and 1817 and also in *Annals of Philosophy,* Sept. 1816. VIII, 173-182. For a critique by Prof. Thomson see *Annals of Philosophy.* XIII, 135-136. Followed in 1820 with 'On the bed of the German Ocean or North Sea' in *Memoirs of the Wernerian Soc.,*1821. III, 314-336, with a chart of the North Sea including depth sections. Also published in *Edin. Philos. J.*, Apr.-Oct. 1820. III, 42-56, 1 pl. [24] Theme continued with 'Remarks upon the wasting effects of the sea on the shore of Cheshire, between the rivers Mersey and Dee.' *Edin. New Philos. J.*, Oct.-Apr. 1828. (IV), 386-389. Read to Wernerian Society on 8 March 1828. Robert continued to propound his belief that coastal erosion was caused by the raising of the sea bed which, in turn, caused the sea level to rise. In 1840 he read a paper to the British Association at Glasgow 'Hints on the state of our knowledge respecting the relative level of the land and sea; and the waste in some places, and extension in other places, of the land, on the east coast of England.'

Articles in *Encyclopedia Britannica*. Supplement to 4th, 5th & 6th eds., 1824:

'Bell Rock Light-House'. II, 253-258, pl.XXXIII. First published Dec. 1816. The fine view was engraved by W. & D. Lizars from a drawing by Robert's assistants W. Lorimer and J. Steedman. Also issued separately in 1816. Robert's second published account of the lighthouse? The first was probably that included in Headrick, J. *A general view of the agriculture of Forfarshire*. Edinburgh, 1813.

'Blasting'. II, 317-321. First published June 1817. Describes rock blasting on land and under water. Includes a description of blasting rock at Calton Hill for the new road.

'Caledonian Canal'. II, 570-579, 1 pl. First published June 1817. Also published separately as *Information relative to the Caledonian Canal*. An authoritative summary of the project and some of its engineering operations.

'Dredging'. III, 671-675, 1 pl. First published Jan. 1819. The plate of dredging apparatus was drawn by Robert's assistant G. C. Scott. Outlines dredging practice from 1736 to 1818. Describes steam dredging on the Caledonian Canal.

'Vertical differences of salinity in water.' *Annals of Philosophy*, July 1817. X, 55-58. Summary of a paper read to the Royal Society of Edinburgh, 19 May 1817.

*Report relative to the line of a canal upon one level, between the cities of Edinburgh and Glasgow, to form a junction with the Forth and Clyde Canal at Lock No. 20 and also with the Port of Leith, and the Broomielaw at Glasgow*. Edinburgh, 1817. With a plan surveyed by John Steedman. Robert's line was more direct than those of Hugh Baird and John Rennie. It had no locks between Edinburgh and Glasgow, but required a 3-mile tunnel under the Bathgate Hills. Written in Dec. 1814. Published Feb. 1817 at the request of interests who hoped for an extension of the canal to Leith. Partly reprinted in Scots Mag., Feb., 1817. Estimated at £491,999. Not executed.

*Instructions for the light-keepers of the Northern Lighthouses*. Edinburgh, 1817. Other editions 1823, 1836 and 1843.

*Report relative to the Strathmore Canal, or inland navigation between the royal boroughs of Forfar and Aberbrothwick*. Edinburgh, 1817. With plan surveyed by John Steedman. Proposing a 16-mile canal with 20 locks for boats of up to 30 ton burden. Robert also considered a cast iron, horse traction, railway, but preferred a canal. Estimated at £88,378. Not executed.

[Engraved plan] *Sketch of the coast from Lincolnshire to Hampshire by Yarmouth Roads & the Downs referring to a memorial relative to the navigation of that coast*. [n.p.], 1818. Envisaging a canal from Blakeney (via the London & Cambridge Junction Canal?) to near London and on to Southampton. Not progressed.

*Report relative to the various lines of railway from the coal-field of Mid-Lothian to the city of Edinburgh and port of Leith, with plans and sections, showing the practicability of extending these lines of railway to Dalkeith, Musselburgh, Haddington and Dunbar, . . .* Edinburgh, 1819. 2 pl. Dated 28 Dec. 1818. Plans surveyed by Robert and John Steedman in 1818. Not executed, apart from Newton colliery railway for which a larger scale plan was printed in 1818.

*The report . . . relative to the improvement of the communication by the ferries betwixt Fife and Forfar*. Edinburgh, 1818. 2 pl. Plans surveyed by Robert and John Steedman in 1818. Recommended that priority be given to pier improvements at Dundee, Newport, Broughty

Castle and Ferry-port-on-Craig. Estimated cost £20,860. Not executed. In 1820 Robert published *'Observations'* critical of a newly projected and costly alternative to the approved parliamentary plan.

*'Journal of a visit to Holland, and part of Flanders, in the months of July and August 1817. In a series of letters to a friend in Edinburgh.' Scots Mag.*, March, June and July 1818; Sept., Oct., Nov. and Dec. 1819; Jan., Feb., April, Sept., and Dec., 1820; and, March 1821. Robert revealed himself as the author of these charming and informative letters to his daughter Jane in the preface to the last letter. In 1848 he published privately for the benefit of the family *a small impression* of the 14 letters. Some copies include plates of Bonaparte's fly bridge on the Scheldt and the medal presented to Robert by the King of the Netherlands. **[13]**

*Report relative to an iron railway, between the port of Montrose and the town of Brechin.* Edinburgh, 1819. 1 pl. **[26]**
Written 31 March 1819. Plan surveyed by John Steedman. Followed by a revised report dated 30 Nov. 1819 with a second state of the plan showing a new line and additional topography.

*Report relative to the compensation reservoirs for the mills on the Water of Leith and Bevelaw Burn,* Edinburgh, 1819. 1 pl.
Recommends a reservoir estimated at £1,884. Discusses the bursting of dams at the Crinan and Huddersfield canals and Cartsdike.

*Memorial relative to opening the great valleys of Strathmore and Strathearn, by means of a railway or canal, with branches to the sea from Perth, Arbroath, Montrose, Stonehaven, and Aberdeen; together with observations on interior communication in general.* Edinburgh, 1821. 1 pl. Written July 1820. Proposing a horse traction railway from Stirling and Perth to Aberdeen, with branches. Not executed.

[Dalkeith, Galashiels & St Boswells Railway report] *To His Grace the Duke of Roxburgh . . .* [Edinburgh?], 1821. 1 pl.

Proposing a horse-traction railway with cast iron rails to connect Dalkeith with Telford's proposed Glasgow to Berwick railway in the Tweed valley. Estimated at £63,631. Neither railway was executed.

*'Description of bridges of suspension.' Edin. Philos. J.,* Apr. to Oct. 1821. V. 237-256, 1 pl. Written 19 July 1821. An authoritative review of early suspension bridge development in Scotland, including Robert's proposal for an underspanned suspension bridge. **[39]** Printed in German [1822,1823], French [1823], and Polish [1824]. Includes a description of Capt. Samuel Brown's Union Bridge, 1820 which is still in use. Robert commented further on this bridge in *Monthly Mag.*, 1822, 54, 117-118.

[Harperrig Reservoir, Midlothian report] *To the proprietors and tenants of the mill property, situate on the course of the Water of Leith . . .* [Edinburgh], 1822. 1 pl. Estimated at £7,149.

*Report relative to the improvement of the communication across the Bristol Channel.* [Edinburgh, 1822]. 3 pl. Proposing improvements to New Passage Ferry between Gloucestershire and Monmouthshire.

*An account of the Bell Rock Light-house . . . To which is prefixed a . . . view of the institution and progress of the northern light-houses.* Edinburgh, 1824. 23 pl. the last mis-numbered XXI instead of XXIII as given in the *Description of Plates.* An engineering classic with engraved frontispiece after a Turner watercolour now in the National Galleries of Scotland. Drawings for other plates were by Jane, and members of staff - W. Lorimer, J. Slight, J. Steedman, G. C. Scott, and D. Logan. Review in *Edin. Philos. J.,* Jan. to Apr. 1825., XII, 18-38, 1 pl.

'Notes by Mr Stevenson, in reference to the essays on railways presented to the Highland Society.' *Prize Essays & Trans. Highland Soc. Scot.*, 1824, VI, 130-146, 1 pl. An adjudication on these important essays.

[East Lothian Railway report] *To the subscribers for the survey of the East Lothian Railway.* Edinburgh, 1825. 1 pl. Two lines had been surveyed from Cow Pits via Haddington to Dunbar. Not executed.

*Report relative to lines of railway, surveyed from the ports of Perth, Arbroath, and Montrose, into the valley of Strathmore; . . .* Edinburgh, 1827. 2 pl. Dated 14 August 1826. *Reduced Plan* surveyed by Wm. Blackadder and John Steedman. An 84-mile length of horse-traction railways with malleable iron rails and steam-powered inclined planes were envisaged costing c. £370,000, including a 350 ft. span suspension bridge over the Tay. Not executed.

[Stirling and Crieff Road. Reports 27 October 1826 & 10 February 1827] *Excerpt from minutes of meeting of the trustees upon the turnpike road from Crieff to Longcauswayhead, held at Balhadie Inn, 26th September, 1825.* [n.p., 1827?] Envisaged improvements estimated at £29,447 to the 22-mile road from Stirling via Dunblane to Crieff, including five substantial new bridges.

'Specification of Hutcheson Bridge over the River Clyde at Glasgow.' [ & plates illustrative of its design & construction]. In: Weale, J. (ed.) *The theory, practice and architecture of bridges,* 1843. I, 106-140, pls 27-33. **[28]** Includes a view of work in progress. **[29]** John Steedman contractor. Cost £23,865.[5] First published 1839.

[With Telford, Thomas & Nimmo, Alexander] 'Intended ship canal between the Rivers Dee and Mersey. The report of . . . recommending two extensive new sea ports &c., on the Rivers Dee and Mersey, adjacent to Liverpool, with a floating harbour or ship canal to connect them.' In: *Appendix No. 37. A report of the proceedings of a Court of Inquiry into the existing state of the Corporation of Liverpool, . . .Liverpool,* 1834?, cxxi-cxxviii, (31)-44. Reprinted with a further report of 14 July 1828 in David's *Life of Robert,* 1878. Estimated at £1.4m. Not executed.

[Forth Navigation report] To the Hon. *The Provost . . . of Stirling . . .* [Stirling], 1838. 1 pl. Dated 26 Nov. 1828, with prefatory note dated 10 Dec. 1838. The 'Reduced plan and section of the Forth from Alloa Pier to Stirling Shore, shewing the means of improving its navigation' surveyed in 1826-27 was drawn by Thomas in 1838. Proposed deepening at fords to accommodate ships of 13 ft. draught. Estimate £10,126. Report reprinted in *Civ. Eng. & Arch. J.,* July 1841, with a preface stating that the firm's experience in improving the Tay navigation by the removal of fords gave them increased confidence to repeat their recommendations. A further plan of the improvements was published in 1842.

[Sunderland Harbour report] *To the Commissioners for preserving and improving the port and harbour of Sunderland.* [Edinburgh? 1829]. 1 pl. Dated 28 Sept. 1829. Estimated at £193,311. Not executed.

[engravings &c.] 'Bridge across the River Forth at Stirling.' In: Weale, J. (ed.) *The theory, practice and architecture of bridges.* London, 1843. pls 62, 63. This publication also includes a schedule of rates and a measurement report by John Duff dated 7 Sept. 1829. Cost about £17,000.

[with Alan] *A chart of the coast of Scotland with part of England & Ireland shewing the positions of the several lighthouses, the principal anchorages, rocks, shoals & soundings, together with the . . . rise of Spring & neap tides.* Edinburgh, 1832. Drawn by J. Ritson. Scale 8 miles to 1 inch.

[with Alan - Ballyshannon harbour improvement report] *To the most noble the Marquis of Ely . . .* [Edinburgh? 1832] 2 pl. Dated 15 June 1832. Estimated at £5,958 and, for the road or railway to Lough Erne, £18,133. A further report dated Dec., 1836 was published at Ballyshannon in 1837.

[with Alan - Perth harbour and Tay navigation improvement report] *To the Lord Provost . . . of the city of Perth.* [Edinburgh? 1834] 2 pl. Dated 22 Jan. 1834. A specification was printed in August 1834. Harbour works estimated at £48,714, but not executed. By 1841, following the partial removal of various fords the depth of the river at Spring tides had been increased from 11 ft. to 16 ft and work was continuing. In 1845 the firm reported to Perth Council with a 'Plan & sections of the junctions of the rivers Tay & Earn shewing the manner in which the proposed Perth & Dundee, and Edinburgh & Northern railways affect the Tay navigation'.

[with Alan - Granton harbour report] *To His Grace the Duke of Buccleugh . . .* [Edinburgh, 1834]. 2 pl. **[44]** Dated 22 May 1834. Plans surveyed by J. Ritson. Partly executed. Various engineers had proposed schemes for improving Leith harbour to the east of Granton including Robert who had proposed an improvement to the entrance in 1824. In February 1835 a rival firm Grainger & Miller alleged in the *Edinburgh Evening Courant* that the water depths and distances in this report were inaccurate and an acrimonious exchange of letters followed. In September 1835 a specification was drawn up for a wharf on Oxcraig rock with a connecting road. **[44]** In 1836-37 David supervised the construction of an 800 ft. length of steamboat pier and Granton Road approach including a long culvert for Wardie Burn.

[with Alan] 'Plan of the Edinburgh & Glasgow Railway; from a survey by Robert Stevenson & Son.' In: *Prospectus of a company to be called the Edinburgh, Leith, & Glasgow Railway Coy. Edinburgh 26th Dec.1835.* [Edinburgh, 1835]. Plan on reverse of prospectus. The proposed line went via South Queensferry, Linlithgow, Falkirk, Kilsyth and Kirkintilloch and included branches to Leith and Broomielaw. Estimated at £704,558. The firm's line via Midcalder, Whitburn and Airdrie surveyed in 1825-31 also shown. Neither was executed.

[with Alan] 'Plan of the Edinburgh & Dundee Railway; from a survey by Robert Stevenson & Son.' In: *Prospectus of a company, to be called the Edinburgh and Dundee Railway Coy. Edinburgh 23rd April 1836.* [Edinburgh, 1836]. Plan on reverse of prospectus. The 38-mile proposed line connected the ferry terminals at Granton, Burntisland, Kinghorn, Kirkcaldy and Dysart and then turned north to Newport ferry, with a branch from part-way via Newburgh to Perth. Estimated at £456,000. Not executed.

[with Alan] *Chart of Skerryvore Rocks lying off the coast of Argyleshire.* [Edinburgh], 1836.

[with Alan - Ribble navigation improvement report] *To the Mayor and Council of the Borough of Preston . . .* [n.p., 1837]. 2 pl. Dated 16 March 1837. Involved deepening by steam dredging from Naze Point to about a mile below Preston quays. [60] Estimated at £16,026. A further report in May explained the practice of jetties in rivers to protect land. Another report in June 1838 recommended building a steam-dredger to the firm's specification.

[with Alan and David] *Chart of the River Lune from Lancaster to Glasson shewing the proposed improvements in the navigation.* Edinburgh, 1838. Drawn by J. Andrews. Engraved for David's *Marine Surveying* treatise in 1842.

[with Alan and David - Dee Navigation improvement report] *Reports of . . .* Chester, 1839. 1 pl. Dated 21 August 1839 and adopted at a public meeting in Chester on 10 September 1839. Recommended steam dredging a new channel about 400 ft. wide between Flint and Connah's Quay to obtain a 16 ft. depth at high water. Estimated at £24,905 of which £9,458 was for a steam dredger with apparatus and punts. In 1845 the firm proposed an entrance lock from the Dee crossing the Queensferry to Chester road by means of a swing bridge with a new dock to the east.

## ALAN STEVENSON

*The British Pharos; or, A list of the lighthouses on the coasts of Great Britain and Ireland, descriptive of the appearance of the lights at night.* Leith, 1828. 2nd ed., 1831.

[with Robert] *A chart of the coast of Scotland with part of England & Ireland . . .* 1832 Op. cit.

[with Robert] - Ballyshannon harbour improvement report 1832]. Op. cit.

*Letter to the author of an article on the "British Lighthouse system" in number CXV of the Edinburgh Review.* Edinburgh, 1833. Defending the system from the calumnies of the reviewer.

[with Robert - Perth harbour and Tay navigation improvement report 1834]. Op. cit.

[with Robert - Granton harbour report 1834]. Op. cit.

*Report to the Committee of the Commissioners of Northern Lights, appointed to take into consideration the subject of illuminating the lighthouses by means of lenses.* Edinburgh, 1835. 6 pl. Influenced the adoption of the brighter dioptric system of lighting in British lighthouses.

[with Robert] 'Plan of the Edinburgh & Glasgow Railway; . . .' 1835. Op. cit.

[with Robert] 'Plan of the Edinburgh & Dundee Railway; . . .' 1836. Op. cit.

*Report to a Committee of the Commissioners of the Northern Lighthouses, appointed to take into consideration the subject of lighthouses by means of lenses, on the new dioptric light of the Isle of May.* Edinburgh, 1836. Describes the first application of Fresnel's diopric system in Britain which proved a great success.

[with Robert] *Chart of Skerryvore Rocks . . .* 1836. Op. cit.

[with Robert - Ribble navigation improvement report 1837] Op. cit.

[with Robert and David] *Chart of the River Lune from Lancaster to Glasson . . .* 1838. Op. cit.

[with Robert and David - Dee Navigation improvement reports 1839] . . . Op. cit.

'Sea Lights.' *Ency. Brit.,* 7th ed., 1840, XX, 15-31, plates CCCCXLI-II. Also published as, *Lighthouses; being the article 'sea-lights,' in the seventh edition of the Encyclopedia Britannica.* Edinburgh, 1840. Reprinted in the eighth edition of *Ency. Brit.* and also separately as *On the theory and construction of lighthouses.* Edinburgh, 1857.

*Observations on the application of catadioptric zones to lights of the first order in the system of Fresnel; . . .* Edinburgh, 1840. 1 pl. Followed by *New tables of the elements of catadioptric zones for lights of the first order. Calculated by Alan Stevenson . . .* Edinburgh, 1841.

*Account of the Skerryvore Lighthouse, with notes on the illumination of lighthouses.* Edinburgh, 1848. 33 pl. An engineering classic and the author's most important publication.

*A letter to Sir John Rennie, F.R.S., civil-engineer, &c. &c.* Edinburgh, 1848. Refuting the claim that John Rennie designed and built the Bell Rock lighthouse and claiming its design and construction for his own father. This and further letters were printed in 'Correspondence between Sir John and Mr Alan Stevenson, relative to the Bell Rock Lighthouse.' *Civ. Eng. and Arch. J.,* May 1849, XII. 1 pl. [15] Also published separately by the Stevensons.

*A rudimentary treatise on the history, construction and illumination of lighthouses, . . .* London, 1850. 14 pl. A valuable text book in its day. Includes most of the 'notes' published in the Account of Skerryvore Lighthouse.

*Biographical sketch of the late Robert Stevenson . . . Read at the Royal Society, Edinburgh . . . February 1851, . . . Edinburgh, 1851.* Another edition of larger, presentation, format with two plates was published in 1861.

## DAVID STEVENSON

'Chart of the Calf Sound . . . Isle of Man, surveyed in 1835 by David Stevenson.' In Jefferson's *Manks Almanack* [Douglas], n.d.

'Observations on the Liverpool and Manchester Railway.' *Edin. New Phil. J.*, April 1835, XVIII, 322-331. 2 pl. Abridged in *Arcana of Science and Art . . . ninth year*. London, 1836, 25-30, 1pl.

'Remarks on the Dublin and Kingstown Railway.' *Edin. New Phil. J.*, April 1836, XX, 320-325. 1 pl. This and the foregoing paper, read to the R.S.S.A. and printed in the first volume of their *Transactions* were also published separately as *Observations on the Liverpool and Manchester Railway with remarks on the Dublin and Kingstown Railway*, Edinburgh, 1836.

*Sketch of the civil engineering of North America, . . .* London, 1838. Map & 14 pl. Also led to R.S.S.A. papers on 'Long's Frame Bridge' (1839) and 'Building materials of the U.S.A.' (1841).

'Description of a cofferdam adapted to a hard bottom, used in excavating rock from the navigable channel of the River Ribble; . . .' *Trans. I.C.E.*, 1842, III, 377-384. pl. XVIII. Read Feb. 1841. An earlier version was published in *Proc. I. C. E.*, 1837, I, 81-83.

*A treatise on the application of marine surveying and hydrometry to the practice of civil engineering.* Edinburgh, 1842. Chart & 13 pl. The first comprehensive treatise on this subject..

*Report relative to the salmon fishings of the Dornoch Firth.* Edinburgh, 1842. 1 pl.

'Description of portable levelling instruments.' *Edin. New Phil. J.*, July 1844, XXXVII, 99-101. 1 pl.

*Remarks on the improvement of tidal rivers*, 1845. 2 pl. Read to the R.S.E. Re-issued with new title and supplement, 1849. 4 pl..

*Report as to the contemplated railway bridges across the River Dee.* Chester, 1845.

*Report in reference to the harbours of Peterhead.* Edinburgh, 1847. 1 pl. Dated 25 Jan. 1847. Evidence in *Report of Select Committee on Harbours of Refuge*. London, [1858?]. Another report, with Thomas, dated 9th Feb. 1858.

'Abstract of exposition of inland navigation.' *Trans. R.S.S.A.*, Feb. 1850. III.

*Lune Navigation. Report . . .* Edinburgh 1851. 1 pl.

[with Thomas] *Sunderland Navigation Act. . .* Preliminary report. Edinburgh, 1852. 2 pl.

[with Thomas] *Report . . . on the Foyle navigation.* Londonderry, 1853.

[with Thomas] *Report to the Commissioners of the River Wear Navigation* [n.p.], 1853. Another report in 1858, with plan.

[with Thomas - Edinburgh & Leith sewerage] *Report to the Police Commission of the City of Edinburgh, . . .* Edinburgh, 1853. In 1861 a further report, jointly with C. Macpherson, was published. The parliamentary plans for the first Act were completed and approved in 1863. The specifications for excavation, masonry, brickwork and tunnelling were ready by Jan. 1865 following which the work was executed. In 1886 the firm reported on the condition of the main sewer between Coltbridge and the sea and two years later proposed a new Water of Leith intercepting sewer in conjunction with the respective burgh engineers. The parliamentary submission of 1888-89 included 27 plans. Implemented. In 1866 the firm reported on Perth sewerage.

*Address delivered at the opening of the thirty fourth session of the Royal Scottish Society of Arts.* Edinburgh, 1854. A review of the Society's achievements from 1820. Also printed in the Society's *Transactions*.

'Remarks on floating and fixed lighthouses.' *Civ. Eng. & Architect's J.,* Jan. 1856.

[with Thomas] 'Report . . . on the comparative eligibility of the catoptric and dioptric systems of illumination of lighthouses.' In: *Papers on the comparative merits of the catoptric and dioptric lights for lighthouses.* London, 1857. 14-19.

[with Thomas] *Report to the Board of Fisheries upon forming a boat harbour of refuge for the coast of Banffshire.* Edinburgh, 1858. 2 pl.

'Inland navigation.' *Ency. Brit.,* 8th ed., 1853-61. Enlarged into Canal and river engineering. Edinburgh, 1858. 2 pl. Canal and river engineering. Edinburgh, 1858. 2 pl. 2nd ed. 1872 13 pl.; 3rd ed., 1886 13 pl. An influential work.

[with Thomas] 'Notes as to the construction of breakwaters for harbours of refuge.' *Civ. Eng. & Architect's J.,* July 1859.

*Reply to Sir David Brewster's memorial to the Lords Commissioners of Her Majesty's Treasury on the new system of dioptric lights.* Edinburgh, 1859. Relates to an acrimonious exchange which had stemmed from allegations of self interest and incompetence against the Stevensons and which was followed by, with Thomas, an *Answer to Sir David Brewster's reply to Messrs Stevenson's pamphlet on Sir D. Brewster's memorial to the Treasury.* Edinburgh, 1860 and an *Appendix to Messrs Stevenson's answer to Sir David Brewster's reply regarding dioptric lights.*

[with James Leslie] *The High Street catastrophe. The report of . . .* Edinburgh, 1861 On the sensational fall of a tenement at Paisley Close, High St., Edinburgh. The sole survivor called out to his rescuers 'Heave awa' chaps, I'm no' dead yet', words which gave the present building its name 'Heave Awa' House'.

'Notice of the ravages of Limnoria terebrans on creosoted timber.' *Proc. R.S.E.,* 1862. IV. Abstract in *Edin. New Phil. J.,* July 1852, XVI, 152. For the effect on greenheart see *Proc. R.S.E.,* 1875, VIII, 182-185.

[with Thomas] *Specification of a harbour to be constructed in Wick Bay, for the British Fisheries Society,* 1862. 3 pl. Work began in 1863. A report with 3 plans was published in 1870.

[with Thomas] 'Report on the harbour lights of Scotland and the Isle of Man.' In: *Copies of three reports to the Board of Trade on local lighthouses,* 1864. 3-11.

*Lighthouses.* Edinburgh, 1864. Anr ed., 1865. First issued as 'Our lighthouses' in *Good Words,* 1864, 105-115, 233-242.

[with Thomas] *Report relative to the capabilities of Salters Bay, at Buckie, Banffshire, for a refuge boat harbour.* Edinburgh, 1865.

[with Thomas] *Report to Duncan Darroch, Esq., relative to a proposed deep water harbour at Gourock.* Edinburgh, 1866.

[with Thomas] *Report to the Secretary of State for India relative to Kurrachee Harbour.* [n.p., dated Edinburgh, 20th February 1866]. Copies at NLS: MS. Acc. 10706, 528 & Mitchell Library.

[with Thomas] *Report on the application of the magneto-electric light to lighthouse illumination.* Edinburgh, 1866. Regarding the introduction of electric light into Scottish lighthouses.

*Memoir of Alan Stevenson, LL.B., M.Inst.C.E.,* 1867.

[with Thomas] 'Report on Kirkcaldy water supply.' [n.p., March, 1867]. NLS: MS. Acc. 10706, 528.

[with Thomas] *Note of trials with the electric and oil lights, which will be shown from the experimental tower at Granton, and will be visible from the Calton Hill.* [Edinburgh], 1868.

'Notice of aseismatic arrangements, adapted to structures in countries subject to earthquake shocks.' *Trans. R.S.S.A.,* 1868, VII, 557-565. Offprint: Edinburgh, 1868.

[with Thomas] *Report on the improvement of the harbour of*

*Berwick.* [Edinburgh?, 1869] In 1872 a *Specification of wet dock and other works to be executed* was printed.

[with Thomas] *Reports. Papers relative to a proposal to substitute gas for oil as an illuminating power for lighthouses.* London, 1869. Also in *Further papers*, 1-4, 23-24.

'Notice of works designed by Sir Charles Hartley, C.E. for the improvement of the Danube.' *Proc. R.S.E.*, 1869, VI, 313-316.

[with Thomas] 'Copy report relative to the first order lighthouse lantern used by the Commissioners of Northern Lighthouses and that to be adopted by the Trinity House.' In: *Lighthouse lanterns. Return to an order of the honourable the House of Commons, dated 9 February 1870.* 16-19. Supplemental Report. 29-30, 32.

[with Thomas?] *Japanese lighthouses. lightships, buoys, and beacons.* [n.p., dated December 1871]. NLS: MS. Acc. 10706, no. 586(I). Relates to the provision of about 20 lighthouses between 1866 and 1871.

[with Thomas] 'Supplementary report on paraffin light.' In: *Correspondence between the General Lighthouse Authorities and the Board of Trade, relative to the proposals to substitute mineral oils for Colza oil in lighthouses*, 1871. Dated Edinburgh 19 October 1870.

[with John Ball] *Report to the Corporation of Bristol on the proposed schemes for the construction of docks at Avonmouth and at Portishead.* [1872].

[with Thomas] *Preliminary report to the Port and Harbour Commissioners of Londonderry.* [Edinburgh?, 1873].

[with Thomas] *Report to the Clyde Lighthouse Trustees.* [Edinburgh?, 1873]. On coordination. Followed by *Report to the Clyde Lighthouse Trustees relative to the dredging at Garvel Point.* [n.p.], 1876. The firm had reported to James Graham on this subject in 1875. Also, *Report to the Clyde Lighthouse Trustees, on the improvement of the navigation of the River Clyde within the limits of their jurisdiction.* [Edinburgh?, 1877]. 4 pl. Another report, 1878.

[with Thomas] *Report relative to the widening of the North Bridge.* Edinburgh, 1873.

[with Thomas] *Report to the Lord Provost's Committee of the City of Edinburgh, relative to the Rivers Manor and Lyne.* [Edinburgh?, 1873].

'Relations of our own and foreign countries as regards arts and manufactures.' *Trans. R.S.S.A.*, 1873, VIII, 102-130.

[with Thomas] *Report to his Grace the Duke of Argyll on the formation of a commercial harbour in Roseneath Bay.* [Edinburgh?, 1874]. 2 pl.

'On the reclamation and protection of agricultural land.'. *Trans. Roy. Highland & Agric. Soc. Scot.*, VI, 132-174. Also published separately, Edinburgh 1874.

[with Thomas] *The report of . . . water supply of the city of Derry.* [Edinburgh?, 1875].

Articles in *Encyclopedia Britannica*. 9th ed., 1875-89. 'Canal', IV, 782-794; 'Coffer-dams', VI, 114-116; 'Diving', VII, 294-300; 'Dredging', VII, 463-467.

[with T. Constable] *Memoir of Lewis D. B. Gordon . . .* Edinburgh, 1877. With 2 photographs.

*Lectures. Canal & river engineering. Delivered at the School of Military Engineering, Chatham.* Chatham, 1877. 8 pl. State of the art lectures, 400 copies printed for private circulation only.

*Life of Robert Stevenson.* Edinburgh, 1878. 13 pl. Contained previously unpublished material.

[with Thomas] *Report relative to Sir William Thomson's proposed changes on the characteristics of lighthouses.* [Edinburgh?, 1880].

[with Thomas] *Report relative to M. Allard's scheme of illuminating the lighthouses of the French coast by electricity.* [Edinburgh?, 1881].

[with Thomas] *Report relative to the fishery harbours on the coasts of Haddingtonshire and Berwickshire.* [Edinburgh?, 1882]. Includes Thomas's evidence.

*Report relative to Ayr Bridge.* [Edinburgh?, 1882].

[with Thomas] *Report regarding the lighting of the west coasts of the Orkney and Shetland Islands.* [Edinburgh?, 1883].

'Obituary notice of Alexander James Adie (1808-1879).' *Proc. R.S.E.,* 1880, X, 329.

Articles by Messrs. D. & T. Stevenson in *Chambers Encyclopedia,* 1888-92. 'Beacon'. I, 812-813; 'Breakwater'. II, 413-415; 'Buoy'. II, 549-550; 'Dock.'. IV, 29-30; 'Harbour'.V, 551-554; 'Lighthouse'. VI, 622-628. In view of the publication date David A. and Charles may have had an involvement. Listed as 'were important articles'. They were probably written in the 1860s.

## THOMAS STEVENSON

'Description of an improved levelling staff, and a modification of the common level.' *Proc. I.C.E.,* 1837, I, 130-131.

'On Dagenham Breach. A brief account of the stopping of Dagenham Breach on the Thames digested from Captain Perry's Narrative, published at London in 1721.' *Civ. Eng. & Arch. J.,* 1840, III, 106-8.

'Account of experiments upon the force of the waves of the Atlantic and German Oceans.' *Trans. R.S.E.,* 1849, XVI, pt 1, 23-32, text illustration of marine dynamometer. Offprint, Edinburgh, 1845. Followed up with Observations read to the British Association at Edinburgh in 1850 and papers in *Edin. New. Phil. J.* in 1852, 1853, 1855 (wind), 1859 and *Proc. R.S.E.* 1862.

'Description of a portable cofferdam, adapted specially for the use of harbour and other marine works in exposed locations'. *Edin. New Phil. J.,* 1848. XLV. 140-147. 1 pl.

'Description of harbour screw-cramps...'. *Edin. New. Phil. J.,* 1850. XLVIII. 41-45. 1 pl. Dated 25 Nov. 1848.

'Description of the holophotal system of illuminating lighthouses.' *Trans. R.S.S.A.,* 1856, IV, 1-20, 5 pl. Paper awarded Keith Gold Medal or plate value thirty sovereigns. Offprint, Edinburgh 1851. Followed by 'On the destructive effects of the waves of the sea on the north-east shores of Shetland.' *Proc. R.S.E.,* 1862, IV, 200-201.

[with David] *Sunderland Navigation Act. . .* 1852. Op. cit.

[with David] *Report . . . on the Foyle navigation.* 1853. Op. cit.

[with David] *Report to the Commissioners of the River Wear Navigation.* 1853. Op. cit.

[with David - Edinburgh & Leith sewerage 1853-89]. Op. cit.

'On dipping and apparent lights for sunk reefs and pierheads of harbours; with description of an apparent light, the illumination of which is derived from a distant lamp situated on the shore, erected . . . in 1851.' *Trans. R.S.S.A.,* 1856, IV, 276-291. 1 pl.

'On a simple method of distributing naturally diverging rays over any azimuthal angle, with description of proposed spherico-cylindrical and double cylindric lenses for use in lighthouse illumination.' *Edinburgh New Phil. J.,* April 1855, I, 273-277. 1 pl.

[with David] 'Report . . . catoptric and dioptric systems of illumination. . .'. 1857. Op. cit.

[with David] *Report to the Board of Fisheries . . . Banffshire.* 1858. Op. cit.

[with David] 'Notes as to the construction of breakwaters for harbours of refuge.'. 1859. Op. cit.

*Lighthouse illumination; being a description of the holophotal system and of azimuthal condensing and other new forms of light house apparatus.* Edinburgh, 1859. 4 pl. Preface dated March 1859. 2nd ed. 14 pl., 1871; enlarged to Lighthouse construction and illumination. Edinburgh, 1881. 37 pl.

[with David] *Specification of a harbour to be constructed in Wick Bay, . . .* 1862. Op. cit.

[with David] 'Report on the harbour lights of Scotland and the Isle of Man.'. 1864. Op. cit.

*The design and construction of harbours. Reprinted and enlarged from the article 'Harbours' in the eighth edition of the Encyclopedia Britannica.* Edinburgh, 1864. 10 pl. 2nd ed., 1874. 20 pl.; 3rd ed., 1886. 24 pl. First published in the *Ency. Brit.* in 1856.

'New description of box for holding thermometers.' *Scot. Meteorological Soc. J.*, July 1864. In new series, 1866, I, 122. With 2 figs. Modifying the end fastenings of the louvre-boards.

[with David] *Report relative to the capabilities of Salters Bay, at Buckie, Banffshire . . .* 1865. Op. cit.

[with David] *Report to Duncan Darroch, Esq., . . . deep water harbour at Gourock.* 1866. Op. cit.

[with David] *Report to the Secretary of State for India relative to Kurrachee Harbour.* 1866. Op. cit.

[with David] *Report on the application of the magneto-electric light . . .* 1866. Op. cit.

[with David] 'Report on Kirkcaldy water supply.' [n.p., March, 1867]. NLS: MS. Acc. 10706, 528.

'On ascertaining the intensity of storms by the calculation of barometric gradients'. *Scot. Meterorological J.*, New Series, 1869. II. 132-136. Read June 1867.

'Description of a holophone or sound reflector for fog signals'. *Trans. R.S.S.A.*, 1868, VII. 204-209.

'Notice as to the electrical and optical arrangements employed . . . in experiments on the illumination of beacons at sea by electricity communicated through wires connected with the shore.' *Trans. R.S.S.A*, 1868. VII, 306-309,1 pl. Read 22nd April 1867. Offprint: Edinburgh, 1867. Reported to British Association at Dundee, September 1867.

'Some new arrangements for lighthouse illumination ... Tay leading lights'. *Trans. R.S.S.A.*, 1868. VII. 540-546, 3 pl. Dated 6 Dec. 1867. This apparatus which contained every kind of dioptric prism then known maximised the lighting power of an oil lamp - See D. Alan's *I.A.L.A.* paper, 1962.

[with David] *Note of trials with the electric and oil lights, . . .*1868. Op. cit.

[with David] *Report on the improvement of the harbour of Berwick.* 1869. Op. cit.

[with David] *Reports. Papers relative to a proposal to substitute gas for oil . . .* 1869. Op. cit.

[with David] 'Copy report relative to the first order lighthouse lantern . . .'. 1870. Op. cit.

[with David] *Japanese lighthouses. lightships, buoys, and beacons.* 1871. Op. cit.

[with David] 'Supplementary report on paraffin light.' 1871. Op. cit.

[with David] *Preliminary report to the Port and Harbour Commissioners of Londonderry.* 1873. Op. cit.

[with David] *Report to the Clyde Lighthouse Trustees.* [Edinburgh?, 1873]. Op. cit.

[with David] *Report relative to the widening of the North Bridge.* Edinburgh, 1873. Op. cit.

[with David] *Report . . . relative to the Rivers Manor and Lyne.* 1873. Op. cit.

[with David] *Report to his Grace the Duke of Argyll . . . Roseneath Bay.* 1874. Op. cit.

[with David] *The report of . . . water supply of the city of Derry.* 1875. Op. cit.

Articles in *Encyclopedia Britannica.* 9th ed., 1875-89. XI. 'Harbours and docks.', 455-471. 2 pl.; 'Lighthouse.', 615-629. Offprint: Edinburgh, 1882.

[with David] *Report relative to Sir William Thomson's proposed changes . . .* 1880. Op. cit.

[with David] *Report relative to M. Allard's scheme . . .* 1881. Op. cit.

[with David] *Report relative to the fishery harbours on the coasts of Haddingtonshire and Berwickshire.'* 1882. Op. cit.

[with David] *Report regarding the lighting of the west coasts of the Orkney . . .* 1883. Op. cit.

*Proposed national harbour of refuge at Peterhead. Report to the Trustees . . .* Edinburgh, 1883.

'On the principal causes of the silting up of estuaries, and the danger, where such causes exist, of employing training walls as a means of improving navigable rivers.' *Proc. R.S.E.,* (1884-86), XIII, 80-91. Read 2.2.1885. Offprint: Edinburgh, 1885. With reference to the proposed Manchester Ship Canal. Based to a considerable extent on David's work.

Articles by Messrs. D. & T. Stevenson in *Chambers Encyclopedia,* 1888-92. Op. cit.

ROBERT LOUIS STEVENSON

'Notice of a new form of intermittent light for lighthouses.' *Trans. R.S.S.A.,* 1873, VIII, 271-275. Paper read in 1871. Reprinted in various editions of the author's Works.

*On the thermal influence of forests.* Edinburgh, 1873. *Proc. R.S.E.,* 1875, VIII, 114-125. Reprinted in various editions of the author's Works.

'Memoirs of an islet.' [Earraid]. In: *Memories and portraits,* 1887, 120-131.

*Familiar studies of men and books,* 1882.

'Letter relating to the Bell Rock Lighthouse.' *Athenaeum,* 11 October 1884, 465. In support of his grandfather rather than Rennie as the designer of the lighthouse. Also, another letter dated 25 October.

'Thomas Stevenson, Civil Engineer.' *Contemporary Review,* June 1887, LI, 789-793. Reprinted in *Memories and portraits, paper IX.* Includes the comment, *Many harbours were successfully carried out* [by D. & T. Stevenson]: *one, the harbour of Wick, the chief disaster of my father's life, was a failure; the sea proved too strong for man's arts; and after expedients hitherto unthought of, and on a scale hyper-cyclopean, the work must be deserted, and now stands a ruin in that bleak, God-forsaken bay, ten miles from John-o'-Groat's.*

'Memoir of Fleeming Jenkin.' In: *Papers literary and scientific by the late Fleeming Jenkin.* Edited by S. Colvin. New York, 1887. Republished London, 1888. First separate edition, 1912.

'Contributions to the history of Fife. Random memories.' *Scribner's Mag.,* October 1888, IV, 507- 512.. [Same as: 'Random memories. I.-The coast of Fife.' In: *Across the plains.* London, 1892.]

'The Education of an Engineer. More random memories.' *Scribner's Mag.,* New York, Nov. 1888, IV, 636-640. [Same as: 'Random memories. II.-The education of an engineer.' In: *Across the plains.* London, 1892.]

*Records of a Family of Engineers.* Edinburgh, 1896. With a reprint of the Memoir of Fleeming Jenkin. First separate edition, 1912. Augmented by *The manuscripts of Robert Louis Stevenson's Records of a family of engineers. The unfinished chapters.* Edited, with an introduction by J. C. Bay., Chicago, 1930.

'Memoirs of himself.' In: *Memories and portraits.* Philadelphia, 1912. On Thomas Stevenson; a fragment.

'To the Commissioners of Northern Lights, with a Paper.' In: *Boston Bibliophile Society, I and II: Poems by Robert Louis Stevenson: hitherto unpublished.* Boston, 1916. A poem. Written c. 1871.

*The Letters of Robert Louis Stevenson.* Edited by Bradford A. Booth and Ernest Mehew. Yale U.P., New Haven, 1994-1995, **1-8.**

*The new lighthouse on the Dhu Heartach Rock, Argyllshire.* Edited with an introduction by Roger G. Swearingen. St. Helena; California, 1995.

## DAVID ALAN STEVENSON

'The Dhu Heartach Lighthouse.' *Min. Proc. I.C.E.,* 1876, XLVI, 1- 19. 2 pl. Awarded the Institution's *Manby Premium* prize.

'On coast fog signals.' *Trans. R.S.S.A.,* 1883, X, 490-506,1 pl. Read 16 March 1881.

'Ailsa Craig lighthouse and fog signals.' *Min. Proc. I.C.E.,* 1887, LXXXIX, 297-303, 1 pl. Awarded the Institution's *Telford Premium* prize.

'Description of the electric light on the Isle of May.' *Proc. I.Mech. E.,* 1887. 38. 347-372

*The principles and practice of canal and river engineering. By David Stevenson . . . revised by his sons David Alan Stevenson ... Charles Alexander Stevenson.* Edinburgh, 1888. *Third edition.*

[With Charles] *Memorandum regarding the formation of a ship canal between the Forth and Clyde, by Messrs. D. & T. Stevenson.* Edinburgh, 1889.

'Notice regarding the proposed Forth and Clyde Ship Canal.' In: *Fourth International Congress on Inland Navigation.* Manchester, 1890. The proposal was for a 30 foot deep canal from Grangemouth along the Forth valley to Loch Lomond with a cut through from Tarbet to Arrochar into Loch Long.

'Recent improvements in the lighting and buoying, etc. of the Scottish and Isle of Man coasts.' *Proc. International Engineering Congress (Glasgow) 1901. Report of the proceedings and abstracts of papers read,* Glasgow, 1902, 85-89. Reprinted London, 1902, 153-156.

'Safety of navigation. Lighted buoys.' *XIIth International Congress of Navigation, Philadelphia, 1912, IInd section: Ocean navigation, 4th communication.* Brussels, 1912.

[With Charles] 'Improvement works on the Clyde estuary.' *International Engineering Congress (Glasgow) 1901. Report of the proceedings and abstracts of papers read,* Glasgow, 1902, 77-79. Reprinted London, 1902, 124-125.

'On the proposed Forth and Clyde Ship Canal.' *Trans. R.S.S.A.,* 1914, XVIII, pt. iv, 265-285, 1 pl. **[93]** Read 31.1.1910. Separately published in 1913.

[With Charles] Report to the Denver Sluice Commissioners on the improvement of the drainage of the Fens by the River Ouse.[Edinburgh, 1918]. 1 pl. Dated 9 February 1918.

CHARLES ALEXANDER STEVENSON

'The earthquake of 28th November 1880 in Scotland and Ireland.' *Proc. R.S.E.*, XI, 176-187, 1 pl. Abstract published in *Nature* 1881, XXIII, 591-592. Updated by a notice of earthquakes in Scotland from 1882-1889 in Proc. R.S.E., 1889, XV, 259-266.

'A new form of seismograph.' *Trans. R.S.S.A.,* 1883, X, 546-549. An abstract was published in Nature, 31.5.1883, XXVIII, 117-118. Followed by 'Seismographs - An apology.' Nature, 13,11.1884, 29.

'Aseismatic tables for mitigating earthquake shocks'. *Nature,* 26.6. 1884.

*The principles and practice of canal and river engineering.* By David Stevenson . . . *Op. cit.*

'On the dredging of the lower estuary of the Clyde.' *Proc. I.Mech.E.*, August 1887. **38**. 386-401, 4 pl. See also 'Correspondence on dredging of lower estuary of Clyde.' *Proc. I.C.E.,* 1887, LXXXIX, 109-110.

*The principles and practice of canal and river engineering.* By David Stevenson . . . *revised by his sons David Alan Stevenson . . . Charles Alexander Stevenson, Edinburgh, 1888. Third edition.*

'On a dipping or fog apparatus for electric light in lighthouses.' *Min. Proc. I.C.E.*, 1888, XCII, 299.

[With David A.] *Memorandum . . . ship canal between the Forth and Clyde, . . .1889. Op. cit.*

'Correspondence on bars at mouths of tidal estuaries.' *Min. Proc. I.C.E.,* 1890, C. 202-203.

'Correspondence on Portland cement and on Portland cement concrete.' *Min. Proc. I.C.E.*, 1892, CVII, 196-197. [Anstruther pier, 1871; Lochindaal pier, 1877; Berwick, 1873; Aberdeen harbour].

'Correspondence on lighthouses.' *Min. Proc. I.C.E.*, 1892, CVIII, 242.

'On the progress of the dioptric lens as used in lighthouse illumination.' *Report of British Association at Edinburgh, August 1892,* 1893, 879-880. Also in *Nature,* 29.9.1892, 514-516.

'Lighthouse refractors.' *Proc. I.C.E.,* 1894, CXVII, 341-352, 1 pl. See earlier publication 'On a new form of refractor for dioptric apparatus.' *Trans. R.S.S.A.,* 1891, XII, 219-220, 1 pl., and 'Note upon mode of calculating spherical refractors.' *Trans. R.S.S.A.,* 1894, XIII, 321-324.

'Induction through air and water at great distances without the use of parallel wires.' *Proc. R.S.E.,* 1895, XX, 25-27. 1 pl. Read 30th January 1893. Proposing a leader cable for guiding ships safely into harbours at night or in fog. Abstract in *Electrical Review,* 10.2.1893, 171-172. Letter from Charles in *Nature,* 1896, LV, 197.

'Telegraphic communication by induction by means of coils.' *Proc. R.S.E.,* 1895, XX, 196-200. 2 pl. Read 19.3.1894. Transmission of speech over a distance of two miles without wires. Reported in *Engineering* 6.4.1894, *Electrical Review,* 13.4.1894, and *Nature* 1896, LV, 197, in a letter from Charles dated 21.12.1896.

'The late Charles Jopp, Civil Engineer.' *Edinburgh Academy Chronicle,* May 1895, 78.

'Distillery pollution.' *Nature,* 4.8.1898

[With Charles] 'Improvement works on the Clyde estuary.' 1902. Op. cit.

*Evidence on Craigenroad and Cluny Harbour Schemes. Full report of Board of Trade Inquiry at Buckie.* Buckie, 1904. 46-57, 83. *Apparatus for lighting lighthouses, beacons, buoys and the like.* Patent no. 5916, 1907.

[With John Moyes] *Improvements in and relating to signalling apparatus. Patent no. 5615, 1910.*

[With David A.] Report to the Denver Sluice Commissioners . . . Op. cit.

DAVID ALAN STEVENSON

'Early Scottish lighthouses.' *Chambers's Journal,* Seventh Series, VII, Feb. 17, 1917, 181-5.

'Aids to navigation during fog.' Report by D. Alan Stevenson. *XIIIth International Congress of Navigation, London, 1923, 2nd Section: Ocean Navigation, 4th Communication.* Brussels, 1923.

*Lighthouses in India, Burma, Persian Gulf and Ceylon. Report of D. Alan Stevenson, 1927.* Delhi, 1927.

'The development of lighthouses.' *Journal of the Royal Society of Arts,* LXXX, Jan.15, 1932, 224-242.

'Telford the engineer.' *Scotland,* Autumn 1934. **1**, No. 3. 23-24.

'The flooded Fens: A tidal river and its control.' *Scot. Geog. Mag.*, May 1937, **53**, 166-175.

'The engineering work of the Clyde Lighthouses Trust.' *Trans. Inst. of Eng. & Shipbuilders in Scot.*, 1945, LXXXIX, 423-441.

*English lighthouse tours 1801 1813 1818 from the diaries of Robert Stevenson with his drawings of lighthouses.* Edited by D. Alan Stevenson, 1946.

*The triangular stamps of Cape of Good Hope.* New York, London & Sydney, 1950.

'Improvements in seamarks before 1840.' *Paper 11 International Association of Lighthouse Authorities.* July 1961.

[Design of a dioptric apparatus installed at one of the Tay leading lights in 1866], *Paper 14, International Association of Lighthouse Authorities.* April 1962.

*The world's lighthouses before 1820, 1959.*

# Appendix 2 - Lighthouses by Smith and the Stevensons [102]

## THOMAS SMITH

Kinnaird Head•, Fraserburgh (NJ 999676) 1787. Modernised 1824, 1851, 1907, closed 1990.

Mull of Kintyre•, Argyllshire (NR 586085) 1787-88. Rebuilt in 1820s, modernised 1906.

North Ronaldsay•, Orkney (HY 785559) 1789. Modernised, 1809, c. 1854.

Eilean Glass•, Scalpay, Harris (NG 247947) 1789. Modernised 1820s, 1907.

Tay Lights, Firth of Tay (NO 4529 & 5431). Already existing, modernised 1789.

Pladda•, Arran, Bute (NS 027191) 1790. Modernised 1820s, 1901.

Leith Pier, Midlothian (NT 272767). Already existing, modernised 1790.

Portpatrick, Wigtownshire (NW 998541) 1790.

Little Cumbrae•, Bute (NS 143515). Already existing. Modernised 1793, 1900, 1906, 1908.

Pentland Skerries•, Orkney (ND 465784) 1794. Rebuilt 1820s, modernised 1929-30.

Cloch•*, Renfrewshire (NS 203759) 1797. Modernised 1825, 1903.

Inchkeith•*, Fife (NT 293828) 1804. Modernised 1815, 1824-25, 1835, 1889, 1899.

Start Point•*, Sanday, Orkney (HY 786435) 1802-6. Replaced 1870, modernised 1913.

• Indicates a major light    * With Robert.

## ROBERT STEVENSON

Cloch•*, Renfrewshire (NS 203759) 1797. Modernised 1825, 1903.

Inchkeith•*, Fife (NT 293828) 1803-04. Modernised 1815, 1824-5, 1835, 1889, 1899.

Start Point•*, Sanday, Orkney (HY 786435) 1802-06. Replaced 1870, modernised 1913.

Bell Rock•, North Sea (NO 760270) 1807-11. Modernised 1901.

Toward Point•, Argyllshire (NS 136673) 1812. Modernised 1877?, 1930.

Isle of May•, Fife (NT 656 998) 1815-16. Modernised 1886, 1924.

Corsewall•, Wigtownshire (NW 981727) 1815-17. Modernised 1891, 1910.

Point of Ayre•, Isle of Man (NX 464048 & 467051 - 2 towers) 1818. Modernised 1891.

Calf of Man•, Isle of Man (SC 149657 - three towers) 1818.

Sumburgh Head•, Shetland (HU 406079) 1821. Superseded by a second tower built 1914.

Rhinns of Islay•, Argyllshire (NR 164514) 1825. Modernised 1895.

Buchan Ness•, Aberdeenshire (NK 137422) 1827. Modernised 1909-10.

Cape Wrath•, Sutherland (NC 259748) 1828. Modernised 1896.

Mull of Galloway•, Wigtownshire (NX 157304) 1828-30. Modernised 1879, 1901.

Tarbat Ness•, Ross & Cromarty (NH 946876) 1830. Modernised 1891-92.

Dunnet Head•, Caithness (ND 203768) 1831. Modernised 1908-09.

Douglas Head•, Isle of Man (SC 391747) 1832. Modernised 1892.

Barra Head•, Barra (NL 549803) 1833. Modernised 1882.

Girdle Ness•, Aberdeenshire (NJ 972053) 1831-33. Modernised 1890.

Lismore•, Argyllshire (NM 778351) 1833. Modernised 1931.


• Indicates a major light   * With Thomas Smith.

ALAN STEVENSON

Skerryvore•, Argyllshire (NL 835260) 1838-44. Modernised 1909.

Little Ross, Kirkcudbrightshire (NX 658432) 1842-43. Modernised 1911.

Isle of May leading light (NT 656 998) 1844. Discontinued in 1887, building still exists.

Covesea Skerries•, Moray (NJ 204713) 1846. Modernised 1911. Associated with an iron beacon on Halliman's Scars 1844.

Chanonry•, Ross & Cromarty (NH 750557) 1846.

Cromarty•, Ross & Cromarty (NH 786678) 1846.

Loch Ryan (Cairn Point) (NX 062687) 1847.

Noss Head•, Caithness (ND 388550) 1849.

Ardnamurchan•, Argyllshire (NM 416676) 1849.

Sanda Island•, Kintyre, Argyllshire (NR 725037) 1850. Modernised 1881-82.

Hoy Sound [Low]•, Orkney (HY 246066) 1851.

Hoy Sound [High]•, Orkney (HY 268061) 1851.

Arnish Point•, Stornoway, Lewis (NB 432308) 1853.

DAVID STEVENSON

Out Skerries• [Whalsay Skerries], Shetland (HU 702718) 1852-54

Davaar•, Campbelltown, Argyllshire (NR 761206) 1854

Muckle Flugga•, Unst, Shetland (HP 605198) 1854 (temporary)

Muckle Flugga•*, 1857 (permanent) Modernised 1927.

Ushenish•*, South Uist (NF 873351) 1857. Modernised 1884-85.

Rona•* [South Rona], Inverness-shire (NG 634611) 1857. Modernised 1949.

Kyleakin*, Syke (NG 745270) 1857.

Ornsay•* [Oronsay], Skye (NG 714122) 1857.

Inchcolm*, Fife (NT 186824) c. 1858.

Rubha Nan Gall* [Runa Gall Rock], Mull (NM 508571) 1857.

Cantick Head*, Walls, Orkney (ND 346 894) 1858.

Bressay•*, Shetland (HU 488376) 1858.

Ruvaal•* [Rubha Mhail], Islay, Argyllshire (NR 426792) 1859. Modernised 1927.

Corran Point*, Inverness-shire (NN 016635] 1860.

Fladda* [Phladda Island] (NM 721123) 1860.

McArthur's Head*, Islay (NR 462598) 1861.

St. Abb's Head•*, Berwickshire (NT 915693) 1862.

Butt of Lewis•*, Lewis (NB 519665) 1862.

Holburn Head•* [Holborn Head; Clett], Caithness (ND 107707) 1862.

Monach* [Heisker], Monach Islands, North Uist (NF 613818) 1864.

Skervuile* [Sgeir Maoile][Iron Rock], Jura (NR 604712) 1865.

Auskerry•*, Orkney (HY 673155) 1866-67. Modernised 1927.

Loch Indaal*, Islay (NR 256589) 1869.

Scurdyness•*, Montrose (NO 734568) 1870. Modernised 1881, 1885. Optical apparatus designed by Alan Brebner jnr., 1885.

Stoer Head•* [Ru Stoer], Sutherland (NC 004330) 1870. Modernised 1909.

Dhubh Artach•* [Dhu Heartach], Argyllshire (NM 120030) 1867-72. Modernised 1883, 1913. Red stripe painted, 1890.

Turnberry•*, Ayrshire (NS 196072) 1873.

Chicken Rock*, Isle of Man (SC 143639) 1874-75.

Holy Island*, Inner, Arran, Bute (NS 063286) 1877. Modernised 1950.

Langness•*, Isle of Man (SC 283653) 1880.


• Indicates a major light   * With Thomas Stevenson.

THOMAS STEVENSON

Muckle Flugga•*, Unst, Shetland (HP 605 198) 1857 (permanent).

Ushenish•*, South Uist (NF 873351) 1857.

Rona•* [South Rona], Inverness-shire (NG 634611) 1857.

Kyleakin*, Syke (NG 745270) 1857.

Ornsay•* [Oronsay], Skye (NG 714122) 1857.

Inchcolm*, Fife (NT 186824) c.1858.

Rubha Nan Gall•* [Runa Gall Rock], Mull (NM 508571) 1857.

Cantick Head•*, Walls, Orkney (ND 346 894) 1858.

Bressay•*, Shetland (HU 488376) 1858.

Ruvaal•* [Rubha Mhail], Islay, Argyllshire (NR 426792) 1859. Modernised 1927.

Corran Point*, Inverness-shire (NN 016635} 1860.

Fladda* [Phladda Island] (NM 721123) 1860.

McArthur's Head*, Islay (NR 462598) 1861.

St. Abb's Head•*, Berwickshire (NT 915693) 1862.

Butt of Lewis•*, Lewis (NB 519665) 1862.

Holburn Head•* [Holborn Head], Caithness (ND 107707). 1862.

Monach* [Heisker], Monach Islands, North Uist (NF 613818) 1864.

Skervuile* [Sgeir Maoile][Iron Rock], Jura (NR 604712) 1865.

Auskerry•*, Orkney (HY 673155) 1866-67.

Loch Indaal*, Islay (NR 256589) 1869.

Scurdyness•*, Montrose (NO 734568) 1870. Optical apparatus designed by A. Brebner jnr., 1885.

Stoer Head•* [Ru Stoer], Sutherland (NC 004330) 1870.

Dhubh Artach•* [Dhu Heartach], Argyllshire (NM 120030) 1867-72.

Turnberry•*, Ayrshire (NS 196072) 1873.

Chicken Rock*, Isle of Man (SC 143639) 1874-75.

Holy Island, Inner*, Arran, Bute (NS 063286) 1877.

Langness•*, Isle of Man (SC 283653) 1880.

Fidra•▲ [Fiddra], East Lothian (NT 512870) 1885.

Oxcars▲, Midlothian (NT 203818) 1886.

Ailsa Craig•▲, Ayrshire (NX 026997) 1886.


• Indicates a major light.  *With David. ▲ With David A.

DAVID A. STEVENSON

Fidra•* [Fiddra], East Lothian (NT 512870) 1885.

Oxcars*, Midlothian (NT 203818) 1886.

Ailsa Craig•*, Ayrshire (NX 026997) 1886.

Grey Rocks, Mull (NM 715399) 1890.

Dubh Sgeir, Barra (NL 667965) 1891. Rebuilt 1995.

Weaver Point, North Uist (NF 955691) 1891.

Sgeir Leadh (Castlebay), Barra (NL 649971) 1891

Calvay, South Uist (NF 821181) 1891

Dunollie, Oban (NM 852311) 1892

Crowlin, Applecross, Ross & Cromarty (NG 681358) 1892. Modernised 1911.

Kylerhea, Skye (NG 788223) 1892. Modernised 1934.

Fair Isle•, South [Skaddan], Shetland (HY 197698) 1892.

Fair Isle•, North [Skroo], Shetland (HY 222741) 1892.

Rèisa an t'Struit, Jura (NR 734989) 1892. Modernised 1944.

Carloway [Loch Carloway], Lewis (NB 172429) 1892. Modernised 1914.

Heliar Holm, Shapinsay, Orkney (HY 484151) 1892.

Heston Island, Kirkcudbrightshire (NX 839503) 1893.

Fugla Ness, Shetland (HU 363361) 1893. Modernised 1936.

Eyre Point, Raasay (NG 580342) 1893. Modernised 1938.

Dunvegan, Skye (NG 235490) 1893. Modernised 1936.

Vaila Sound, Shetland (HU 246462) 1894.

Loch Eribol, Sutherland (NC 458618) 1894. Modernised 1937.

Rattray Head•, Aberdeenshire (NK 111577) 1892-95.

Skerry of Ness, Orkney (HY 254076) 1895.

Hillswick Ness, Shetland (HU 278745) 1895. Modernised 1937.

Balta Sound, Shetland (HP 658069) 1895. Modernised 1938.

Sule Skerry•, West of Orkney (HX 624242) 1892-95.

Tod Head•, Kincardineshire (NO 870769) 1896.

Stroma•, Caithness (ND 354792) 1894-96.

Scarinish•, Tiree, Argyllshire (NM 044446) 1897. Modernised 1936.

No Ness, Sandwick, Shetland (HU 4422) 1897. Modernised 1938. Disused.

Muckle Roe, Shetland (HU 304630) 1897. Modernised 1936.

Cava, Orkney (HY 323006) 1898. Modernised 1935.

Noup Head•, Westray, Orkney (HY 393499) 1896-98.

Flannan Isles•, Ross & Cromarty (NA 730475) 1897-99. Disappearance of the keepers 15.12.1900.

Killantringan•, [Blackhead], nr. Portpatrick, Wigtownshire (NW 981564) 1898-99. Superseded Portpatrick lighthouse.

Tiumpan Head•, Lewis (NB 573377) 1897-1900.

Greinam, Lewis (NB 200358) 1900.

Duart Point, Mull (NM 754343) 1900-01. Built as a memorial to William Black (1841-1898), novelist. The architect was William Leiper (1839-1916).

Bunessan, Mull (NM 361249) 1901. Modernised after 1954.

Hoxa Head, Orkney (ND 404932) 1901. Modernised 1934.

Bass Rock, East Lothian NT 602872) 1900-02.

Barns Ness, East Lothian (NT 723772) 1899-1901. Modernised 1966.

Scalasaig, Colonsay (NR 398938) 1903.

Lady Isle, Ayrshire (NS 274294) 1903.

The Garvellachs, Firth of Lorn (NM 633093) 1904. Modernised 1946.

Suther Ness, Shetland (HU 551655) 1904. Modernised 1936.

Whitehill of Vatsetter, Shetland (HU 547889) 1904. Modernised 1937.

Sgeir Bhuidhe, Port Appin (NM 905462) 1904.

Mull of Eswick, Shetland (HU 499535) 1904. Modernised 1935.

Craigton Point, Inverness (NH 662478) 1904.

Symbister Ness, Shetland (HU 533623) 1904.

Rova Head, Shetland (HU 475455) 1904.

Hyskeir• [Oigh-sgeir], Inverness-shire (NM 156962) 1904. Mercury flotation 1911.

Roseness, Orkney (ND 521987) 1905. Modernised 1911.

Holy Island, Outer#, Arran, Bute (NS 068292) 1905. Modernised 1954.

Swona, Orkney (ND 381838) 1906.

Green Island [Eileanan Glasa] (NM 595453) 1906.

Ruadh Sgeir, Jura (NM 722928) 1906.

Eigg (NM 488830) 1906.

Lady Rock, Lismore (NM 772343) 1907.

Eilean a' Chuirn, Islay (NR 473492) 1907. Modernised 1950.

Papa Stronsay, Orkney (HY 669299) 1907. Modernised 1935.

Canna (NG 292038) 1907.

Elie Ness•, Fife (NT 496993) 1908.

Ornsay Beacon, Skye (NG 714131) 1908.

Eilean Trodday, Skye (NG 442789) 1908.

Firths Voe•, Shetland (HU 453748) 1909.

Cairns of Coll, Coll (NM 280658) 1909.

Ruff Reef, Orkney (ND 347897) 1909.

Ness of Sound, Shetland (HU 447824) 1909.

Calf of Eday, Orkney (HY 580390?) 1909. Modernised after 1954.

Dubh Sgeir, Luing (NM 727121) 1910. Modernised 1990.

Sandaig, Glenelg (NG 761146) 1910.

Lowther Rock, Orkney (ND 434829) 1910.

Neist Point•, Skye (NG 127471) 1910.

Na Cuiltean, Jura (NR 547646) 1911.

Rubha Reidh• [Rhu Rhea], Gairloch, Ross & Cromarty (NG 740919) 1912.

Milaid Point, Lewis (NB 422115) 1912.

Crammag Head•, Wigtownshire (NX 089341) 1913.

Cairnbulg Briggs, Aberdeenshire (NK 036661) 1914.

Maughold Head•, Isle of Man (SC 498914) 1910-14.

Copinsay•, Orkney (HY 615014) 1911-15. Architect: Mr Taylor.

Clythness•, Caithness (ND 291364) 1914-16.

Vaternish [Waternish], Skye (NG 233670) 1924. Modernised 1946.

Duncansby Head•, Caithness (ND 405734) 1924.

Brough of Birsay•, Orkney (HY 234286) 1925. Modernised 1931.

Ardtornish, Morvern, Argyllshire (NM 692425) 1927. Modernised 1950.

Carragh Mhor, Islay (NR 433684) 1928.

Esha Ness•, Shetland (HU 205785) 1929.

Sleat Point, Skye (NM 562993) 1933-34.

Torness, Orkney (ND 251886) 1937.

Rubh Uisenis, Lewis (NB 354031) 1938.


• Indicates a major light.   * With Thomas.

## Appendix 3. David Stevenson's apprenticeship indenture 10 July 1834

*It is contracted and agreed upon between the parties following vizt. Robert Stevenson Civil Engineer residing in Edinburgh on the one part and David Stevenson third son of the said Robert Stevenson with consent of Adam Warden Doctor of medicine as Cautioner and taking burden upon him for the said David Stevenson on the other part in manner following That is to say the said David Stevenson with consent foresaid hereby becomes bound Apprentice to the said Robert Stevenson  for carrying the art and practice of a Civil Engineer as exercised by him and that for the space of five years from and since the term of Martinmas [11 November?] one thousand eight hundred and thirty notwithstanding the date hereof during which whole space the said David Stevenson and the said Adam Warden as Cautioner for him Bind and Oblige themselves and their heirs and successors conjuctly and severally, that the said David Stevenson shall faithfully diligently and Honestly attend his said masters service by night and by day, and shall not absent himself therefrom without leave asked and given, and that he shall not hear or see his masters skaith without hindering and preventing the same to the utmost of his power and timeously acquainting his master therewith, and that he shall not divulge any secret or secrets with which his master may intrust him And further the said David Stevenson and his Cautioner Bind and Oblige themselves and their foresaids conjunctly and severally to repeat and refund to the said Robert Stevenson any loss damage or expence which he may happen to incur or sustain through the omissions or default of the said David Stevenson at any time during his apprenticeship For which Causes and on the other part the said Robert Stevenson Binds and obliges himself to teach and instruct the said David Stevenson his apprentice in the foresaid art and practice of a Civil Engineer in all its branches as practised by him the said Robert Stevenson during the foresaid space in so far as he knows and the said David Stevenson is capable to learn and the said David Stevenson Binds and obliges himself and his foresaids to warrant, free relieve harness and skaithless keep his said Cautioners of all cost damage interest and expence which they or any of them may anyways sustain or be put to by being bound and obliged for him in manner foresaid And lastly both parties Bind and oblige themselves and their foresaids to implement and fulfill the premises to each other hinc inde under the penalty of Fifty pounds sterling to be paid by the party failing to the party performing or willing to perform over and above perfomance and both parties Consent to the Registration hereof in the Books of Council and Session or others competent therein to remain for preservation and that letters of Horning on six days charge and all other necessary execution may pass upon a Decree to be interponed hereto in common form and thereto Constitute their Procurators.*

*In witness Whereof these presents written upon Stamped paper by James Gordon Apprentice to Charles Cunningham and Carlyle Bell Writers to the Signet Are Subscribed by the said parties at Edinburgh on the tenth day of July eighteen hundred and thirty four before these witnesses James Falconer Writer in Edinburgh,and Thomas Stevenson residing in Baxters Place Edinburgh. [signatures].*

This document was signed after the apprenticeship had already run for nearly four years. On completion of the apprenticeship in 1835 Robert gave the following discharge:

*I Robert Stevenson within designed in respect that the also within designed David Stevenson has served me as my apprentice in terms of the within Indenture during the whole period therein stipulated properly and faithfully, Therefore I do hereby Exonerate and Discharge him and the within designed Adam Warden his Cautioner, of the said Indenture whole purport and effect thereof so far as the same were incumbent on them and I oblige myself to warrant this discharge to be good and sufficient at all hands. In witness whereof I have subscribed these presents written on the back of the said Indenture by James Falconer Clerk to Cuninghams & Bell Writers to the Signet at Edinburgh.*

## Appendix 4. The Stevenson Family Tree

**Thomas Smith (6.12.1752-21.6.1815)**
m. 1st Elizabeth Couper (d. 1786)
m. 2nd, Mary Jack (d. 1791)
m. 3rd, Jean Lillie (1751-1820)
Son in law: Robert Stevenson (1772-1850)

**Robert Stevenson (8.6.1772-12.7.1850)**
m. Jane Smith (1779-1846)
Jane Warden (1801-1864)
Alan Stevenson (1807-1865)
David Stevenson (1815-1886)
Thomas Stevenson (1818-1887)

**Alan Stevenson (28.4.1807-23.12.1865)**
m. Margaret Scott Jones (1813-1895)
Robert Alan Mowbray Stevenson (1847-1900)

**David Stevenson (11.1.1815-17.7.1886)**
m. Elizabeth Mackay (1816-1871)
David Alan Stevenson (1854-1938)
Charles Alexander Stevenson (1855-1950)

**Thomas Stevenson (22.7.1818-8.5.1887)**
m. Margaret (Maggie) Isabella Balfour (1829-1897)
Robert Louis Stevenson (13.11.1850-3.12.1894)

**David Alan Stevenson (21.7.1854-3.12.1938)**
m. Anne Roberts (c. 1862-1945)

**Charles Alexander Stevenson (23.1.1855-9.5.1950)**
m. Margaret (Meta) Sherriff (1863-1945)
**David Alan Stevenson (7.2.1891-22.12.1971)**

**Descendants of David Alan Stevenson:**

### Dorothy Emily Stevenson (later Peploe) (1892-1973)

m. James Reid Peploe (d. 1969)
Annie Patricia Peploe (1917-1928)
James Robert Stevenson (Robin) Peploe (b. 1918-1995)
Rosemary Fleming Peploe (later Bevan) (b. 1922)
John William Peploe (b. 1930)

### Katheleen Elizabeth Stevenson (later Chambers) (1898-1978)

m. Reginald Stuart Chambers (1888-1940)

**Descendants of Charles Alexander Stevenson:**

### David Alan Stevenson (1891-1971)

m. Jessie Laura Margaret Maclellan (1891-1975)
Helen Rhoda Laura Stevenson (later Shepherd) (b. 1924-1995)
Margaret Joyce Beryl Stevenson (later Will) (b. 1927)
Robert Quentin Charles Stevenson (b. 1932)

### Frances Margaret Stevenson (later Douglas; later Richardson) (1892-1974)

m. 1st, David William Sholto Douglas (d. 1916)
Evelyn Margaret Isobel (Bettina) Douglas (later Thomson) (b. 1914)
Jean Frances David Douglas (later Leslie) (b. 1916)
m. 2nd, James Smith Richardson (1883-1970); divorced 1943

### Evelyn Mary (May) Stevenson (later Yeoman) (1897-1972)

m. Thomas Yeoman (1897-1956)
Zara Caroline Yeoman (later Groundes-Peace) (1924-1966)
m. John Victor Groundes-Peace (b. 1919)
Roderick Jonathan Groundes-Peace (b. 1952)

# INDEX

Notes: The illustrations, in square brackets, are preceded by their page numbers - e.g. **[92]** is on page 119. The chronological lists of lighthouses and publications in the appendices are generally not included.